THE MESSIANIC PILGRIMAGE

a journey of discovery

Stan Nussbaum & Richard J Fairhead
with other pilgrims

First published - July 2022
Reprinted September 2022 - typgraphical corrections

Published by
Ushaaqallah Community Benefit Society Ltd
info@ubs.ngo

Stan Nussbaum and Richard J Fairhead assert their moral right to be identified as the authors of this book.

Design and layout by Richard J Fairhead.

Publisher's Cataloging-in-Publication data

Names: Nussbaum, Stan. | Fairhead, Richard J.

Title: The Messianic Pilgrimage: a journey of discovery / Stan Nussbaum and Richard J Fairhead with other pilgrims

Description: Anthology of thoughts about the Messianic Pilgrimage from a loose community of people who are passionate about God | Summary: Introduction to the eight seasons of the Messianic Pilgrimage, followed by details about each of the eight seasons including materials used on the ushaaqallah.com website and linked material from the SYNCx.org website

Identifiers: ISBN 979-8-7724-5546-3 (softcover)

LC Subjects: Religon-Worship-Devotional Exercises

LC Classification: BV5-530

Dewey Decimal Classification: 204

Contents

How to use this book

To use this book to your advantage, you should realise one thing about it. It is not your guide. The living Messiah himself is your guide, and he is the perfect guide for pilgrims.

The Messiah knows you and all your relatives. He knows your dreams, your language, your schedule and your bank balance. He knows which part of your body hurts right now and why.

The Messiah knows you are holding this book. If you keep reading, you will discover whether this is part of his communication to you or not. His voice in your soul will tell you. His Spirit may cause certain pages or words to jump out at you.

You will notice that this printed book isn't the usual shape of a novel or a nonfiction book, which may give you an idea that it is neither. It is more like a series of blog posts on a theme than a normal book.

It's an anthology of thoughts about what we call the 'Messianic Pilgrimage' from the two of us and a few friends who are as passionate as we are about the Messiah whom God sent to lead humanity.

We use this term Messianic Pilgrimage to be as inclusive as possible when communicating with Arabic speakers in the Middle East and North Africa. A pilgrimage is a well-known term for a journey with a purpose—physical or spiritual. The Messianic Pilgrimage is a pilgrimage led by Jesus, who is respected as the Messiah by Muslims and Christians.

Websites

Most of the material was adapted from one of two websites: In Part One most of the material is from the ushaaqallah.com Arabic website and all of the material in Part Two is from the syncx.org website. Some introductory and bridge material was added for the printed version.

Not a programme or an organisation

There is no 'Messianic Pilgrimage' organisation to join. We are not a new religion. We have no new sacred book, no new prophet and no new religious label like 'Muslim' or 'Christian' that you have to use instead of those.

Our prayer is that no matter how you decide to label yourself, you would take this pilgrimage with Jesus the Messiah and discover his guidance for each remaining day in your life. That is what we are doing. This book is work in progress rather than definitive or finalised. Though the core has been used for some years, we keep discovering things as we walk with the Messiah. Sometimes he gives us new ways to say things. If you listen to him, you will see how he does this in your case.

Articles used from our websites will be indicated at the bottom of each page
Articles new to this book will have nothing at the bottom of the page

BEFORE WE START   7

Missing out on life's most important journey

(or, What's really wrong with the world and how you can help fix it)

There are a few bad people in the world but not many and none of them are reading this. They skip over pages like this because they already have decided that the only way to get what they want out of life is what we call the Dagger or DAG approach—Dominate, Attack and Grab.

Of course, we all have a little bit of that in us, but most of us do not let it turn us into aggressive, heartless Dagger people. Instead we take a normal, reasonable approach to life most of the time. All we want is to stick with the same default settings all humans are born with—the ordinary desires to manage our own lives, escape pain and enjoy the things we want to enjoy.

This is realistic. It doesn't mean we will get our own way all the time. It means we expect reasonable freedom to set our own goals, boundaries and schedule and choose our own relationships and obligations.

While we do that, we would like to make a positive difference in the world too. We may not be as good as people like Mother Teresa who sacrifice their whole lives for others but we admire them and lean as far as we can in being like them.

We could be a lot more like them if it weren't for those nasty Dagger people. Our big problem in life, as we learn at about the age of two, is that even though there are only a few real Dagger people in the world,

from https://syncx.org

everybody has a Dagger streak in them.When people show that streak, inflicting pain on us or interfering with what we want to enjoy, we learn to fight back. We exclude them from our group, retaliate against their attacks and guard our things more the next time. We call this growing up, gaining adult levels of suspicion and self-defence.

The change we would love to see in the world would be for people in general to suppress their Dagger streak more, and maybe even for some of the Dagger people to get a total personality makeover. Oppression and crime would drop. Cheating and abuse would die down to manageable levels. We wouldn't have to be so defensive all the time: A better world would arrive.

But Jesus says our analysis is all wrong. According to him the real problem with the world is not the few Dagger people or even the Dagger streak in the rest of us. It's the whole approach to life that masses of normal people see as realistic, grown-up and good.

What's wrong with growing up?

The so-called grown-up approach to life has adult levels of suspicion and self-defence, but as we all know, it isn't perfect. It involves inflicting pain in order to teach other people not to inflict pain on us. Sometimes this fails or even backfires.

We retaliate to teach people a lesson, but they are such slow learners. Oppressors don't want to learn they are oppressive. Racists don't want to stop denying their racism. Prisoners can all tell us why they don't belong in prison. When ordinary people occasionally act like Dagger people, they usually find an excuse for it.

If we retaliate against people when they don't think they did anything wrong, they think we are the Dagger people. We know they are wildly misjudging us and our motives because all we are doing is self-defence. When we remind them that they deserved our retaliation, they get even more upset with us. This goes

into a downward spiral of accusation and counter-accusation and it produces the world as we know it.

Self-defence turns out to be a full-time job. We don't have time or energy to do even half of the good we would like to do for the world, and the little good we get done often gets undone by the Dagger people. We settle for managing our own lives in our own interests, including other people's interests as far as possible except for the real Dagger people, whom we condemn and exclude. The world is what it is and we are stuck in it with each person and group trying to make the best of a bad situation, looking out for their own welfare.

But are we missing something? Is our 'realistic grown-up' view actually unaware about a way this could all change? Suppose the human default settings we were born with, the ones that were reinforced in preschool, the ones that look justified and mostly harmless, the ones we take for granted about our own welfare—suppose there was a way they could be flipped to a position that would change the world as we know it into a world that would be better for everybody.

What way? Clue me in.

You may not like the sound of this, but it is not our idea as writers of this book. It is the high risk, counter-intuitive approach to life that Jesus summed up in this amazing double oxymoron, *'If you try to hang on to your life, you will lose it. But if you give up your life for my sake, you will save it.'* (Luke 9:24)

Many people have no idea that Jesus ever said any such thing. When they first hear it, they are unsure what he meant by it. What life was he talking about? How do we hold onto it or give it up for his sake? What does it mean to lose it or save it?

The life we lose is a life unaffected by Jesus, the life we just described as the 'grown-up' life. We lose the self-centred pattern we were born with, looking out for our own welfare as best we can and using as much self-defence as necessary. To give up that life for the sake of Jesus means to get connected to him through the Holy Spirit, following his guidance on a daily basis. It is listening to his voice inside us rather than our own ideas about what is best.

If we accept his call, we embark with him on the Messianic Pilgrimage, a journey away from our human default settings through unexplored territory into the territory he rules. This is a long pilgrimage of discovering in our daily experience what Jesus meant by losing and finding life, moving from darkness to light, from the world as it is to the world as it will be.

From our first step on this pilgrimage, we are leaving our old life of self-management and self-defence behind. We stop making our own calculations about how best to avoid pain and enjoy our lives. We stop trying to develop and defend our own little kingdoms. We stop living like people who are clueless that there even is a Messiah who is on the move and who is calling us to move with him.

In other words, pilgrims fall in love with the resurrected, living Jesus, with his pilgrimage and with other pilgrims. *This is life's most important change—from clueless to clued in, from managing life in our own interests to letting the Messiah give us our assignments as part of his campaign for a better world.*

Our pilgrimage of discovery is our new life, or the start of it. The pilgrimage leads to the ultimate life that will be ours when we see the Messiah face to face instead of only through his Spirit or in visions. But we already are getting more and more connected as we walk along with the Spirit and our fellow pilgrims, all of us connected, all trusting the Messiah to lead us into a new life that really is life.

Don't expect an easy pilgrimage. The Messiah's route may take us into a lot of pain, suffering and undeserved disgrace. Some pilgrims may give up because the Messiah's path is too painful for them. They turn their backs on the Messiah and resume managing their own lives so they have less pain. But the true pilgrims see the journey through to the end, and they discover that the pilgrimage is worth it, the Messiah is reliable and the life we discover beyond the pain is far more soul-satisfying than the life we had when we were focused on avoiding pain.

So life comes down to one huge question: Do we trust Jesus enough to let him lead us on his Messianic Pilgrimage even though it may be very hard? If we do, we swap our current self-managed life for a new connected life, led by the Messiah's Spirit one day at a time. *Jesus the Messiah promises it will be our best swap ever. Why bet our life against him?*

So how do I join the pilgrimage?

It's all about listening. Jesus is still alive, still calling people who are more passionate about his pilgrimage than anything else.

We tell Jesus we have heard his call to leave our old independent life and follow him on his pilgrimage. He can hear us any time, anywhere, in whatever words we want to use.

It might be as short and personal as, 'OK, Jesus, I'm listening. Please sign me up for the pilgrimage. Where do I start?' Some other things you may want to say as you sign up:

- Get me off to a good start. This seems overwhelming

- I don't have what it takes to do this on my own. Give me strength.

- Please connect me to a few fellow pilgrims I can share the journey with and learn with. Keep me from letting the group down or bringing any shame on you as our guide.

- Please make me fit to be called a member of your pilgrim band.

- Change my attitudes. Get my focus off myself and onto connecting, healing, and blessing

- Forgive me for not listening to your guidance before. I was all wrapped up in my own little world. I'm leaving that now.

- Develop my skills so I can follow your instructions well and be an asset to the whole group.

Maybe we have never said any of these things before. We either didn't hear him calling us to the pilgrimage or we didn't pay attention.

But now we are getting serious, committing to listen to whatever he tells us as the Guide, not arguing with him about the best path or causing trouble in the group. We have given up building our personal kingdoms. We will leave that all behind. His guidance is now more important to us than our own power or welfare. Life means listening for that.

FAQs

How do we listen for Jesus?

Jesus guides us on the pilgrimage in two ways—written and unwritten. We read the written guidance in the Bible.

The unwritten guidance is personal and different for each person each day. The unwritten guidance tells us what our personal assignments are in God's campaign. We get this step-by-step guidance as we listen to the Spirit of God, sent by Jesus to live in us and keep us in touch with him.

The Spirit puts these assignments into our minds and hearts. We can look at them as errands that Jesus tells us to do for the good of the other pilgrims or the people whose territory we are passing through.

The Spirit's voice is like the voice of our conscience but more like a coach than a judge. The Spirit talks to each of us in just the right tone, telling us whatever we need to know at each phase of the journey.

As we read the Bible and listen to the Spirit, other pilgrims listen with us. At the start, pilgrims may be totally clueless about the Bible, the Spirit or how to discuss things with other pilgrims, but we get better at it.

As we continue reading the Bible we learn from the stories of pilgrims who have gone before us, even those before the Messiah lived on earth. They had the same struggle we do—how to change their default independent settings and enter the new life God wanted them to live.

We also learn that our original human settings were actually to connect, heal and bless others. Our forefathers switched them to independent (self-manage, escape pain and enjoy what we want). We need to restore those original defaults, looking forward to the new world—the connected, healed and blessed world—that is described at the end of the Bible.

Will this mean I have to become all religious?

Does 'losing my life' mean I won't use a smartphone, watch movies, stay in fashion, get an education, raise a family or respect the government?

No, but it means we will change the way we look at all those things now. For example, when we were self-managing our life, our smartphone was a huge help. We could always go onto our phone to escape pain and boredom, choose whatever we wanted to enjoy and communicate our wishes or instructions to anyone.

On the Messianic Pilgrimage we do not see our phone that way. Now we see it as something that sometimes helps us carry out the things the Messiah is telling us to do but at other times interferes with hearing and obeying him. When he gives us an assignment to help someone, we should not answer, 'Just as soon as I finish this level!'

from https://syncx.org

What about all the other people working for a better world?

Is the Messianic Pilgrimage one of many ways of working for a better world? We all know of people who lay down their self-managed lives not for Jesus but simply for the good of others. They may throw their whole lives into the good cause they adopt. Often they do a lot of good in the process but their passion for their cause can also carry them away, making them self-righteous, pushy or even violent about it.

There is an ugly lesson from history about this. It was not Dagger people who killed Jesus. Nor was it people who were just minding their own business and trying to do their best in managing their lives. The killers were people defending causes and power systems they thought were good for the world. They saw Jesus as a threat and they stopped at nothing to eliminate him.

We still see this pattern. Some people who support good causes start demonising their enemies, seeking more power and dominating others. They become the problem while seeing themselves as the solution.

Jesus had a very specific technique to keep his followers from falling into those traps as they supported his cause but it can't be summarised easily. We will explain it later in the book.

Other reasons to join?

- **Neutralise the Dagger people.** The pilgrimage works for us no matter how the Dagger people respond. Jesus does not guarantee that they will change or that we will be protected from all their attacks. He guarantees that in the pilgrimage we will find a new life, and we do.

- **The world gets better.** By changing our approach to life we break the cycle of accusation and counter-accusation that plagues the world as we know it. We never get misjudged to be Dagger people because we don't rely on self-defence the way they do.

- **It's free.** The new life is all free to pilgrims. We don't have to earn it or create it. Jesus puts it there for us on a platter. We simply open ourselves up to the influence of his Spirit and start going where the Messiah instructs us to go.

Do we trust Jesus enough to let him lead us on his Messianic Pilgrimage even though it may be very hard?

Preparation: A different kind of pilgrimage

A pilgrimage has been part of the religious side of human life for centuries, be it the pilgrimage to Mecca every Muslim should make, Catholic pilgrimages to places like Lourdes, Hindu pilgrimages to places like Puri, Rameswaram, Dwarka and Badrinath or Buddhist pilgrimages to Lumbini and… the list goes on.

The Messianic Pilgrimage is a different kind of pilgrimage.

1. **It has no geographic destination.** It is a lifelong journey from our old self to our new self. We were in our own personal 'kingdoms', running our own lives for our own interests. Now we are listening to the Messiah as he guides us to discover his life and his kingdom.

2. **The destination fulfills our new desire not our old ones.** When we reach his kingdom where our new self is at home, it will not be a life of enjoying whatever we want to enjoy. That was the goal of the old independent life we left behind. The new goal is to be caught up in the Messiah and his purpose to connect, heal, and bless the world. That is the new kind of pilgrim life that Jesus gives. We start enjoying some of it with the Messiah and our fellow pilgrims during the pilgrimage.

3. **On this pilgrimage we care about the welfare of the local residents.** Pilgrims usually avoid locals because pilgrims have only one thing on their minds—getting to their destination. Maybe they stop to buy a few supplies but that is only for their own benefit as travellers. They don't delay their trip by taking any interest in the lives of the local people. But our Messiah keeps sending us out among the local people to listen to them, feel their pain, heal them and bless them. He says we have plenty of time for that.

4. **On this pilgrimage we recruit more pilgrims.** The Messiah passionately wants more pilgrims. It's not that he is trying to impress anyone with the size of his group or that he needs a bigger group in order to conquer something. He wants more pilgrims because he knows that all the locals along the pilgrimage route are doomed if they stay where they are. He wants them to join him for their own good.

But can local people ever trust a passing foreigner who wants to recruit them? Does the Messiah really have their good in mind? Will they really have full rights as new citizens in the land at the end of the Messianic Pilgrimage, which he claims is his kingdom? Or is the whole thing a trick like the trick of foreign recruiters who promise young women good jobs in a foreign country but trap them in prostitution when they get there?

And is their homeland really doomed as he says? Isn't staying put in their familiar locality the safest thing to do, the most likely way to save their lives in the long term? It feels much safer than a pilgrimage through unknown territory.

The Messiah knows that to win the trust of suspicious locals he has to do more than talk. That is why he sends his pilgrims to take time with locals, to listen and help them. The locals notice this, of course, and they get curious. They have never seen any pilgrims like the Messiah's pilgrims. Their suspicions die down and their ears are opened up for the Messiah's call to join him.

And the call is extremely interesting. It is about the difference between reality and illusion. The Messiah claims that things are not what they seem. He says that people are living with illusory life, illusory honour, illusory identity, illusory freedom, illusory power, illusory mercy, illusory rest and illusory vision. The real versions of all those things are found by connecting with the Messiah during and after the Messianic Pilgrimage.

The illusory versions will all turn out to be empty, and those who trusted them will lose everything. The Messiah does not want that to happen to anyone and neither do his pilgrims. They call people to find real life, real honour, etc by joining the Messiah on his pilgrimage and leaving their illusions behind.

The pilgrim recruitment strategy gets described a little differently in each area along the route so it is more convincing to the people of that area. For example, people concerned with Freedom think freedom is the most important thing in life, and they work hard to get it and keep it. Among them the pilgrims go into more detail about real freedom that is only found in the Messiah. Among those driven by Honour we go into details about real honour. (We call these areas seasons of the pilgrimage—the season of Life, the season of Honour, the season of Freedom, etc).

That is what the rest of this book is about—details about the way the Messiah exposes illusions of honour, freedom, power, in fact, everything we thought mattered in life. He replaces them with the realities that save peoples' lives.

When people first join the pilgrimage, it may seem odd to them to have to take time with locals and try to recruit them. It feels like a distraction from the pilgrimage. Gradually they realise that the Messiah, their leader, cares as much about how they act during the pilgrimage as he cares about them reaching the destination.

During the pilgrimage they are already becoming the new people they will be fully when they reach their destination. The process of the pilgrimage changes them.

If one of these values is most important to you: life, honour, identity, freedom, power, mercy or vision, you may want to go to that chapter of the book first. Any chapter may be read alone.

Preparation: Cost of the journey

We are used to the cost of journeys these days – paying for air fare, train fare or the petrol for our vehicle. Often there may be hotels or AirBnB and food to pay for. Sometimes we need to find someone to look after our house or pets while we are gone.

As we prepare for the Messianic Pilgrimage the first command we need obey is to count the cost and then follow him.

'But don't begin until you count the cost. For who would begin construction of a building without first calculating the cost to see if there is enough money to finish it? Otherwise, you might complete only the foundation before running out of money, and then everyone would laugh at you. They would say, "There's the person who started that building and couldn't afford to finish it!"'

'Or what king would go to war against another king without first sitting down with his counselors to discuss whether his army of 10,000 could defeat the 20,000 soldiers marching against him? And if he can't, he will send a delegation to discuss terms of peace while the enemy is still far away. So you cannot become my disciple without giving up everything you own.'

Luke 14:28-33

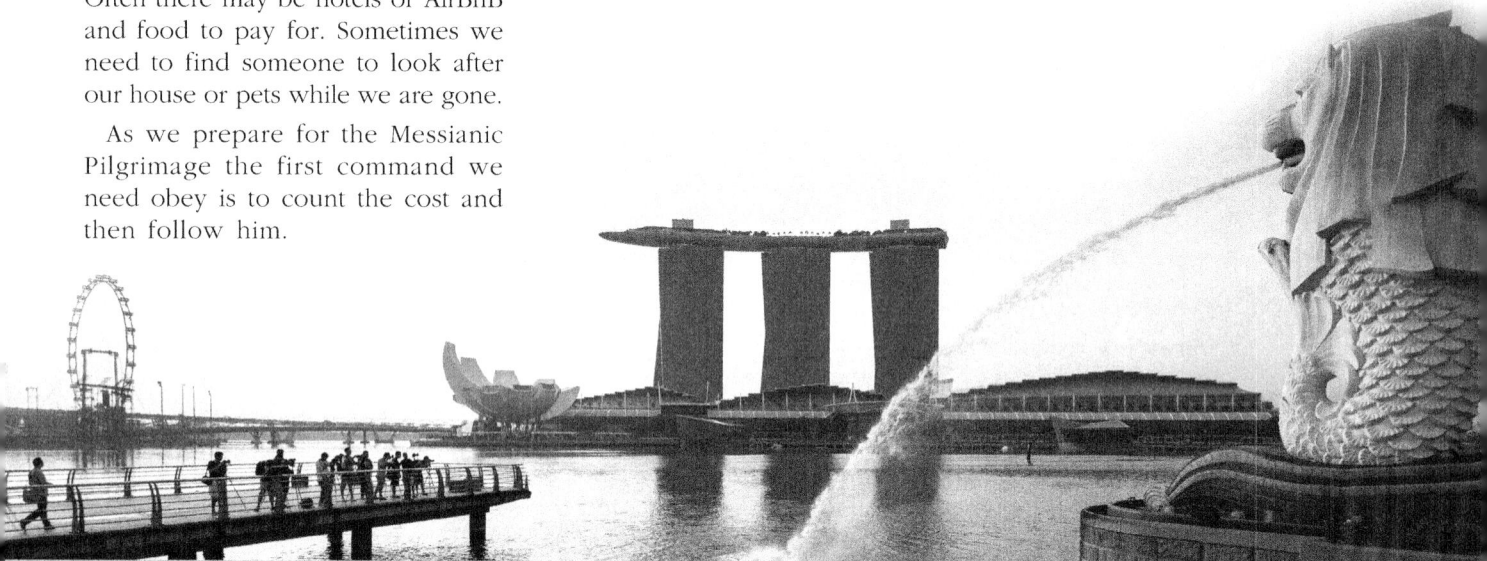

Going with the Messiah on his pilgrimage may make our lives more difficult. Some of our family and friends may oppose the whole idea. We might lose our jobs. The Messiah said the pilgrimage is not an easy path and few follow it.

> 'If you love your father or mother more than you love me, you are not worthy of being mine; or if you love your son or daughter more than me, you are not worthy of being mine. If you refuse to take up your cross and follow me, you are not worthy of being mine. If you cling to your life, you will lose it; but if you give up your life for me, you will find it.'
>
> Matthew 10:37-39

The cost of the Messianic Pilgrimage may be very high, but the cost of not taking it may be even higher. The Messiah warns that we can lose everything if we do not come on the pilgrimage.

To go or not to go? It is a huge decision.

> 'Anyone who listens to my teaching and follows it is wise, like a person who builds a house on solid rock. Though the rain comes in torrents and the floodwaters rise and the winds beat against that house, it won't collapse because it is built on bedrock. But anyone who hears my teaching and doesn't obey it is foolish, like a person who builds a house on sand. When the rains and floods come and the winds beat against that house, it will collapse with a mighty crash.'
>
> Matthew 7:24-27

Preparation: Who will join you?

As we have seen, the Messiah's first command to potential pilgrims was 'Come along with me' having counted the cost of doing so. His second was 'Count the cost'. Now we come to his third, 'Bring others with you'.

We may be glad to hear this third command since a pilgrimage isn't something we want to do alone. It can be fascinating, scary and sometimes long. We want some company.

One of the Messiah's main purposes for coming to earth was to connect people to each other, uniting them around him and his pilgrimage. You can start doing that now, if you wish, by choosing friends or family members you would like to join you as you explore this book. Bringing friends is a way of honouring the Messiah as you set out on the pilgrimage yourself.

This is precisely what Andrew, one of the first followers of the Messiah did: *'Andrew, Simon Peter's brother, was one of these men who heard what John said and then followed Jesus. Andrew went to find his brother, Simon, and told him, "We have found the Messiah" (which means Christ). Then Andrew brought Simon to meet Jesus.'* (John 1:40-42)

The Messiah has designed the pilgrimage experience to bond you with the fellow pilgrims you bring. In fact, we could describe it as a pilgrimage of 'life, liberty and the pursuit of harmony'. We seek to harmonise our lives with the Messiah and the others on the journey as he leads us to freedom and life in all its fullness. Don't you have some friends who would love to be part of that with you?

A pilgrim gets connected in three ways: Firstly directly to the Messiah, secondly to other pilgrims and thirdly to other people from our country or culture and those we interact with on the way.

Of course, during a pilgrimage we meet all kinds of people. Some are like us. Some are very different from anyone we have met before. This is one of the amazing things about the Messiah—he can connect with all kinds of people himself and he can bring them into peace with each other as fellow pilgrims, even those who have been hating each other.

'I have other sheep that are not of this sheep pen. I must bring them also. They too will listen to my voice, and there shall be one flock and one shepherd.' (John 10:16).

If you want to keep hating people or groups whom you have always hated, do not join the Messianic Pilgrimage. The Messiah will tell you not to hate them. He may even connect you with some of them. Then you will have to defy him and leave the pilgrimage in disgrace. It is better not to join in the first place.

Even during the pilgrimage the people who are not like us may not be doing the pilgrimage exactly like we are. The Messiah knows each pilgrim and he directs each pilgrim in

Get Connected!

the way that is best for him or her. Each pilgrim listens to the Messiah. No pilgrim tells another pilgrim, 'You are wrong because you are not following the Messiah the way he told me to follow him'.

For example, we may come to a hill. The Messiah may tell one of us to take the path around the right of the hill and the other around the left of the hill. He knows the paths will meet on the other side. We trust what he knows, and we don't tell the other person he is on the wrong path.

Sometimes these different paths relate to different cultures. What Jesus tells pilgrims in one culture to do may look wrong to pilgrims from another culture. But each culture only sees part of the picture while the Messiah sees the whole thing. He knows exactly what he is doing and it is beautifully flexible so it can include people from all cultures.

For example, Middle Eastern and North American cultures are very different. The main part of this book (Part One) uses 'Messianic Pilgrimage' language to help Middle Easterners follow the Messiah. The supplement (Part Two) uses 'SYNC' language (See Yourself iN Christ) which is more appropriate for North American cultures. We have included both parts to show that following the Messiah is similar in each culture but not exactly the same. This paradox of all being pilgrims, harmonised with each other, yet all following slightly different paths is something unique to the way of Christ.

Even within one culture, the paths of different individuals will be a little different. This does not mean we each may choose the path we like best and any path we choose will be fine. No, we must each listen to the Messiah about the path he has for us, even the parts of the path that we may not like.

Preparation: A clean start

Ritual or spiritual washing

A psalm of David says, *'Who may climb the mountain of the LORD? ...Only those whose hands and hearts are pure'* (Psalm 24:3-4). Many religions have forms of ritual washing: Muslims, for instance, before each time of prayer.

The Messiah undertook a form of ritual washing before starting out on his pilgrimage. It was not by running water over parts of his body but a total immersion in the river Jordan (Matthew 3:13-17). This he did as an example of how we should also prepare ourselves.

The ritual body washings remind us that we must be clean in our hearts as we approach God. We must be spiritually ready. That is what the Messiah's example shows us—being ready for God to guide us and work through us by his Spirit.

The Spirit of God came down on Jesus like a dove when he was immersed. After he completed his time on earth, he sent the same Spirit onto his followers, not as a dove but like a fire on their heads (Acts 2:1-40). Then they were spiritually ready for their pilgrimage—cleansed by God's forgiveness and empowered by God's Spirit.

That is how we make a clean start to our pilgrimage too. We ask for and accept the two gifts that only the Messiah can give us—God's forgiveness and his Spirit.

How do we do that? Not by a bodily washing but by a prayer from our hearts. We use the one prayer that the Messiah taught his pilgrims to pray. See next page.

A prayer before we start

This prayer is the start of our pilgrimage and we will keep praying it all the time as we travel. It keeps us respectfully in touch with the Messiah and his mission, listening to his voice and depending on his strength.

Some pilgrims may desire to practise some form of ritual body washing as they use the Pilgrim Prayer. Others may not. Either is fine as long as we use the prayer he gave us to clean up our hearts. It focuses us on him and the pilgrimage he has for us.

The Pilgrim Prayer
aka the Lord's Prayer,
paraphrased by Stan Nussbaum.
See Part Two on SYNCx
for more details.

Our Father in heaven,

please light up our pilgrim path just as you light up heaven.

May all of us pilgrims honour you,

stick together under your leadership

and carry out all your assignments.

Please give us all enough to eat as we travel

and don't make us pay for wronging you

like we don't make people pay for wronging us.

Don't put us into situations along the way that will test our limits

but set us free from evil inside and out.

Yes, come King Jesus and be our Guide!

You are the Messiah, the Light who connects, heals and blesses the world.

You have the power. You get the glory now and forever.

Bring it on!

PART ONE
a journey of discovery for pilgrims and potential pilgrims

The first part is aimed at giving a flavour of what the Messianic Pilgrimage is about for the average pilgrim. It is culturally orientated towards the Middle East and North Africa. It's starting from basics and introduces people to the ideas, assuming little or no knowledge of the Messiah or the Bible.

Alongside this in the second part is SYNC which is the same ideas but contextualised for North America. This gives you some idea how it can be approached in radically different societies.

WHERE TO NOW?

The Messianic Pilgrimage is a pilgrimage through time we celebrate on a repeating cycle every year. Because we're trying to encourage Arabic speakers and Muslims in this pilgrimage we follow the Hijri calendar which has 12 lunar months. Each season in the pilgrimage lasts either one or two lunar months.

Jesus referred to himself as the 'Light of the World' and each season reflects something of that light.

The sequence starts at creation and ends at the vision of the return of the Messiah in glory.

In this book each season will have a section dedicated to it: Within each season there is a miscellany of materials, some we have used in the past and some are new to this book.

Whatever you call youself —a Christian or a Muslim or something else— we hope you can use these in your lifelong Messianic Pilgrimage.

Messianic Pilgrimage

VISION · LIFE · HONOUR · IDENTITY · FREEDOM · POWER · MERCY · REST STOP

There are seven main seasons taking us from life in creation through to the vision before us of the coming of the Messiah in glory when we will continue sharing eternity with him and other pilgrims.

Alongside this there is a season we call the Rest Stop: Contemplation, counting the cost of the pilgrimage and thinking of the journey ahead.

We repeat this cycle each year as a circle around the Messiah sharing the journey with him; both the joys and the struggles.

We could see this as a spiral rather than a cycle as we grow closer to the Messiah, yet when we receive the power of the Holy Spirit maybe the spiral is outwards. To be passionate for God means to participate passionately in what he is passionate about, and that is about going out to connect, heal, and bless the world.

Eight ground-breaking acts of God

	Ground-breaking event	Before the event	After the event
Life	God created the universe	There was nothing	We live in an amazing world
Honour	Jesus predicted persecution for his followers	We thought honour and shame were always earned	Undeserved shame may be part of our assignment or mission
Identity	God created his own nation/people	God dealt with all peoples on the same basis	God has a special assignment for each particular people/group
Freedom	Jesus launched the freedom era	Control was oppressive (unless we had it)	Control is liberating (we don't need to have it)
Power	The Holy Spirit was poured out	We tried to be good	We open up to God's influence
Mercy	Jesus presented the final sacrifice	We focused on justice for ourselves	We overflow with mercy for others
Rest Stop	God rested and ordained rest	Work was central to our lives	We have time to ponder why we are here
Vision	Jesus will return to make the world perfect	We couldn't see God or his perfect world	We partly see the perfect world arriving but one day we will see it totally

Taking ground-breakers personally

Each season has a ground-breaking event linked to it. To sync with these ground-breaking events means that we take them seriously and personally. As we do, we begin to see how they change the way we have been answering many other basic questions about life:

1. Where did everything we see come from?

2. Whose honour do we seek most? Whose shame do we fear most?

3. What do we belong to that is bigger than we are? How did we get in?

4. What guarantees that we can live our lives as free people?

5. How do we find the strength to make a difference in the world?

6. What kind of terms are we on with God, and how did that happen?

7. When may we rest? How do we rest?

8. What is our destiny? How do we know we will reach it?

As we discover new answers to these questions, we also discover that we are becoming new people. The new me realises that life is a pilgrimage and we are on it.

Jesus the Messiah is our guide, holding us all together. Under his direction we participate in it, trusting him to bring us safely to our destination. Meanwhile we enjoy the benefits of being in sync with the Messiah—security, significance, goodness, self-respect and much more. This is the way to live!

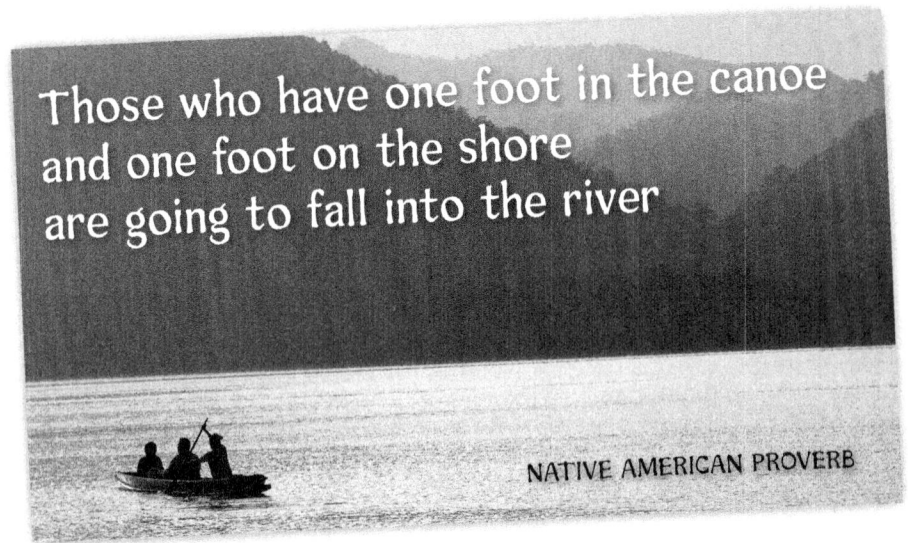

Those who have one foot in the canoe and one foot on the shore are going to fall into the river

NATIVE AMERICAN PROVERB

1

LIFE SEASON

GOD SAW EVERYTHING THAT HE HAD MADE AND IT WAS VERY GOOD....-

The Life Rhythm we focus on during Life Season

God is a life-giver, the source of everything we see--our bodies, our planet, our universe.

God loves life, and he loves to give it. To him the universe is like a flower garden or a playground. He is creative and he is good to the core. He loves to promote life in all its forms, and he sets himself up against anything that demeans, reduces or destroys what he has created.

The Bible is more about life in this world than it is about religion and the afterlife. The biblical story is much more about how to live in this world than how to prepare for the next one.

The other half of the big idea of Life Season

The forces of death are running loose in our world, and people don't agree on who to blame or what to do about it.

The world as we see it today is obviously messed up. The forces of death are doing their worst, and they seem to be getting away with a lot of it. Why doesn't God do something about it?

Actually he is, but it's not the quick fix that people are looking for from him, so lots of people conclude he isn't doing anything at all. Or perhaps they think all he is doing is a little damage limitation by sending a few

religious leaders like Jesus to urge people to be better and kinder.

They do not see that God is furious about every attack of death against life and he has master-minded a global campaign to deal with it. The Bible tells us how he is executing his plan through Jesus and the Holy Spirit continuing till today.

Why hasn't God's campaign succeeded yet? Because timing is everything. On God's calendar we are living in a global grace period. God's campaign strategy for the present time is to hand out second chances and third and fourth and fifth... It looks like the forces of evil are getting away with everything but when the grace period ends they will be wiped out and everything else will be connected, healed and blessed.

In the meantime our job is to listen to God and carry out the assignments he gives us to promote authentic life. We already have one foot in that glorious future life, and we get to show the world some of what it will look like.

THE BIG IDEA

Of course, that puts a target on our backs because the forces of death don't like us saying their days are numbered. They promote their own views of who to blame and how to make a better world.

Bottom line of the big idea

We see ourselves in Christ as life-bringers, participating in God's campaign to reconnect the world with his Life, to heal all wounds and to bless everyone we can, even if we have to give our lives in the process.

In sync with Jesus, we are connected to life itself. *'Whoever has the Son has life; whoever does not have God's Son does not have life.'* (1 John 5:12)

When we SYNC (See Yourself iN Christ) as a life-bringer, we realise we are participating in the life-giving, life-healing, life-restoring campaign of Christ. That is our cause. We are caught up in it, energised by it and delighted every time we have even a small success.

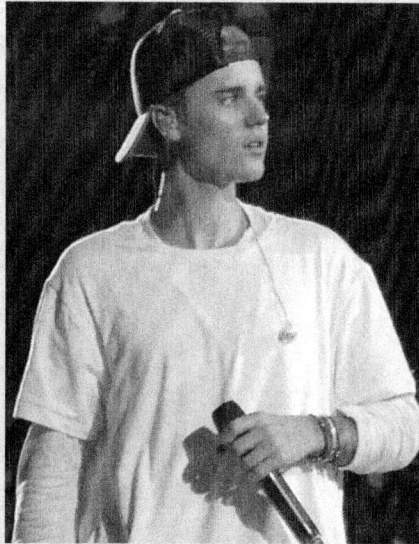

'Many people would mistake me for a religious man, which I am not.'

Bieber is a Canadian singer. He was born in 1994, in London, Ontario. He is the son of Jeremy Jack Bieber and Pattie Mallette. Mallette's mother Diane and stepfather Bruce helped her raise her son.

Although Bieber says he's not religious, he does claim, 'I am however

PILGRIMS
alongside us
Justin Beiber

in love with the one who created me. I believe Jesus is the saviour of humanity and that His love is what changes us. I believe that the brokenness of humanity pains God and that He sent an answer and provided hope in Jesus… my advice is to steer clear of religion, but put your hope in the eternal one who died an excruciating death so that you and I could truly live on for eternity.'

When faced with facial paralysis in 2022, Beiber didn't avoid the reality of it but shared his journey through it. 'I'm reminded he [Jesus] knows all of me. He knows the darkest parts of me… and he constantly welcomes me into his loving arms.'

'This has given me peace during this horrific storm that I'm facing.'

The story of creation

The oldest myth or story of creation comes from the Enuma Eliš – stone tablets on which is inscribed the Babylonian story of creation.

The story tells of the gods, but not how they came into being. Before anything existed there was Apsû from whom everything was begotten through Tia-mat. From these two all the gods were born. There was disorganised matter and from this confusion of matter the gods created everything we know as the universe. There is a battle between some of the gods and Apsû is killed. This results in a war among the gods. In the death of Tia-mat tears come from her eyes as the river Tigris and the river Euphrates.

Quingu, the god who instigated the war among the gods is tried, found guilty and executed. From his remains humanity is created:

'I will bring together blood to form bone, I will bring into being human being, whose name shall be "man". I will create a human—man—on whom the toil of the gods will be laid that they may rest...'

From his blood he (Ea) created human beings, on whom he imposed the service of the gods, and set the gods free. After the wise Ea had created humanity and had imposed the service of the gods upon them—that task is beyond comprehension.'

The story has some similarities to the story in Genesis, enough to suggest that the writers of Genesis were familiar with the Enūma Eliš. But... and there is a big but... the stories also show significant variance. The Biblical version centres on one true God. But the core difference is the place of human beings.

In the Babylonian version humanity is created to serve the gods

In the Babylonian version, human beings are created to serve the gods and it is an ongoing burden for people. In the Biblical version God created the universe and brought order out of chaos with a greater ease than Apsû or Marduk (his successor) could have imagined.

Then God said, 'Let us make human beings in our image, to be like us. They will reign over the fish in the sea, the birds in the sky, the livestock, all the wild animals on the earth, and the small animals that scurry along the ground.'

So God created human beings in his own image.

In the image of God he created them; male and female he created them.

Then God blessed them and said, 'Be fruitful and multiply. Fill the earth and govern it. Reign over the fish in the sea, the birds in the sky, and all the animals that scurry along the ground.'

Then God looked over all he had made, and he saw that it was very good!

Genesis 1: 26-28, 31

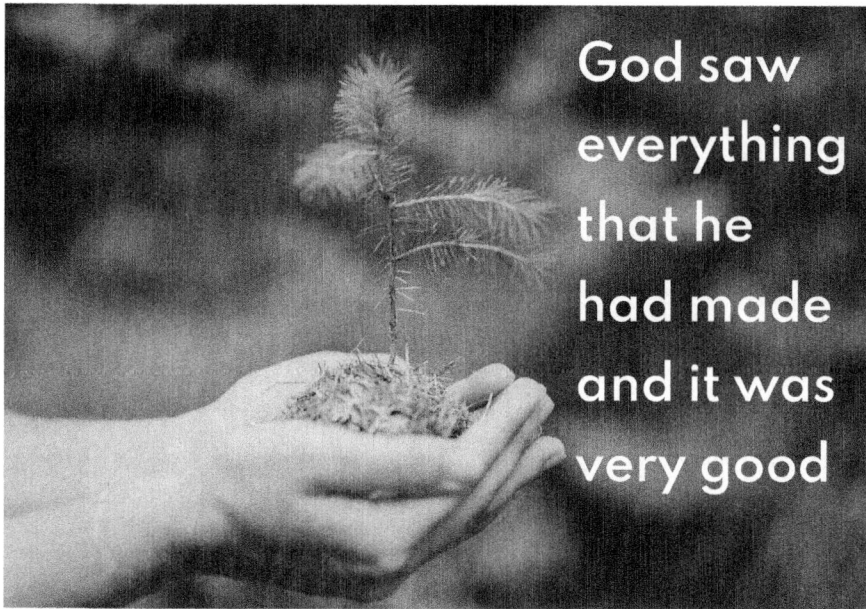

God saw everything that he had made and it was very good

The biblical story shows God walking and talking with the first people as friends. Whereas the Enūma Eliš shows people as slaves of the gods, having little value. The biblical story shows people as the climax of creation, with a very special relationship to the one true God.

In this first phase of the Messianic Pilgrimage, the season of Life when we celebrate creation, we need to remember that though God created everything, we are the pinnacle of creation and we can enjoy a very special relationship with God.

The moon is born anew, يولد القمر من جديد

washed with the sun, مغسولا بالنور

and showered with starlight. ورذاذ النجوم

The world becomes green, يغدو العالم أخضر

winter solstice abandoned. فالشتاء قد راح إلى حال سبيله

And so, I look toward the sun. وأقبل المصيف

I listen gently to the earth. أرهفْ سمعك للأرض

It spins. وهي تدور

Its axis tilting to the sun, إنها محور الشمس

endowing seasons. هبة الفصول

Oh God, we hear you, أرهف سمعك لله

constant as forever. ثابت هو إلى الأبد

And here we dance a pirouette ها نحن نرقص دوّارين

around the seasons of our soul. حول مواسم روحنا

Our back to darkness, ظهرنا إلى الظلام

the light inviting us to follow, وأمامنا النور ينادينا

and join the dance of life. لرقصة الحياة

We are the lesser light, نحن القمر

born anew! وهذا ميلادنا الجديد!

The birth of a lesser light

مولد القمر

THOUGHTS
from Uncle Azis

About two years ago I drove from Fes into the Atlas Mountains. I remember coming round one corner in the road and looking down into the valley and being amazed at the beauty. It was breathtaking.

Years earlier, I had driven up into the mountains of Kurdistan in northern Iraq. So different yet so beautiful.

Years earlier still, I also drove in the Rocky Mountains in America and saw the Grand Canyon. Even the splendour of Gibraltar rising from the sea on the south of Spain gives me a shiver of delight. Mountains are a marvel of God's creation. How great is God that he made all this.

Water has such amazing power. The waterfalls around the world rush tonnes of water gushing over the precipice to tumble and crash below. I've sailed in a storm. The power of the wind and the water terrify me as I realise how small I am in the wide ocean… How great is God that he made all this.

There is a salt lake near us and every year flamingos arrive in the late autumn. The lake usually dries out in the summer and has water in the winter. How do the flamingos know there will be water here? Where have they come from? How did they navigate?

Slowly as they eat the crustaceans in the lake they turn pink. The lake becomes a stunning swathe of colour… How great is God that he made all this!

Yet in all this God cares for you and me. He loves us. Each of us individually. Like a father loves his child. He is our father in heaven. He created this earth for us to enjoy. How great is God!

PILGRIMS *before us?*

'Yes, but…'

Einstein, God and creation

For a very long time there has been a debate between some scientists and those classified as 'religious' who believe in creation. Often they are seen as complete opposites: If you believe in science, you cannot believe in creation and if you believe in creation you cannot believe in science. To each side I have wanted to say 'Yes, but…' In other words it's complex.

Did creation happen in six twenty-four-hour periods as some Muslims and some Christians claim? Was there a 'big bang' that started it all off? Did we evolve, or were we created exactly as we are today?

Recently I came across an article about Albert Einstein. He was possibly one of the foremost scientists of the last century and did a lot of the thinking about how the universe came into being. He didn't reject God and mentioned him many times in his talks and writing. Reading more about him, I'm sure he too would have responded 'Yes, but…'

For example in 1926 he wrote to another physicist Max Born: 'Quantum mechanics is certainly imposing. But an inner voice tells me that this is not yet the real thing. The theory yields much, but it hardly brings us closer to the Old One's secrets. I, in any case, am convinced that he does not play dice.' He is referring to the 'inner voice' of God who is 'the Old One'.

Einstein wondered whether everything was predestined, or whether there was any choice in the cosmic blueprint: 'What really interests me is whether God could have created the world any differently; in other words, whether the requirement of logical simplicity admits a margin of freedom.' That 'margin of freedom' allows us to care for or destroy the earth.

However, to Einstein himself I would also say 'Yes, but…'

An inner voice tells me that this is not yet the real thing

He admired the Dutch philosopher Baruch Spinoza, and wrote: 'I believe in Spinoza's god, who reveals Himself in the lawful harmony of the world, not in a god who concerns himself with the fate and the doings of mankind.'

Translated from Arabic

PROVERBS
about Life

What is life? It is the little shadow which runs across the grass and loses itself in the sunset. NATIVE AMERICAN

Life is already half spent before we know what it is. ITALIAN

God made us and we wonder at it. CUBAN

God often visits us but most of the time we are not at home. FRENCH

How lovely to live for those whom you love. ARABIC

The deep sea can be fathomed, but who knows the hearts of human beings? MALAYSIAN

Yes, but... God is interested in us as human beings, he is interested in the world he created. He is interested in how we treat his creation, his gift to us.

As we celebrate God's creation in this Life Season let us go further than Einstein, remember that God loves us and follow his leading daily on the pilgrimage.

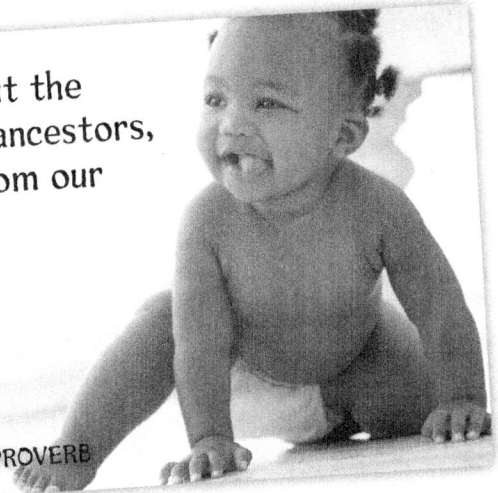

We do not inherit the earth from our ancestors, we borrow it from our children

NATIVE AMERICAN PROVERB

'Whenever I see the suffering that COVID has created—every time I read about the latest death toll or hear about someone who lost their job or drive by a school that is closed—I can't help but think: We don't have to do this again.'

PILGRIMS
alongside us?
Bill Gates

Bill Gates is sometimes criticised as purely motivated by being politically liberal. But maybe he is actually following the Messianic Pilgrim path.

He is without doubt one of the richest men in the world, but stands out as a humanitarian. For example, he gave $400 million to help poor countries in their vaccination programmes. This is the largest single donation by any individual in human history.

Nobody is denying Microsoft's role in transforming the computer from a corporate machine to an affordable family friend. The company is in constant development, but what is greater and more permanent than the company are those human qualities that its founder enjoys.

So who is this Bill Gates?

He is an American citizen born in Seattle, Washington in 1955 of Irish-Scottish descent. Bill Gates was brilliant at maths and science, and his parents recognised his special abilities, so after he finished elementary school they sent him to the prestigious Lakeside Prep School. In 1968 the school decided to buy a computer, a decision that changed the course of life for 13-year-old Bill Gates.

After leaving school Bill Gates entered Harvard, the best university in the United States. But he found that he was not the best at Harvard in mathematics, and his reaction was: 'If I am not the best at mathematics, why should I continue in this field?'

So he left, and with a friend from school started Microsoft. Their motto was: 'Work hard, improve your products and win.'

Ironically, everyone was working hard, day and night, and everyone was wearing jeans and a T-shirt! While going to the meeting with IBM to make the deal that launched Micro-

Translated from Arabic

soft as an empire, Bill Gates realised he was without a tie. So he went to the market and was late for the meeting. He commented, 'It is better to be late than to go (to IBM) without a tie'.

In 1986 Microsoft entered the stock market and he and his business partner Paul Allen became overnight millionaires.

Bill Gates married Melinda Frances Dallas in 1994 and they have three children - Jennifer, Rory and Phoebe. They divorced in August 2021. The family home overlooking Lake Washington was one of the most expensive houses in the world, valued at $113 million in 2002.

Despite this he realised his responsibility: 'Is the world of the rich conscious of how 4 or 6 billion people live? If he is conscious, then the rich should intervene and help them.'

He and Melinda created a foundation with their wealth. In 2000 the Foundation awarded Cambridge University $210 million to the annual Gates Scholarship for students and the Foundation spent more than $7 billion in other aid. According to a

report published by Forbes magazine in 2005, Gates spent more than $28.4 billion on charitable projects and institutions, thus spending a third of the wealth on charitable work.

About creation Bill Gates said 'The mystery and the beauty of the world is overwhelmingly amazing, and there's no scientific explanation of how it came about.' He went on to echo the feelings many people have: 'I think it makes sense to believe in God, but exactly what decision in your life you make differently because of it, I don't know.' (Rolling Stone interview March 2014)

He does not say he receives guidance about life's many decisions from the Messiah, yet he is doing many of the things the Messiah wants people to do. Let us as pilgrims share Bill Gates' concern for the world, and at the same time let us listen to the Spirit of the Messiah guiding us in our decisions all the time.

Creation shows us the Creator who shows us love

Nader Abdel Amir

In my simple understanding of the issue of creation in the Bible, I see that the doctrine of creation does not primarily seek to explain the manner or formation of the existence of the universe. Rather, it seeks, in my opinion, to first reveal the meaning of existence and to clarify that this existence stems from God who is the source of all existence. And science, despite its development, has not been able to explain how the world was formed rationally. It is only able to present theories about how this formation was. Faith explains the intimate relationship between this universe and its Creator.

The Abrahamic religions all tell us in detail about that relationship between the universe and its Creator, which can be summed up in one word: love. Almighty God ascribed love to himself, so one of his names was 'the affectionate one' and he is also the lover. There are many verses in the Qur'an in which Almighty God mentions his love for his pure servants, the repentant, the trustworthy, the patient, and other good qualities of the believers. The Muslim mystics elaborated on the relationship of divine love with the issue of creation. The Bible demonstrates God's love for everyone, good and bad alike. And as the Bible also tells us, people were created not only from a loving Creator, but were created in the image of the loving Creator.

The essence of humanity's existence and the motive for him is love, with all that it means of things. The Apostle Paul expounded on this in his beautiful hymn about love, especially when he says:

> If I had the gift of prophecy, and if I understood all of God's secret plans and possessed all knowledge, and if I had such faith that I could move mountains, but didn't love others, I would be nothing. If I gave everything I have to the poor and even sacrificed my body, I could boast about it; but if I didn't love others, I would have gained nothing.
>
> Love is patient and kind. Love is not jealous or boastful or proud or rude. It does not demand its own way. It is not irritable, and it keeps no record of being wronged. It does not rejoice about injustice but rejoices whenever the truth wins out. Love never gives up, never loses faith, is always hopeful, and endures through every circumstance.
>
> 1 Corinthians 13:2-7

Translated from Arabic

If love is the essence and motive for human creation, then what is the way to make it a daily focus in our lives to ensure the abundant life that God wanted for us on earth? There are three main points:

1. The living relationship between God and humanity, according to John's words in his first epistle: *'We proclaim to you what we ourselves have actually seen and heard so that you may have fellowship with us. And our fellowship is with the Father and with his Son, Jesus Christ.'* (1 John 1:3) and Paul also said, *'May the grace of the Lord Jesus Christ, the love of God, and the fellowship of the Holy Spirit be with you all.'* (2 Corinthians 13:14)

2. The living relationship between people is consistent with the Almighty's saying in the Book of Genesis: *'Then the Lord God said, "It is not good for the man to be alone. I will make a helper who is just right for him."'* (Genesis 2:18) Confirming it in the second great commandment that Jesus said, *'A second is equally important: "Love your neighbour as yourself."'* (Matthew 22:39)

3. Relationship with other creatures: Because human beings have bodies created from the clay of the earth, they are able, capable, and qualified to deal with the rest of the creatures that God created. For this reason God blessed people and gave them authority over the rest of the creatures, as he told in the book of Genesis, where we read: *'Be fruitful and multiply. Fill the earth and govern it. Reign over the fish in the sea, the birds in the sky, and all the animals that scurry along the ground.'* (Genesis 1:28)

THOUGHTS
from Uncle Azis

I love this world that Almighty God created with a paternal feeling towards human beings. I especially love the sea. I believe that God also loves it because more than two thirds of the earth is covered by the sea.

One of the amazing things I do is lie on my back at sea on a clear night and look up at the sky. There you don't see any other light around you but the light from not only the planets and the moon, not just a few stars but millions of millions of stars... or what we call the Milky Way. Almighty God created it all!

Sometimes I am disgusted with what we have made of this world. We who were created by God in his image have done terrible thing. When I travel at sea I see piles of trash floating on the face of the most beautiful seas. In the world news I hear about the devastating wars in Ukraine,

Creation...
and I feel
like crying

Yemen, Syria and Libya. What have we done with God's trusted gift to us, which is the world?

The Internet and social media are littered with news of the fires that broke out in the Amazon rainforest, and no one is interested in addressing the matter. The same can be said about the melting of ice in the polar regions. Although a 19 year-old Swedish student, Greta Thunberg, is educating young people and calling for action to save our planet, we see many people criticising and attacking her as a result. Why don't we pay attention to this world?

There are days when I feel depressed, and I tend to read a type of literature called pathos. It is an emotional expression of pain and pity. It represents more than half of the Psalms of David. This helps me somewhat but it never totally resolves things for me. In my sadness I feel like a person who is on a journey; not a person who has arrived.

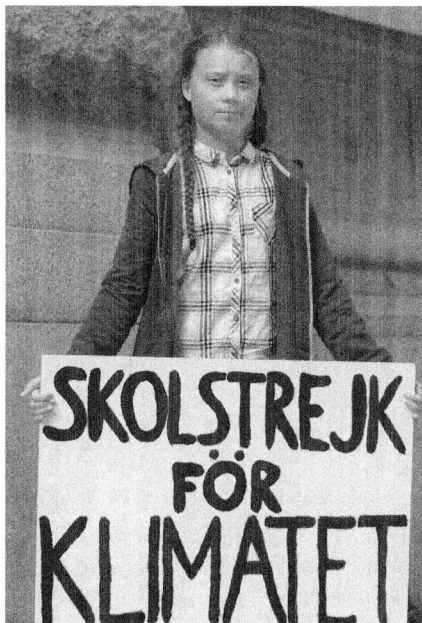

SKOLSTREJK FÖR KLIMATET

The Life season is when we celebrate God's gift of life from creation through to his gift of life to every baby born. It's the starting point for all of us. It's a time of immense joy, and a time of heartache seeing what we are leaving for the next generation.

Remember God created everything and we live in his image

Use the reminder daily to remember the theme of the season. Share it as a greeting in emails, with friends and relatives... wherever you need to focus on the pilgrimage.

THOUGHTS
from Uncle Azis

In the image of a creative God

Creativity is one of those words bandied around to the point where it becomes almost meaningless. What do we actually mean by creativity and why is it important?

We have to go back to the start, where God created the universe and life.

We were created. And we were created in the image of God. God who creates. So we are implicitly creative in the core of our being. And that is important.

Creativity is about making things and about communicating things. When we are thinking about a band of pilgrims then communicating between them is important.

How do we express what we are perceiving on the pilgrimage to others?

There are many ways we human beings communicate: words, stories, music, painting, photography (itself almost a form of painting with light), dance and sculpture.

Some people like to communicate in a structured way, deconstructing ideas to explain the pilgrimage like the mechanics of a car engine. That suits some people but also leads to arguments as life is a lot more complicated than a car engine. Sometimes this is helpful, sometimes not.

Mankind has told myths and stories since the start of time when language existed. We know from cave paintings in South Sulawesi in Indonesia that there were stories, some relating to spirituality. Through carbon dating those paintings are shown to be as old as 44,000 years.

On a journey, we may wish to express to fellow travellers what we are learning. In this book we can only use a limited range of communications: words and pictures. In the words it is mainly stories. And the pictures are only black and white.

But sound, music and moving pictures (video and film) play an important part in our communication. By all means and in every way we should see creativity in what we do. We are after all created in the image of a creative God.

Celebrate Life

So let's get the party started, celebrating with a huge 'Yes' to all five of these things:

Yes, God is proactively bringing heaven's life to earth. He isn't just keeping score and reacting to what we do.

Yes, Christ has put his Spirit, life, and power into his followers, plugging into the life-giving movement that goes all the way back to Abraham.

Yes, I realise my life may get very hard because some people don't want the life I am bringing, but I am trusting Christ and his Spirit to get me through the pain.

Yes, God's whole life-giving plan revolves around the Messiah, the rescuer who makes earth more like heaven and less like hell.

Yes, I am taking my first life-giving step by the Spirit's power — forgiving others like the Messiah has forgiven me.

Each season has a celebration where we say 'Yes' to 5 things about being a pilgrim.

Sing a new song to the Lord! Let the whole earth sing to the Lord! Sing to the Lord; praise his name. Each day proclaim the good news that he saves. Publish his glorious deeds among the nations. Tell everyone about the amazing things he does. Great is the Lord! He is most worthy of praise! He is to be feared above all gods. The gods of other nations are mere idols, but the Lord made the heavens! Honour and majesty surround him; strength and beauty fill his sanctuary.

O nations of the world, recognise the Lord; recognize that the Lord is glorious and strong. Give to the Lord the glory he deserves! Bring your offering and come into his courts.

Worship the Lord in all his holy splendour. Let all the earth tremble before him. Tell all the nations, "The Lord reigns! The world stands firm and cannot be shaken. He will judge all peoples fairly. Let the heavens be glad, and the earth rejoice! Let the sea and everything in it shout his praise! Let the fields and their crops burst out with joy! Let the trees of the forest sing for joy before the Lord, for he is coming! He is coming to judge the earth.

He will judge the world with justice, and the nations with his truth.

(Psalm 96: 1-13)

Readings for this Season

Genesis 1:1-13 Creation, part one

Genesis 1:24-2:3 Creation, part two

Psalm 96:1-13 What life is supposed to be like

Genesis 3:1-9 Death gets its foot in the door

Deuteronomy 30:11-20 The choice of life or death

John 10:1-10 The shepherd of life

Revelation 22:1-7 The river of life and the tree of life

John 1:1-14 The source of Life

2

HONOUR SEASON

A BATTLE BETWEEN LIGHT AND DARK

The Honour Rhythm we focus on during Honour Season:

God is on a campaign to turn his team members into honourable people. The centre of his campaign strategy is Jesus carrying his cross. He inspires us to carry our cross, to honourably endure the world's shame for the sake of his campaign.

The Bible is one long coherent story. The sad pattern repeated through most of this story is that we humans keep disgracing ourselves. Adam and Eve did it, Moses did it, David did it, Israel did it as a nation, even Jesus' followers did it when he was arrested.

Jesus broke that pattern. He was an honourable finisher, faithful to death. He showed us how it is done by following his God-given mission and refusing to let human shame and violence influence him.

By itself, his courageous example does not guarantee we will have what it takes to copy him. But he gives us more. He promises to be with us continuously as we go about our risky, painful mission (Matthew 28:20). He moves into our lives by putting his Spirit into us, connecting us to him constantly.

After he sent the Spirit his followers acted honourably, enduring beatings, mobs, court room trials and even execution. His presence gave them courage and it does the same for us.

The other half of the big idea of Honour Season:

God's campaign strategy for our era is to impress the world with the courage that Jesus puts into his pilgrims. He empowers them to rise above ridicule and opposition from the campaign's enemies. It is impressive that Jesus could do that himself, but if he can empower other people to do it too, that takes amazing to a whole new level.

It is easy to think that Jesus had the courage and faith to carry his cross because he was the Son of God, but that we don't have that courage because we are not God. So we point people to Jesus carrying his cross and deflect attention from ourselves. His courage is admirable whether ours is or not.

But if we think this way, we are out of sync with God's strategy. He already showed the world how much loyalty and courage Jesus had. Now he wants to show the world what ordinary people can do when they hit opposition as his campaign team members. Their loyalty and

THE BIG IDEA

courage show that Jesus is still alive, still empowering people to do things they could not do on their own. It's not just his ancient example but his spiritual power today.

This reassures us, but it also puts an uncomfortable responsibility on us. We have to endure opposition honourably. If we fearfully shirk our assignments in God's campaign, we bring disgrace on ourselves and the Messiah. He said he would give people courage. Our failure makes him look like a liar or a weakling. That is a much greater shame than anything other humans may throw at us.

Bottom line of the big idea of Honour Season:

We see ourselves in Christ as honourable finishers, showing the world that no shame or violence will break our loyalty to the campaign that Christ died for. He was raised to keep leading the campaign team and we live in sync with the personal instructions that he still gives us one day at a time.

Our campaign message is that Jesus the Messiah deserves more honour than anyone else who ever lived. He connects humanity to God. He is the key to global unity, healing and blessing. He is seated on the throne of the universe! (Hebrews 12:2)

But on his way to the throne, he out-suffered us all. He took more physical, legal and personal abuse than we will ever know. And through it all, he never wavered in his commitment to his excruciating assignment as the campaign spearhead. That is heroic and God honoured it.

Jesus defended his honour by not defending it. That is, he showed true honour not by using violence against those who shamed him, but by disregarding the shame, not reacting to it at all. He was focused on God the Father's assignment for him--announcing the beginning of the reign of God on earth through him as the Messiah. He was sentenced to death for this, but even that didn't stop him.

People around us may say we are a disgrace for going on the Messi-anic Pilgrimage, but we don't have to defend our honour by force. The Messiah showed us that the true defence of honour is not violence. It is submission to the will of God, continuing the pilgrimage no matter what, because God wants us on this pilgrimage.

We accept it as our cross, carry it quietly and let worldly people call us losers, if they do. Jesus did, and he is with us by his Spirit, giving us whatever it takes to keep going despite whatever shame we have to get through.

And that is why we stay focused on Jesus, '*the champion who initiates and perfects our faith*'. (Hebrews 12:2) Our faith or trust comes from him and leads us to him. This is the trust that '*defeats this evil world*'. (1 John 5:4) When we look at Jesus carrying the cross, we see God's great paradox. The Messiah looked like a hopeless loser but actually he was on his God-appointed way to his destiny as the ultimate winner.

Chess is a battle of logic between two players. It rarely ends in a draw, usually one side—white or black—must win. It's easy to see history as a game of chess, a battle between good and evil, between God and Satan. We believe the story ends with God winning and good triumphing over evil. In this game we can sometimes see ourselves as the pawns, castles, bishops, knights, kings and queens in this giant game of chess with God and Satan the players with different honour attributed to different pieces.

We always hope we are on the winning side and will end up in heaven or that we won't be sacrificed as a pawn to enable God to win the game. If God is playing this game with us as the pieces we can see everything as being what he determines and we have no control over anything... he decides what we eat, what clothes we put on, whether we are happy or sad...

However, this isn't a game, nor are human beings mere pieces on the board. When damaged, they hurt or die. If it were a game with the result predetermined, then the damage to those players lost even on the winning side is cruel in the extreme.

Is history more than a game? About 5,000 years ago there were cities on the side of evil that were so depraved that God, as a sort of game player on the side of good, decided not merely to remove the pieces from the game board but destroy them entirely.

Ibrahim, a kind and compassionate person, interceded for the righteous living in those cities. Starting at 50, he argued God down to not destroying the cities if there were only ten upright people in them. The story goes that there were not even ten, though Ibrahim's relative Lot and his family survived except for Lot's wife, who perished.

Before that, God had promised to bless all people on earth through Ibrahim. These are not the actions of a puppeteer and marionette. Indeed the prophet Isaiah described Ibrahim as a *'friend of God'*. (Isaiah 41:8) But, being a 'friend of God' is not just for prophets but everyone.

What happens after the game of life is over?

Is it paradise for some and burning in hell for others?

Jesus announced, *'I no longer call you slaves, because a master doesn't confide in his slaves. Now you are my friends, since I have told you everything the Father told me.'* (John 15:15) He gave us honour which we now fulfil walking in his footsteps.

Nevertheless, the idea of a game raises a larger question 'What happens after the game is over?' Is it paradise for some and burning in hell for others? What does paradise mean?

Ibrahim gives us the answer. God promised Ibrahim that he would bless the whole world through him. Ibrahim was described as a 'friend of God' and that tells us this is what God desires to be spread throughout the world—friendship with him! The end of the game, therefore, is about an eternal relationship: sharing food, interdependence and kinship with others and also enjoying this relationship with God.

The idea of a battle (struggle/ jihad) between good and evil, between God and Satan has been around since the beginning of time. But to see history or life as a grand game of chess is to completely and dangerously misunderstand God and history. As a metaphor it simplifies things to the point it can trivialise and hurt those who are suffering. It only tells part of the story. It would be better to see it as a symphony conducted by God looking for harmony in the orchestra. We, as the orchestral players, are God's friends.

Apollo 13 splashes down in the South Pacific on 17 April 1970

There is a difference between daring and courage. Daring is the ability to face danger, pain or attempts to intimidate without any sense of fear. Courage is the ability to do something very difficult or face excruciating pain despite the presence of fear. In both cases it is about our attitude to fear.

Personnel and equipment in the entrance chamber of Tham Luang cave during rescue operations during 26-27 June 2018

In April 1970, the world held its breath as the brave Apollo 13 astronauts returned to Earth. And more recently, in June 2018, I felt the world hold its breath again as we prayed to God for the success of the brave rescue attempt of the children of the Thai soccer team.

Sometimes things happen to us and we have no choice but to bravely confront them. Other times, as happened with the football rescuers, we are faced with a choice that is not imposed on us. Were the rescuers fearlessly brave when entering the cave to save the children, or were they fearful upon entering the cave but facing it with courage?

When we make a decision about something, it has consequences. Major decisions have major consequences and repercussions as well. Sometimes those results are good and other times they are bad. More than 40 years ago I decided to marry the woman who is now my wife. The results and consequences of this were more than good. She has always been a wonderful wife.

Some people have made the decision to follow the Messiah. This is exactly what he called us to do. But what did Jesus say and what did he mean when he asked us to follow him? Sometimes the consequences of following Christ are difficult and require great courage.

Our Lord Jesus Christ said to a wealthy young man, 'Go and sell all your possessions and give the money to the poor, and you will have treasure in heaven.' (Mark 10:21-22)

I have a friend who never gives up the responsibility of zakat. Zakat is the obligation upon all Muslims to give part of their wealth to the poor.

He gives zakat every year to the poor. But he always likes to do it directly, not through any of the charitable groups. So he seeks out and honours needy people. I greatly respect this friend and the way he applies zakat and charity. My friend did not sell everything he had and give it to the poor. I am not sure that Jesus called us all to do this, but he said exactly that to someone who was not only wealthy but lacked the courage to face life without his wealth.

Jesus also says in the Gospel of Matthew 16:24. 'If any of you wants to be my follower, you must give up your own way.'

We know from the news that some people, whether Christians or Muslims, are being killed because of their faith. Are we safer if we are Christians or Muslims? The answer is no. Christ asks us not to hold on to our lives too tightly and but to live them with courage. Why? Is it because there is a paradise waiting for those who are killed because of their faith? No never! Jesus Christ never promised paradise to anyone. But he promised eternal life in the midst of the community of those who love God.

This is one of my favourite passages in the Scriptures:

'For we are both God's workers. And you are God's field. You are God's building. Because of God's grace to me, I have laid the foundation like an expert builder. Now others are building on it. But whoever is building on this foundation must be very careful. For no one can lay any foundation other than the one we already have—Jesus Christ.

Anyone who builds on that foundation may use a variety of materials—gold, silver, jewels, wood, hay, or straw. But on the judgment day, fire will reveal what kind of work each builder has done. The fire will show if a person's work has any value. If the work survives, that builder will receive a reward. But if the work is burned up, the builder will suffer great loss. The builder will be saved, but like someone barely escaping through a wall of flames.' (1 Corinthians 3:9-15)

Even if our lives count for nothing, if we have joined the campaign we're in—even if just barely.

PILGRIMS *before us*

Auschwitz... giving someone freedom cost Kolbe his life

It's over 75 years since the freeing of the Auschwitz Concentration Camp in Poland. Auschwitz was actually a complex of 40 concentration and extermination camps operated by the Nazi party in Germany. More than a million people were killed at that camp.

On the 27th January 1945 the Russian and Ukrainian armies freed the concentration camps. Georgii Elisavetskii, a Soviet soldier who entered one of the barracks, said that he could hear other soldiers telling the inmates: 'You are free, comrades!' But they did not respond, so he tried in Russian, Polish, German and Ukrainian. Then he used some Yiddish (a sort Jewish): 'They think that I am provoking them. They begin to hide. And only when I said to them: "Do not be afraid, I am a colonel of Soviet Army and a Jew. We have come to liberate you." Finally, as if the barrier collapsed... they rushed toward us

shouting, fell on their knees, kissed the flaps of our overcoats and threw their arms around our legs.'

There is one man who could have been free on that day but died in the place of another in Auschwitz. That was Father Maximilian Kolbe, a Franciscan Monk who volunteered to die in the place of a stranger on the 14th August 1941.

Rajmund Kolbe was born on 8th January 1894 in Zdu´ńska Wola, in Poland, which was then part of the Russian Empire. He was the second son of weaver Julius Kolbe and midwife Maria Dąbrowska. His father was of German descent and and his mother was Polish. He had four brothers. Shortly after his birth, his family moved to Pabianice.

Kolbe's life was strongly influenced in 1906, when he was 12, by a vision of the Virgin Mary. He later described this incident:

'That night I asked the Mother of God what was to become of me. Then she came to me holding two crowns, one white, the other red. She asked me if

I was willing to accept either of these crowns. The white one meant that I should persevere in purity and the red that I should become a martyr. I said that I would accept them both.'

In 1907 Kolbe and his elder brother Francis joined the Conventual Franciscans. They enrolled at the Conventual Franciscan minor seminary in Lwow later that year. In 1910, Kolbe was allowed to enter the novitiate where he was given the religious name Maximilian. He professed his first vows in 1911 and final vows in 1914.

Between 1930 and 1933, Kolbe undertook a series of missions to East Asia. He arrived first in Shanghai in China but failed to gather a following there. Next he moved to Japan where, by 1931, he had founded a Franciscan monastery, Mugenzai no Sono, on the outskirts of Nagasaki, the city later wiped out by an atom bomb in the war.

Meanwhile, in his absence the monastery at Niepokalanów began to publish a daily newspaper, Mały Dziennik (the Small Diary), in alliance with a political group, the National Radical Camp (Obóz Narodowo Radykalny). This publication reached a circulation of 137,000 and nearly double that, 225,000, at weekends.

After the outbreak of World War II, Kolbe was one of the few monks who remained in the monastery, where he organised a temporary hospital. After the town was captured by the Germans he was arrested by them on 19 September 1939 but released on 8 December. He refused to sign the Deutsche Volksliste which would have given him rights similar to those of German citizens in exchange for recognising his ethnic German ancestry. Upon his release he continued work at his monastery where he and other monks provided shelter to

refugees from Greater Poland, including 2,000 Jews whom he hid from German persecution in the Niepokalanów Monastry. Kolbe received permission to continue publishing religious works, though significantly reduced in scope. The monastery continued to act as a publishing house issuing a number of anti-Nazi German publications.

On 17 February 1941 the monastery was shut down by the German authorities. That day Kolbe and four others were arrested by the Gestapo and imprisoned in the Pawiak prison. On 28 May he was transferred to Auschwitz as prisoner 16670.

Continuing to act as a priest, Kolbe was subjected to violent harassment including beating and lashings. Once he was smuggled to a prison hospital by friendly inmates. At the end of July 1941 one prisoner escaped from the camp prompting SS-Hauptsturmführer Karl Fritzsch, the deputy camp commander, to pick ten men to be starved to death in an underground bunker to deter further escape attempts. When one of the selected men, Franciszek Gajowniczek, cried out, 'My wife! My children!', Kolbe volunteered to take his place.

According to an eyewitness, who was an assistant janitor at that time, in his prison cell Kolbe led the prisoners in prayer. Each time the guards checked on him he was standing or kneeling in the middle of the cell and looking calmly at those who entered. After they had been starved and deprived of water for two weeks only Kolbe remained alive. The guards wanted the bunker emptied so they gave Kolbe a lethal injection of carbolic acid. Kolbe is said to have raised his left arm and calmly waited for the deadly injection.

Translated from Arabic

Prisoner 16670

'Pick ten men to be starved to death...'
One cried out... 'My wife! My children!'
Kolbe volunteered to take his place.

PROVERBS
about Honour

Gold when beaten shines. PERUVIAN

The hammer shatters glass but forges steel. RUSSIAN

Victory belongs to the most persevering. RUSSIAN

To endure what is unendurable is true endurance. JAPANESE

When the bitters of adversity are exhausted, then come the sweets of happiness. JAPANESE

The gem cannot be polished without friction nor the person perfected without trials. CHINESE

It is a rough road that leads to the heights of greatness. LATIN

No one has done good who has not suffered disillusionment. NICARAGUAN

Who loses honour can lose nothing else. LATIN

It is easy to be brave from a distance NATIVE AMERICAN

Better suffer for the truth than be rewarded for a lie. SWEDISH

God sells knowledge for labour and honour for risk. ARABIC

He who wants to sell his honour will always find a buyer. ARABIC

Bitter pills may have blessed effects. RUSSIAN

Success consists of getting up just one more time than you fall

CELTIC PROVERB

Footprints In The Sand

One night a man had a dream. He dreamed
he was walking along the beach with the
LORD.

Across the sky flashed scenes from his life.
For each scene he noticed two sets of
footprints in the sand: one belonging
to him, and the other to the LORD.

When the last scene of his life flashed before
him,
he looked back at the footprints in the sand.

He noticed that many times along the path of
his life there was only one set of footprints.

He also noticed that it happened at the very
lowest and saddest times in his life.

This really bothered him and he
questioned the LORD about it:

'LORD, you said that once I decided to follow
you, you'd walk with me all the way.
But I have noticed that during the most
troublesome times in my life,
there is only one set of footprints.
I don't understand why when
I needed you most you would leave me.'

The LORD replied:
'My son, my precious child,
I love you and I would never leave you.
During your times of trial and suffering,
when you see only one set of footprints,
it was then that I carried you.'

Author disputed

Jesus, founder and perfecter of our faith

Therefore, since we are surrounded by such a huge crowd of witnesses to the life of faith, let us strip off every weight that slows us down, especially the sin that so easily trips us up. And let us run with endurance the race God has set before us. We do this by keeping our eyes on Jesus, the champion who initiates and perfects our faith. Because of the joy awaiting him, he endured the cross, disregarding its shame. Now he is seated in the place of honour beside God's throne. Think of all the hostility he endured from sinful people; then you won't become weary and give up. After all, you have not yet given your lives in your struggle against sin.

And have you forgotten the encouraging words God spoke to you as his children? He said,

'My child, don't make light of the Lord's discipline,
    and don't give up when he corrects you.
For the Lord disciplines those he loves,
    and he punishes each one he accepts as his child.'

As you endure this divine discipline, remember that God is treating you as his own children. Who ever heard of a child who is never disciplined by its father? If God doesn't discipline you as he does all of his children, it means that you are illegitimate and are not really his children at all. Since we respected our earthly fathers who disciplined us, shouldn't we submit even more to the discipline of the Father of our spirits, and live forever?

For our earthly fathers disciplined us for a few years, doing the best they knew how. But God's discipline is always good for us, so that we might share in his holiness. No discipline is enjoyable while it is happening—it's painful! But afterward there will be a peaceful harvest of right living for those who are trained in this way. So take a new grip with your tired hands and strengthen your weak knees. Mark out a straight path for your feet so that those who are weak and lame will not fall but become strong.

Hebrews 12: 1-13

PILGRIMS
alongside us?

Patrick Hutchinson

In June 2020 Patrick Hutchinson's act of bravery saving the life of a white right wing person became one of the definitive moments of a summer of protest with the slogan 'Black Lives Matter'. He carried the injured white protester over his shoulder getting him to safety during a rally to protect British monuments.

A statue of slave trader Edward Colston had been toppled in Bristol a week earlier. As a result gangs of drunk, angry, white men claimed they were in London to protect British monuments.

Hutchinson grew up on a south London council estate with his older sister Pauline. He was looked after by his Jamaican mother who had to work several jobs to support the single parent family. He only got to know his estranged father when he discovered he had two other brothers living nearby.

Hutchinson is both a father and grandfather of three. He first became a father at 20 and worked in IT in the city of London before becoming a sports coach. A group of four other fitness enthusiasts with years of mar-

tial arts training had formed a group called 'Ark Security'. Their aim was to protect young black protesters from getting caught up in violence.

The Mayor of London had warned people to stay away but Hutchinson and his four friends went to central London 'just in case'. They had seen 'senseless white rage' before and they 'knew how aggressive it could be: 'We knew we had to be there to protect vulnerable Black Lives Matter protesters and to protect our black boys from harm.' But they didn't expect to have to save Bryn Male, a retired transport police officer who was part of the white anti-protest group and who had reportedly been drinking heavily before he was abandoned by his friends and injured in the fray.

'I always like to hear the stories where someone's life has been changed, when an ordinary person gets recognised for something. They made me smile. I didn't think I could have the same effect.'

When interviewed by CNN, Hutchinson said 'My real focus was on avoiding a catastrophe - all of a sudden the narrative changes into "Black Lives Matters Youngsters Kill Protesters." That was the message we were trying to avoid.' He said he saw the man lying in a fetal position surrounded by protesters and it never crossed his mind whether the man might be for or against the movement. He just wanted to get him out safely. 'I had no idea who this man was. All I know is that he was there, up to no good!'

He and his friends saw the man and formed a cordon around him, then Hutchinson picked him up to take him directly to the police. While they were doing this protesters were still trying to hit him. 'I am carrying him, my friends are protecting myself and the man on my shoulder. He was still receiving blows, you can feel people trying to hit him,' he said. There were people trying to protect him at the same time as he carried him over to the police.

'Some people have asked me why I bothered saving him and I understand their frustration,' he said. 'But my natural instinct is to protect the vulnerable. If that man had died, the whole Black Lives Matter movement would have been torpedoed. Young black men would have gone to prison and had their lives ruined. I wasn't just protecting that guy – I was protecting us.'

'My natural instinct is to protect the vulnerable'

In hearing about the actions of Patrick Hutchinson one realises how behaving honourably releases identity, brings mercy, freedom and life.

The actions of Hutchinson mirror those of the 'Good Samaritan' that Jesus spoke about. At the protest, the police authorities filmed the event, but didn't intervene to protect the injured counter-protester. This is like those who walked past the injured man in Jesus story.(Luke 10:25-37)

Hutchinson hasn't publicly made any mention of God or following the Messiah, so we have no idea of his deeper motivation. For us, the honourable path we follow on this pilgrimage is to bring the same freedom and mercy the Messiah brought, to protect the vulnerable and to be the peacemakers who become the Messiah's hands to those we meet on the journey.

Courage is the door to honour

Nader Abdel Amir

Translated from Arabic

Since humans became sentient – aware of their existence on earth – that existence has been fraught with danger from birth to the time of their death. Natural disasters, wars, diseases, epidemics, hostilities and evil of all kinds are not just today. The mechanisms of evil may differ from time to time, but the evil is the same. Throughout the ages, what has distinguished humans from the other animals is the power of exploration and discovery, allowing them to overcome all the difficulties and challenges faced. And the difference between societies and peoples is their degree of success or failure in overcoming these challenges. However, it is only a difference in the methods of perseverance and approach.

Therefore, central to God Almighty's dealings with us was not to let us stumble randomly in the face of our destiny on earth, but rather to guide us to ways to do so through teaching, example and the prophets. The virtue of courage is, like all virtues, a middle ground between two opposing and conflicting ideas; on the one hand fear or trepidation; impulsiveness or recklessness on the other. Down through the ages philosophers defined the essence of this virtue as a middle route between these two opposite sides. Courage, in this sense, is the self-control when faced with the feelings of fear, or the state of reckless rush to confront it. We often call it 'flight or fight'. The role of the virtue of courage is to urge us to overcome the state of fear in front of an obstacle, difficulty, or evil and at the same time restrain oneself and dis-courage it from jumping between the jaws of evil or the enemy in an unreasonable and useless manner, often with terrible consequences.

Therefore, the Bible teaches us not to live in a state of anxiety, convulsion, aggression and shutdown in anticipation of a possible attack. Rather, it teaches us through Jesus,

> Look at my Servant, whom I have chosen.
>   He is my Beloved, who pleases me.
> I will put my Spirit upon him,
>   and he will proclaim justice to the nations.
> He will not fight or shout
>   or raise his voice in public.
> He will not crush the weakest reed
>   or put out a flickering candle.
>   Finally he will cause justice to be victorious.
>
> Matthew 12:18-20

to be like him; patient, calm and restrained, as well as courageous at the same time. Because in the Bible meekness does not detract from courage but rather accompanies it like her twin sister.

Is there a better description of meekness than this? Isn't this what a believer's behaviour should be? Meekness does not mean submission or silence over lies or falsehood, because this is Christ, the person who *'entered the Temple and began to drive out all the people buying and selling animals for sacrifice. He knocked over the tables of the money changers and the chairs of those selling doves. He said to them, The Scriptures declare, "My Temple will be called a house of prayer," but you have turned it into a den of thieves!'* (Matthew 21:12-13)

The disciples and the apostles after him followed him in this combination of meekness and courage. They did not remain silent, despite their memorable meekness, about telling the truth, as Paul often did, as he directed in one instance to Peter himself, saying in front of everyone:

'Since you, a Jew by birth, have discarded the Jewish laws and are living like a Gentile, why are you now trying to make these Gentiles follow the Jewish traditions?' (Galatians 2:14).

Jesus was patient, calm and restrained as well as courageous at the same time

Then we can go on to consider Jesus during his trial or being led to the cross; as well as the apostles in the face of death, which they faced with all determination, patience, and confidence in the promises of the Lord, even in the darkest and most difficult moments of life. It is exactly what Jesus meant when he spoke of the narrow and wide paths, when he said:

'You can enter God's Kingdom only through the narrow gate. The highway to hell is broad, and its gate is wide for the many who choose that way. But the gateway to life is very narrow and the road is difficult, and only a few ever find it.' (Matthew 7:13-14)

REMINDER *for Honour*

Remember Jesus carried his cross and calls us to carry ours

Use the reminder daily to remember of the theme of the season. Share it as a greeting in emails, with friends and relatives… wherever you need to focus on the pilgrimage.

Celebrate Honour

So let's get the party started, celebrating with a huge 'Yes' to all five of these things:

Yes, God can be trusted 100% of the time to take people like Abraham and the Messiah from shame to honour as they show him respect by trusting him and doing things his way.

Yes, Christ has put his Spirit into us to overpower our fears and give us the strength it takes to trust God no matter who tries to shame me.

Yes, we will trust Christ and his Spirit to give us whatever it takes to endure shameful and unfair attacks as unflinchingly as the Messiah did.

Yes, God's whole plan revolves around the heroic courage and perseverance of the Messiah to face the shame of execution on a cross. He calls us to trust him as sacrificially as he trusted God, his Father.

Yes, we are going on a dangerous mission—showing mercy to everybody for everything like Christ has shown mercy to me, and trusting God to honour me even if others despise us.

Each season has a celebration where we say 'Yes' to 5 things about being a pilgrim.

from https://syncx.org

So to pacify the crowd, Pilate released Barabbas to them. He ordered Jesus flogged with a lead-tipped whip, then turned him over to the Roman soldiers to be crucified.

The soldiers took Jesus into the courtyard of the governor's headquarters (called the Praetorium) and called out the entire regiment. They dressed him in a purple robe, and they wove thorn branches into a crown and put it on his head.

Then they saluted him and taunted, 'Hail! King of the Jews!' And they struck him on the head with a reed stick, spit on him, and dropped to their knees in mock worship. When they were finally tired of mocking him, they took off the purple robe and put his own clothes on him again. Then they led him away to be crucified.

A passerby named Simon, who was from Cyrene, was coming in from the countryside just then, and the soldiers forced him to carry Jesus' cross.

Mark 14: 15-21

Readings for this season

Mark 15: 15-21 Jesus is beaten and mocked

Hebrews 12: 1-13 We look to Jesus as our example of honour

Luke 14: 25-33 Jesus demands total exclusive loyalty

John 15: 18-25 The world hates those who honour Jesus

Philippians 1: 20-30 Facing opposition fearlessly

Matthew 5: 1-12 Jesus blesses those who suffer for him

James 1: 2-12 The beneficial effects of suffering

Luke 9: 20-26 Saving our lives by losing them

1 Peter 4: 12-19 Suffering according to God's will

3

IDENTITY SEASON

CONNECTED
EVERYWHERE

The Identity Rhythm we focus on during Identity Season:

God is proactively running a campaign to connect, heal and bless everyone on earth. He isn't just making rules and measuring how people do so he can split the good ones from the bad ones.

When people assume God is basically a scorekeeper and judge they read the Bible as the book that tells us how he will keep score. How much will that good deed raise my score? How badly will that bad deed hurt it?

People may read the Bible that way for a whole lifetime without realising that something different and bigger is going on. The Bible as a whole is not a glorified list of God's rules and standards. It's a story: the story of God proactively working his campaign strategy to bless the world.

The other half of the big idea of Identity Season:

God's campaign strategy is to create his own campaign team, connect it tightly to himself and bless the whole human race through it.

God does send some of his blessing directly to the whole human race but most of the really important blessings he gives to his team to spread. We call this the 'Abraham Strategy' not because Abraham invented it, which he didn't, but because he was the person through whom God launched it.

The Abraham Strategy involves God in human life at the group level. He puts his own group (his campaign team) in among all the other groups, and in the end, it will bless them all and unite or connect them all.

Bottom line of the big idea of Identity Season:

We sync to God's ancient promise to bless the world through Abraham's descendants. We live in sync with God's intentions when he made that promise.

In sync with Jesus, we are rooted in Abraham. *'And now that you belong to Christ, you are the true children of Abraham. You are his heirs, and God's promise to Abraham belongs to you.'* (Galatians 3:29)

When we sync with the Messiah we become a fulfilment of God's promise to Abraham, we are participating in the work of Abraham's descendants, which is to bless everybody. That is what it means to SYNC (See Yourself iN Christ). That is our cause. We are

THE BIG IDEA

caught up in it, energised by it, and delighted every time we have even a small success.

Do you want a better world? So does God. Have you got a plan for a better world? So does God. What are the odds that syncing with his plan will do more to improve the world than continuing with any other plan?

We have to be careful here. People who support good causes often go too far. They start demonising their enemies, seeking more power and dominating others. They become the problem while seeing themselves only as the solution.

The Messiah teaches his followers that the way we work for his cause is just as important as the cause itself. We do not try to force things. We do not demonise our enemies or even retaliate against them. That is not who we are.

Instead we peacefully and honourably endure the opposition we face as we work for the cause. We saw more about this in the Honour Season.

God is proactively running a campaign to connect, heal and bless everyone on earth.

The Covid-19 lockdown was difficult for me. At times very difficult. It made me think about prisoners, locked up sometimes for years on end. There were times I got very depressed.

We were locked down in our homes. We were disconnected from friends and family. I don't think any of us liked it. Relationships are important, whether close family or friends. We live in community, we enjoy community. When we have that taken from us, it hurts and life gets difficult.

Some people we relate to because we have to… they are our family. Sometimes it's easy and sometimes it's really difficult when they do things that hurt us. I know brothers who have not spoken to each other for years because of something they did. It's the same with friends. Sometimes we just stop seeing some people because of what they do. There's one friend I had for many years whom I had to stop seeing, and it was very painful.

These human relationships are mirrors of our relationship with God and His relationship with us. That relationship is, at the same time, similar and very different. That is because we are similar to God and at the same time very different.

The Qur'an in Sura 42 affirms that 'There is nothing whatsoever like God' yet the Hadith states that 'God created Adam in His image'. This seems like a contradiction.

The Holy Scriptures also say in Genesis: *Then God said, "Let us make human beings in our image, to be like us. They will reign over the fish in the sea, the birds in the sky, the livestock, all the wild animals on the earth, and the small animals that scurry along the ground."'*

Translated from Arabic

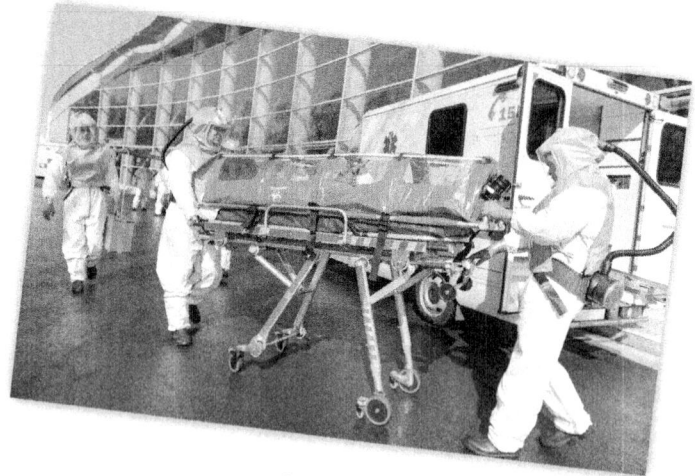

Separated by COVID?

'God created human beings in his own image. In the image of God he created them; male and female he created them.

Then God blessed them and said, "Be fruitful and multiply. Fill the earth and govern it. Reign over the fish in the sea, the birds in the sky, and all the animals that scurry along the ground."' (Genesis 1: 26-28)

So what does it mean to be made in the image of God? The core to this is an understanding that God is who submits himself to Allah; while at the same time being a doer of good. He follows the religion of Abraham. And Allah took Abraham as an intimate friend.'

We who are Abraham's children follow in his steps. We seek intimate friendship with God as much as he seeks it with us. And that is why the Messiah came - to demonstrate that relationship in a way that we can follow. We listen to his Holy Spirit whispering in our hearts and telling us the

So what does it mean to be made in the image of God?

personal and communicates with us. Not only does he love us, he longs to have a relationship with us. He longs to listen to us and to speak to us.

If it hurt us when we were cut off from our friends and families due to Covid-19, just imagine what it feels like to God to be cut off from us. But then let us think about what it means to be a friend of God. Sura 4 says 'And who is better in religion than one

way of God. What we call ourselves is less important than listening to that voice that tells us what God is doing today. Some of what he is doing might surprise us, and some might challenge us to love our enemies as much as our friends!

So in this the Identity season we celebrate both our connection with God and his connection with his people down through the ages.

PROVERBS about Identity

A paradise without people is not worth stepping foot in. ARABIC

A people without a history is like the wind over buffalo grass. NATIVE AMERICAN

Go back to your kith and kin lest you perish from without and within. ARABIC

As the root, so the sprout. SERBIAN

No branch is better than the root. JAPANESE

When the neighbour's house is on fire you put yourself in danger if you don't help extinguish it. CHINESE

In unity there is strength; in discord destruction. FILIPINO

A paradise without people is not worth stepping foot in. ARABIC

A people without a history is like the wind over buffalo grass. NATIVE AMERICAN

Go back to your kith and kin lest you perish from without and within. ARABIC

As the root, so the sprout. SERBIAN

No branch is better than the root. JAPANESE

When the neighbour's house is on fire you put yourself in danger if you don't help extinguish it. CHINESE

In unity there is strength; in discord destruction. FILIPINO

If two brothers have only the head of a fly they will divide it equally between them. BOTSWANA

The pup barks as it hears its elders bark. RUSSIAN

The cat sees mice in her sleep. RUSSIAN

A human being is human only in a community. Alone we become wild animals. SWAHILI

When the elephant is slain all the tribes gather together to eat of it. SOUTH AFRICAN

One grain doesn't fill the granary but it helps its companion. BOLIVIAN

Brothers and sisters are like hands and feet. VIETNAMESE

The men are the wool of the tribe, but the women are the ones who weave the pattern. ARABIC

Everyone likes to be with his own kind best. SERBIAN

A crowd is not company. RUSSIAN

Sheep from the same stable know each other. SERBIAN

I curse my own child but I hate whoever says 'amen' ARABIC

The dog and the fox are cousins yet they aren't too friendly. ARABIC

The wrath of brothers is the wrath of devils. VENEZUELAN

Bare is the back of a brotherless man. NORSE

One must howl with the wolves one is among

DANISH PROVERB

Am I the victim?

Years ago I remember discussing with a business colleague who came from the USA about guns, knives and other ways that we could get killed on the streets. Since he was from the USA he was saying how bad the gun deaths were in the USA and I was saying that it was worse where I lived because of knifing and other forms of being killed which were more brutal. Both of us were saying how bad our respective countries were.

More recently I was chatting with a colleague; we were talking about the health effects on us of pollution. She lived in a country with very bad pollution, and that winter it had a bad effect on the health of her family and friends.

Over the previous year or so I had been struggling with a number of things, potentially life-changing things. It felt like the world was against me. When that happens I tend to behave like a victim. Sometimes I become paralysed, unable to do normal things, because of these feelings that the world is against me. It is easy to blame it on fate. If it is fate there is nothing I can do about it. If God has destined for me to receive all these bad things, then that is what I have to accept. And I begin to feel other people owe it to me to look after me.

the guilty?' God was gracious and said, 'If I find fifty righteous people in the city of Sodom, I will spare the whole place for their sake.'

Abraham continued to dialogue with God. And the dialogue seemed almost like the bargaining in a market (souk). From 50, Abraham came down to 45, then 40, 30, 20 and finally God agrees not to destroy Sodom if there are 10 righteous people in it.

It's very easy to slip into 'victim mentality'

We call this 'victim mentality'. It's easy for any of us to slip into that.

When I feel like I am a victim I like to remind myself of Abraham and his nephew Lot. Abraham lived close to a very evil city called Sodom, in which his nephew and his family lived. Because Sodom was so evil God decided it needed to be destroyed. Knowing his family members lived there, Abraham pleaded with God, 'If there are 50 righteous people in Sodom, will you destroy them with

Sadly, we read that there were not even 10 righteous people in Sodom and the city was destroyed. But Lot was given a way out. God sent angels to warn him and help him. But in the process he lost everything, including his wife.

There is this connection between humanity and God. It's not that a person is merely a slave of God, as God has this desire to bless. It is Satan who wishes to curse. God is good, all the time.

So how does this connection work out for us in practice? Abraham gives us the clue. Abraham entered into dialogue with God. He remonstrated with God. He pleaded with God. And because God desires this connection with us, he listened and he entered into dialogue with Abraham. It was a two-way dialogue.

And we are Abraham's spiritual descendants and heirs. We inherit that intimate relationship with God as our father.

Life is never easy. Sometimes it is horribly bad. But we need to remember that God is there, and that he desires to wrap his love around us… and to dialogue with us and involve us. We are not victims but children of God and our lives are a journey exploring that relationship.

Struggling to connect with God

Nader Abdel Amir

There is no argument that belief in God essentially requires building a strong connection with him because belief will be meaningless apart from this connection. What does the connection with God mean? It means being close to him, the Most High, and building a very natural relationship with him, a relationship that, in turn, is based on foundations and pillars that are the same as the foundations and pillars of faith.

Among these foundations we can mention first the certainty of his existence, presence and covenants, then secondly obeying him, trusting in him and submitting to him and thirdly learning to see the world through his angle of view and to reflect on the actions of his hands, his will and his purposes as the Almighty. When our relationship with God becomes strong, our relationship with our sur-

> Those who are dominated by the sinful nature think about sinful things, but those who are controlled by the Holy Spirit think about things that please the Spirit. So letting your sinful nature control your mind leads to death. But letting the Spirit control your mind leads to life and peace. For the sinful nature is always hostile to God. It never did obey God's laws, and it never will. That's why those who are still under the control of their sinful nature can never please God.
>
> But you are not controlled by your sinful nature. You are controlled by the Spirit if you have the Spirit of God living in you. (And remember that those who do not have the Spirit of Christ living in them do not belong to him at all.) And Christ lives within you, so even though your body will die because of sin, the Spirit gives you life because you have been made right with God. The Spirit of God, who raised Jesus from the dead, lives in you. And just as God raised Christ Jesus from the dead, he will give life to your mortal bodies by this same Spirit living within you.
>
> Therefore, dear brothers and sisters, you have no obligation to do what your sinful nature urges you to do. For if you live by its dictates, you will die. But if through the power of the Spirit you put to death the deeds of your sinful nature, you will live."
>
> Romans 8: 5-13

Translated from Arabic

roundings improves and strengthens, whether it is relationships with people, animals or the environment. Because then we become one of God's campaign members acting according to his will, seeing things through his point of view, and refraining from doing things that anger him or offend his creation.

But such a connection does not come voluntarily without any effort on our part. Man is weak and quick to fall, many times. As for sin... the soul goes through moments of spiritual weakness that lead to apathy of faith and distance from God, or the body prevails and we begin to retreat from our obedience to God and our obligations before him, because *Temptation comes from our own desires, which entice us and drag us away. These desires give birth to sinful actions. And when sin is allowed to grow, it gives birth to death.'* (James 1:14-15).

...constantly examining our motives ...seeking righteousness ...readiness to repent

Therefore, the relationship with God requires a gradual battle for the soul through resisting its dependence on bodily desires and submitting it through constantly examining our motives, controlling our feelings, seeking righteousness and persevering in seeking forgiveness and constant readiness to repent.

We as human beings and as Messianic pilgrims also have to know that no matter what we do, we will not reach the required degree that we want in our closeness to God. The reason, as I said, is our human weakness, which was also experienced by the prophets and men of God before us, and they continued to resist it. This is not something that discourages us from attempting to rise to those levels of connection with God. On the contrary, it will remain our constant motivation to build the full relationship with God, which will be achieved when we find ourselves with him in glory.

The Apostle Paul himself, who built a strong connection with God and reached a level that only a few believers have attained after him, throughout his life yearned for a closer, stronger and more intimate connection with God, as he says about that.

> Yes, everything else is worthless when compared with the infinite value of knowing Christ Jesus my Lord. For his sake I have discarded everything else, counting it all as garbage, so that I could gain Christ and become one with him. I no longer count on my own righteousness through obeying the law; rather, I become righteous through faith in Christ. For God's way of making us right with himself depends on faith. I want to know Christ and experience the mighty power that raised him from the dead.
> Philippians 3:8-10

No matter how strong our relationship with God and our closeness to him may be, it will always be possible to reach a closer proximity and a stronger and stronger connection. Then in heavenly glory, we will have eternity with its majesty and infinity so that we may transcend more and more in our relationship with him.

PILGRIMS before us?

Gandhi

Translated from Arabic

Could a Hindu be a lover of God and a fellow pilgrim of ours?

That question is hard to answer when a person says, as Gandhi is often quoted, 'I am a Christian and a Hindu and a Muslim and a Jew.' Who could say that? Why would he say it?

Gandhi was born on 2 October 1869 in a family of merchants. His childhood is characterised by seriousness with a tinge of shyness. At the age of thirteen, he married a girl of the same age - a marriage arranged by the two families as was usual at that time.

He studied law in England and upon his return to India was unsuccessful in finding a suitable job but he found an opportunity to work in a South African law firm and take on the cases of Indians. As imported labourers Indians were an oppressed minority in that new country, which had just been granted independence from Britain in 1910.

In 1915 he returned to his native country of India, and within five years became a leader of the national movement demanding the liberation of India from British colonialism.

Gandhi established a unique style of non-violent but strategic resistance to the British through the idea of hand weaving. That is, he proposed that every Indian should weave the cloth he needed with his own hands and not buy it from factories of the coloniser. With this strategic idea he dealt a powerful blow to oppressive colonialism, restored pride and a sense of value to every Indian and at the same time instilled hope for freedom. He also led the Indians in the 'March to the Sea', a march he organised with his people to extract the salt every Indian needs from sea water as a response to the colonisers' control over the distribution and trade of salt in India. With that strategic march Gandhi again succeeded in painting a smile of pride and victory for his people who had felt defeated by colonialism.

Rejection of violence against other people, even if it is colonial and oppressive, was crucial to Gandhi. He called for following the policy of non-violence, claiming that violence would lead to counter-violence and the cycle of violence would continue.

In 1945 the policy of non-violence finally succeeded and the British colonisers left India. But the new nation soon was swept by a tidal wave of violence, a civil war between Hindus and Muslims. In spite of Gandhi's resistance, India divided into the two states of India and Pakistan in 1947.

A few months later he was killed by a Hindu extremist who believed he was a traitor to India because he had been too sympathetic to Muslims during the creation of Pakistan. It is said that as he lay after being shot he told his killer: 'It is my fault that I did not teach you love.'

Gandhi had many friends who were Muslims or Christians. He was very familiar with the Qur'an and the Bible and often cited their teachings on non-violence and peace. He also gave his whole life to helping victims find a non-violent path to freedom from oppressive power structures. He shared God's passionate concern for victims, which is what distinguished the God of Abraham from all other gods and idols of ancient times.

Ghandi was against violence and for the victims. In these two important ways Gandhi walked the pilgrim path that the Messiah calls people to walk on. But he did not pledge his loyalty to Jesus the Messiah as the guide for his pilgrimage because he thought that total loyalty to any Messiah or any religion inevitably leads to violent conflict between the religions. Can we find what he missed— loyalty without violence? We think we can if we keep listening to the Messiah through all the seasons of the Messianic Pilgrimage.

PILGRIMS *alongside us*

Alice Cooper

'Shock Rock' is not a music style that some of us would normally associate with. And Alice Cooper is considered by music journalists and peers to be 'The Godfather of Shock Rock'. He has a raspy voice and a stage show that features numerous props and stage illusions, including pyrotechnics, guillotines, electric chairs, fake blood, reptiles, baby dolls and duelling swords.

He was born in Michigan and named Vincent Furnier. His father was a pastor and his grandfather an evangelist in that church. They moved to Phoenix in Arizona where the teenager set his eyes on being a 'million dollar record seller'. As a result of a Number 1 hit 'Don't Blow Your Mind', the band that started out as a high school

talent show band turned professional. They chose the name 'Alice Cooper' because it sounded innocuous and wholesome, in contrast to the band's brand of psychedelic rock!

The band hit the news when it was claimed that Alice Cooper tore the head off a chicken and drank its blood. Though this was completely untrue, it set the tone for their Shock Rock performances where he wore androgenous costumes which were

more shocking in the early 1970s than they might be in the 21st century.

By the 1980s Cooper was so into alcohol and illicit substances that he cannot remember recording any of the albums he recorded at that time. They were not successful in record sales either.

'There's nothing in following Jesus that says I can't be a rock star.'

In 1983 he had his second hospitalisation for alcoholism and cirrhosis of the liver. He then spent a lengthy time away from the music business dealing with personal issues. His wife and he filed for divorce and then decided not to finalise it. The couple reconciled a year later.

By 1986 he was back touring with his brand of Shock Rock to the extent that when they planned to tour the UK an MP called for it to be banned

Alice Cooper band performing live in London in 2012

since, he said, 'I'm horrified by his behaviour – it goes beyond the bounds of entertainment.'

The show was dangerous and in the London leg of the tour Cooper met with a near fatal accident during rehearsal of a hanging execution sequence at the end of the show.

But his stage persona and the real person are very different. Vincent is the person and he refers to 'Alice' in the third person to distance himself from the artiste he performs as.

Cooper was not a Messianic Pilgrim when he gave up drinking, but stated that he thanks God for taking it away, saying, 'I mean, if he can part the Red Sea and create the universe, he can certainly take alcoholism away from somebody.'

'I grew up in the church, went as far away as I could from it—almost died—and then came back…'

He continues with his Shock Rock performances but he said he doesn't have trouble reconciling his musical persona with following Jesus.

'There's nothing in Christianity that says I can't be a rock star. People have a very warped view of Christianity. They think it's all very precise and we never do wrong and we're praying all day and we're right-wing. It has nothing to do with that.'

Cooper has two identities – like all pilgrims – an identity of his culture and the new identity as as follower of the Messiah.

As part of this new identity Cooper tries to bring freedom to others trapped in different ways. He helped Dave Mustaine of the Magadeth who was struggling with alcohol and drug abuse to the point that Dave now refers to him as his 'godfather'.

Life is but a Weaving

by Corrie ten Boom

My life is but a weaving
Between my God and me.
I cannot choose the colors
He weaveth steadily.

Oft' times He weaveth sorrow;
And I in foolish pride
Forget He sees the upper
And I the underside.

Not 'til the loom is silent
And the shuttles cease to fly
Will God unroll the canvas
And reveal the reason why.

The dark threads are as needful
In the weaver's skillful hand
As the threads of gold and silver
In the pattern He has planned

He knows, He loves, He cares;
Nothing this truth can dim.
He gives the very best to those
Who leave the choice to Him.

All the world's a stage,
And all the men and women merely players:
They have their exits and their entrances;
And one man in his time plays many parts,
His acts being seven ages. At first the infant,
Mewling and puking in the nurse's arms;
And then the whining school-boy, with his satchel
And shining morning face, creeping like snail
Unwillingly to school. And then the lover,
Sighing like furnace, with a woeful ballad
Made to his mistress' eyebrow. Then a soldier,
Full of strange oaths, and bearded like the pard,
Jealous in honour, sudden and quick in quarrel,
Seeking the bubble reputation
Even in the cannon's mouth. And then the justice,
In fair round belly with good capon lin'd,
With eyes severe and beard of formal cut,
Full of wise saws and modern instances;
And so he plays his part. The sixth age shifts
Into the lean and slipper'd pantaloon,
With spectacles on nose and pouch on side;
His youthful hose, well sav'd, a world too wide
For his shrunk shank; and his big manly voice,
Turning again toward childish treble, pipes
And whistles in his sound. Last scene of all,
That ends this strange eventful history,
Is second childishness and mere oblivion;
Sans teeth, sans eyes, sans taste, sans everything.

All the world's a stage
William Shakespeare

Celebrate Identity

So let's get the party started, celebrating with a huge 'Yes' to all five of these things:

Yes, God has provided a new spiritual root to unite and bless humanity, and it all goes back to Abraham.

Yes, the key to God's whole strategy is Christ, the King of blessing, whose wrongful death created a way for people like us to become spiritual descendants of Abraham.

Yes, Christ puts his Spirit, life, and power into us, rooting us in Abraham and giving us a share in the mission of Abraham's family, blessing the whole world.

Yes, I am blessing others right now—forgiving everybody for everything like the Messiah has forgiven me. My identity gives me strength to trust God about that.

Yes, I am trusting Christ and his Spirit to help me rise above any rejection I face for him. I know my roots in Abraham. I know I am one of the many citizens of the Messiah's kingdom.

Each season has a celebration where we say 'Yes' to 5 things about being a pilgrim.

from https://syncx.org

The Lord had said to Abram, 'Leave your native country, your relatives, and your father's family, and go to the land that I will show you. I will make you into a great nation. I will bless you and make you famous, and you will be a blessing to others. I will bless those who bless you and curse those who treat you with contempt. All the families on earth will be blessed through you.'

So Abram departed as the Lord had instructed, and Lot went with him. Abram was seventy-five years old when he left Haran. He took his wife, Sarai, his nephew Lot, and all his wealth—his livestock and all the people he had taken into his household at Haran—and headed for the land of Canaan. When they arrived in Canaan, Abram travelled through the land as far as Shechem. There he set up camp beside the oak of Moreh. At that time, the area was inhabited by Canaanites.

Then the Lord appeared to Abram and said, 'I will give this land to your descendants.' And Abram built an altar there and dedicated it to the Lord, who had appeared to him. After that, Abram travelled south and set up camp in the hill country, with Bethel to the west and Ai to the east. There he built another altar and dedicated it to the Lord, and he worshiped the Lord.

Genesis 12: 1-8

Readings for this season

Genesis 12: 1-8 Abraham, the root of the whole family tree

Exodus 6: 1-12 Why Abraham's descendants owed God their loyalty

Ephesians 2: 11-22 How Jesus enlarged the family tree

Romans 11: 17-24 Being grafted into the tree (adopted into the family)

Galatians 5:16-26 The fruit growing on the family tree

John 15: 1-8 The power to bear fruit as a person attached to the Messiah

Colossians 3:11-17 The DNA of the new family of the Messiah

PILGRIMS TOGETHER

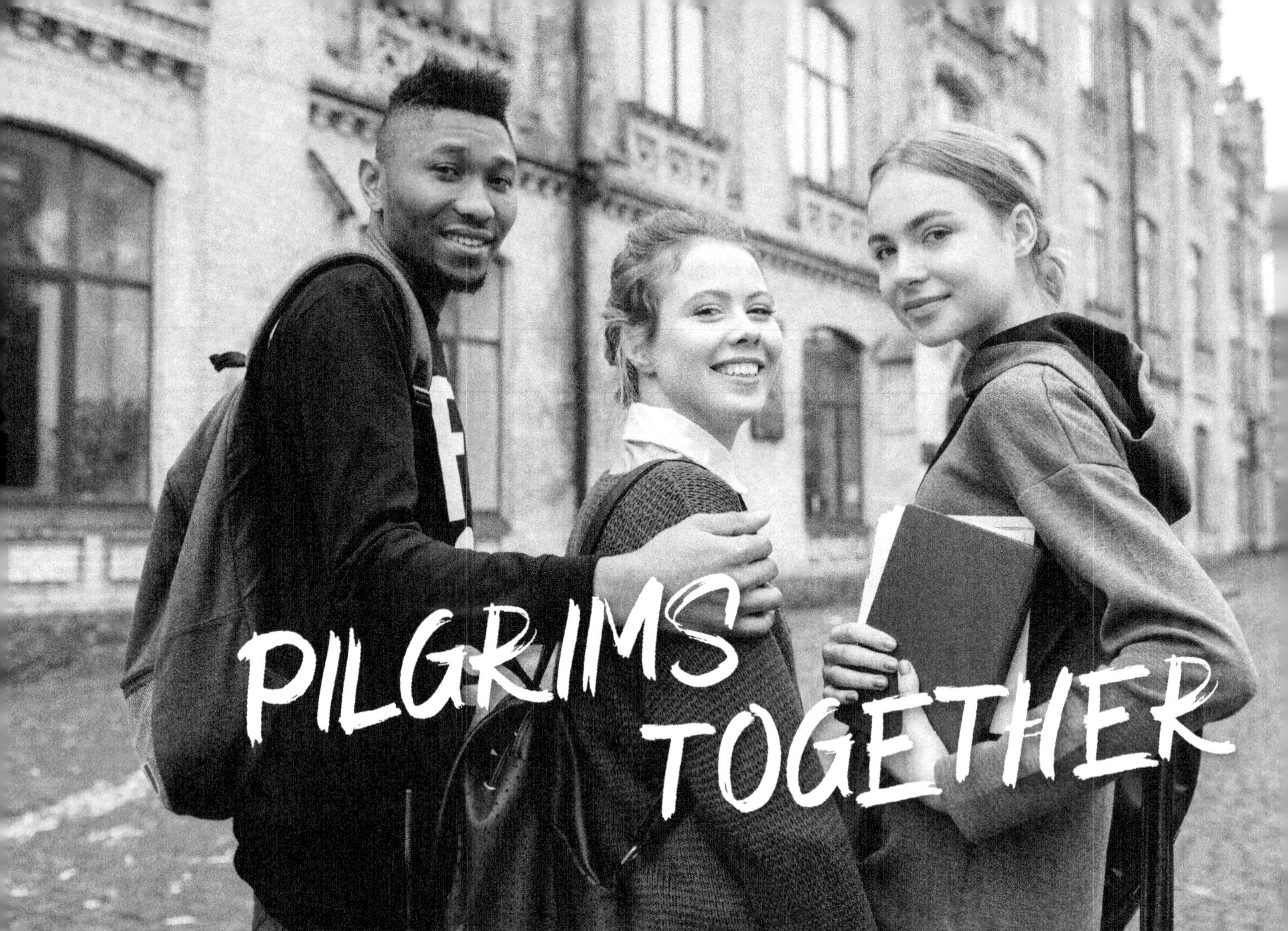

Groups of pilgrims

Dunbar's number

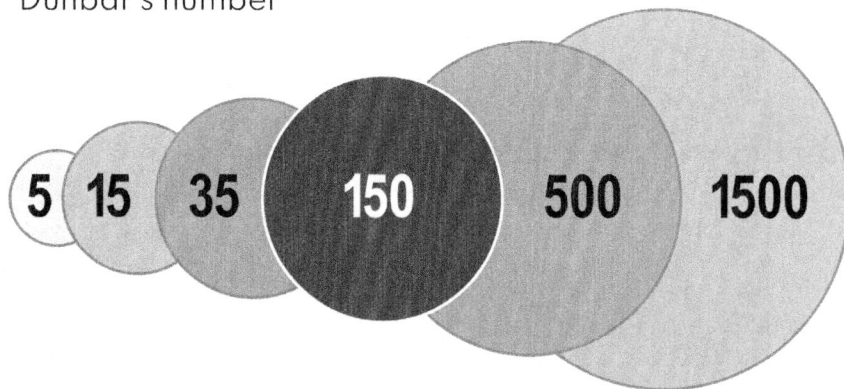

Large or small?

In the 1990's a British Anthropologist called Robin Dunbar found there was a correlation between the physical size of a primate brain and the average social group size. He then did calculations based on the average human brain size and suggested that human beings can comfortably maintain a maximum of 150 stable relationships.

Dunbar explained it informally as 'the number of people you would not feel embarrassed about joining, uninvited, for a drink if you happened to bump into them in a pub or bar'.

Numbers larger than this usually require more restrictive rules to the relationships or some sort of enforced norms to maintain a stable, cohesive group.

So what does this mean on the pilgrimage?

It means that we don't expect large pilgrim groups to function cohesively. Because journeying together is helpful, we deliberately try to maintain small groups in all we do.

This isn't a concert or spectator sport, it's a pilgrimage. There may be millions of others on the pilgrimage and as we meet them we may build relationships with them, but we don't structurally try to maintain a cohesive group with all the pilgrims on the journey.

Other pilgrims may have very different culture or interests and so we may or may not feel comfortable within their group. But we don't have to. We find other pilgrims for the journey or else the Messiah brings them to us, and those are who we travel with. And that group may change over time.

Pilgrim Pubs

The British Pub or Public House can be traced back to the time of the Messiah when the Romans occupied what is now the UK. Though originally ale houses or taverns or inns, they became, quite literally, houses open to the public, offering food and drink. The synagogues of Jesus' time often functioned as inns and places to stay en route on a journey. They were a meeting place for the community as much as a building for religious worship. As such, they were both close to home or work, providing a social atmosphere with the presence of friends and acquaintances. It was the community that made them what they are, rather than the food and drink.

So what has all this to do with a pilgrimage?

As we journey on our pilgrimage, we need fellow pilgrims to encourage us. We need points of contact with others so we can share our difficulties and our joys. It will include the 'religious' but not be limited to that, so that what we see as 'religious' will be grounded in reality rather than removed from it.

We tried this out almost by accident with an online virtual pub where people gather and build community. Above all it functions as an encouragement to each other to carry on. We're frequently in contact with each other during the week, sharing ideas, thoughts and struggles. Sometimes one of us is low and another can help, then it swaps around. In our case it's usually about 6–12 people meeting via Zoom and it's relational rather than structural.

'Pilgrim Pubs' is just putting a name to something we do naturally rather than creating something to fit with the name. We don't find it works well with over about 12–15 people.

Not everyone in the pub is on the Messianic Pilgrimage—much like the eclectic group one might meet in a British pub. That does two things: One is that the non-pilgrims keep our feet on the ground rather than getting too spiritual. We've all met people who come over as being so spiritual to the point that it doesn't feel like they are connected with real life. The second is that we can comfortably share our journey on the pilgrimage with others in a natural way. This isn't structured. We don't plan it. It just happens because as followers of the Messiah he is so central in our lives.

Pilgrim companions

The Pilgrim pubs are small communities and may include people who are not pilgrims yet but are hearing about the pilgrimage and may become pilgrims in the future. But alongside the Pilgrim Pubs it is good to have one or two people we can share the pilgrimage with on a deeper level.

A key part of the pilgrimage is listening to God and doing what he tells us to do. Companions help us to check if we have heard God correctly and can help us during the hard times on the pilgrimage.

Depending on our personality we may wish to make a companion group structured or not. Some of those who have it structured focus on a weekly meeting where they read the Scriptures together, pray together and listen to God's direction. It is a place to share God's ideas and give encouragement for the coming week.

If we do decide to make it structured, we don't need a specific leader for this sort of group, we can take it in turns leading. Each meeting doesn't have to be more than 60 minutes, nor does it have to be limited to once per week. Our companions on the pilgrimage are those we can contact at any time and share our blessings or needs.

With modern communications, that group doesn't have to be physically together because we can easily communicate via the Internet wherever they are: text, audio or video links.

Sharing meals together

When the Messiah was on his earthly pilgrimage we read many, many accounts of him sharing meals with other pilgrims, or others considering the pilgrimage, or just people he met on the journey. Sharing meals together is important. It breaks down barriers in a way that other activities don't.

It can also be an indicator of a problem relationship between people. Many years ago we were filming a dramatised documentary and a tension developed between two of the actors. It got to the point they wouldn't share a meal together until the tension was resolved.

We can also have special meals for each season, with a food that reminds us of the season or milestone.

We also share meals to remember the Messiah. At the very last meal he shared with people before they killed him he instigated two things to remember him by. He said to share a cup of wine to remember that he shed his blood for us fellow pilgrims. He said to to share a piece of bread to remember that he gave his body—his life—for us. We are part of a single body of pilgrims travelling this journey following him, and with him as our guide.

You can read more about this memorial meal on page 164.

Open up vs. be good

Jesus' main teaching was about opening up to God's restoring influence. His message was not what many people think, 'Be loving. Be good. Be kind. Etc.' But his message was more along the lines of: 'God is taking over now, bringing his influence to earth in a new way. Open up to that! Forget whatever else we were doing and align ourself with the plan God is unfolding.' (authors' paraphrase)

Of course, if we do open up to that influence, we are likely to end up being more loving, good, and kind, but we realise that we got there because we opened up, not because we tried harder. His influence does what we can't do.

So the whole point of life is to align or synchronise with his influence and to thank him for the results. Since his plan and intentions are so good, why would we not want to throw ourselves totally open to his influence and participate in the restoration he is carrying out?

Opening up vs. being overpowered

We are not forced to open up. God has set his goal as winning our hearts like a young man who wins the heart of his bride, not forcing us to submit. God wants our love, not merely our acquiescence. His aim is to fulfil us, not to use us.

As we open up freely to him and let his love influence our lives, we get swept up into a new kind of living. God syncs us with his grand plan to restore the world to what it was meant to be and can be. He restores us and draws us into his restoration of the world.

FREEDOM SEASON

4

FREE AT LAST?

The Freedom Rhythm we focus on during Freedom Season:

God is proactively working a strategy to bring freedom, healing and deliverance to everyone on earth. Jesus launched it with the Freedom Declaration which is still in force.

Many people assume God is basically a killjoy, making rules and then making sure people keep them or else. They think of the Bible as the rule book, so they don't read it much. Or if they do read it, they feel bad, getting reminded of all the rules they broke.

They don't get the basic idea of the Freedom Season. Something different and bigger is going on in the Bible which is really one long story, not a patchwork of rules. In the story, the victims get delivered from their cruel master by the liberator, the rightful heroic king, but not as in a predictable fairy tale. The Bible's story is more of a down to earth thriller with some amazing twists and turns in the plot.

The Freedom Season celebrates the biggest twist of all—Jesus, the spearhead of God's Freedom Campaign, is rejected and executed but God brings him back to life. That holds the entire biblical story together from Genesis to Revelation and it puts freedom, healing and deliverance within reach of all of us.

The other half of the big idea of Freedom Season:

God's strategy is to have his kingdom of freedom go viral. The free citizens of his kingdom spread the news and infect others with their freedom until the whole world is drawn to Jesus, the Freedom King.

When someone is freed from prison, addiction, illness or danger there is always a huge sense of relief and joy. There is also gratitude to anyone who helped get the person free. God's strategy banks on that relief, joy and gratitude.

As people accept the Freedom Declaration of Jesus and honour him as their King, they experience his deliverance. Often this is so thrilling and life-changing that they never get over it. It is like being scarred for life but in a good way. They are permanently relieved and full of joy and they keep trying to pay off their debt of gratitude to Jesus.

THE BIG IDEA

How does he tell them to pay it? Pay it forward! Become freedom activists, telling our freedom story so that others want some of the relief and joy we have. Your freedom infects them, they join his kingdom, they experience his freedom and their story infects others. This has exponential growth potential.

What works against God's strategy for exponential growth? Self-quarantine. When we say, 'Yes' to the freedom of Jesus but we do not become freedom activists, we get out of sync with the essence of God's strategy. He wants the freedom to spread; we bottle it up for ourselves.

This is extremely dangerous. God has a strategy, we know what it is and we are working to sabotage it? That does not sound like we are free citizens of Jesus' kingdom. More like traitors. But we will excuse that behaviour if we do not realise that God has viral intentions for his kingdom.

Bottom line of the big idea of Freedom Season:

We see ourselves in Christ as freedom activists, calling the world into the new era of freedom. We live in sync with God's intentions when he sent Jesus to issue the Freedom Declaration.

In sync with Jesus we are rooted in Abraham: *'And now that you belong to Christ, you are the true children of Abraham. You are his heirs, and God's promise to Abraham belongs to you.'* (Galatians 3:29)

When we SYNC, when you 'See Yourself iN Christ' as a freedom activist, we realise we are participating in the new era that Jesus launched with his Freedom Declaration. That freedom is for everybody but not everybody knows it. Not everybody has bought into it yet, activated it, experienced it. That is our cause. Give everybody a chance to get free in Christ. We are caught up in that cause, energised by it and delighted every time we have even a small success.

You want a freer world? So does God. Why not get on board with his plan instead of trying to work some other plan? Of course, you have to get over the view (if it is your view) that God is the great restrictor of freedom.

If you are stuck there, read the whole story of Jesus for yourself in the Gospel of Mark which is only a 30 minute read. See if he looks like a freedom restrictor to you and go from there.

O questioner, what is freedom?

By Ahmad Shawqi

يا أيها السائل ما الحرية

أحمد شوقي

O questioner, what is freedom?
You ask about the jewel of the sun

يا أيها السائل ما الحرية
سالتَ عن جوهرة سنيه

It lights up our pure souls
A blissful life of freedom

تضئ أرواحا لنا زكيه
يا نعمت الحياة بالحريه

Pleasure, pure pleasure
Sending warmth in our hearts

لذاذة طاهرة نقيه
تبعث في قلوبنا الحميه

Evoking echoes of our father
Forging spiritual from mundane

تبعث فيها الهمة الأبيه
فتأنف المواقف الدنيه

Houses are built upon it
Splendour of the glory of freedom

وتألف المنازل العليه
العز كل العز في الحريه

God has given a gift to us
An instinct of his essential nature

االله أعطاك لنا عطية
غريزة في خلقه فطريه

We would be a victim without her
Offspring of the soul and of The Soul

لنبذلنّ دونها ضحية
النفس والنفيس والذرِّيه

I'm free…

Except…

I need to do all my religious duty. Everybody has these duties and nobody can escape. Fasting. Prayers. It can be a burden and sometimes I fail to fulfil all my duties. Duty. Duty. Duty. God seems to put such a burden on us.

I'm free…

Except…

My family need me and I have to provide for them. I work six days a week but it feels like every day without a day off. My employer decides when I work. I cannot chose. And my wife is the same; she works and works… washing, cleaning and providing food.

And then when my mother calls I have to go and help her. Of course I love her but it's another job. And my brother calls with a problem so I need to help him too… Our family seems to put such a burden on us.

I'm free…

Except…

I have to follow all the laws of our country. I cannot drive how I please and I have to pay my taxes.

Every year there seem to be more laws to follow. I'm always worried I may forget one of them and get into trouble. Society seems to put such a burden on us.

I'm free…

Except…

I live with the perceptions I have of myself and those of how other people see me.

I'm free…

Well, maybe I'm actually drowning in the swamp of burdens we call life.

When the Messiah said he came to bring freedom, what did he really mean?

I'm free… Except…

THOUGHTS
from Uncle Azis

More than six million people in North Africa are trying to smuggle their way into Europe

We are told there are more than six million people in North Africa trying to smuggle their way into Europe. Of those, half may succeed this year. Somehow they feel they will be free if they can do so. Many of those will then be returned to where they came from because they are not true refugees.

Everyone wants to be free. But what does freedom mean? Does it mean that I am not a slave to someone else? This freedom means I have access to a range of desirable opportunities and that is what drives people to risk so much to reach Europe. That is freedom from something. It is negative.

Freedom and Responsibility

There is also a positive freedom. A freedom to... I am my own master and I can do what I like. Positive freedom only happens when there is negative freedom. But it also brings responsibility. I might be free to say something nasty about a particular group of people but I am free to direct my own life and so I should not. I should act positively not negatively.

I don't know if you've noticed while travelling, but some of the people in the west I have met have a bracelet with the letters WWJD on it. I asked them what it meant. They

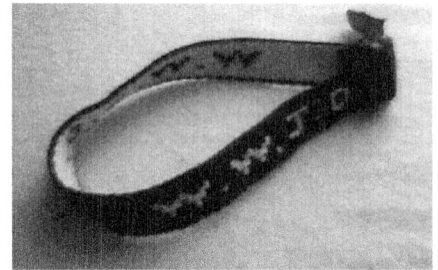

said it meant 'What Would Jesus Do?' and they said it was to remind them to think what he would do every time they needed to make a decision. It got me thinking. I would never wear a bracelet like that and my thoughts are really not 'What would Jesus do?' but more 'What did Jesus do?'

When I think about the Messiah I always remember just how humble he was. He was very unlike many of the leaders we see today. One time when having a meal with his followers he got a bowl of water to wash their feet. Indeed a lot of what he did was to serve others. It is why I try every day to think, 'How can I bless other people today?'

To give blessing is better than to receive blessing

How can I bless other people today? That seems unlike most people today who want the blessing rather than to give the blessing. It is giving up something for others. Indeed we follow in the steps of Abraham who, when God said he would have offspring as many as the stars in the sky, also committed him to become a blessing to the whole world.

Blessing others expresses just how much we value God and it is true worship. When I bless I am exercising my positive freedom.

The prophet Isaiah said *'The Spirit of the Sovereign Lord is upon me, for the Lord has anointed me to bring good news to the poor. He has sent me to comfort the brokenhearted and to proclaim that captives will be released and prisoners will be freed. He has sent me to tell those who mourn.'* (Isaiah 61: 1-2)

700 years later the Messiah repeated those words, giving them true meaning. What did Jesus do? He announced freedom: Freedom from and freedom to. If we want to follow in his footsteps, we too need to bring freedom. Light has overcome darkness.

REMINDER *for Freedom*

Remember Jesus came back to life and his freedom campaign isn't over yet!

Use the reminder daily to remember the theme of the season. Share it as a greeting in emails, with friends and relatives... wherever you need to focus on the pilgrimage.

PILGRIMS *before us*

Dr Martin Luther King

Martin Luther King was born on 15 January 1929 in Atlanta, Georgia and his father, Martin Luther King (Senior) was a Baptist pastor.

In 1947 he graduated from a theological seminary in Atlanta and was appointed as an assistant to his father. He was ordained a pastor himself the following year. He married Corota Scott in Alabama in 1953.

On 17 May 1954 black people won an important victory when the USA Supreme Court ruled that racial discrimination against black students in public schools was unconstitutional— the first step in the Thousand Miles March.

However, later that year the state of Alabama ruled that blacks were not allowed to sit in places where whites sat on buses. On 1 December 1955 a black woman refused to give up her seat on a bus to a white man and the police arrested her.

All the anti-racism movements met in the city on the same day and their members unanimously elected Martin Luther King Jr. as president of their group called the Montgomery Development Association. They decided to file a lawsuit to prove the unconstitutionality of racial discrimination laws on buses. The company responded by halting routes to predominantly black neighborhoods.

Six months later, the court ruled that racial segregation on buses was unconstitutional and before the end of that year blacks had the right to sit in the same place as whites.

Martin Luther King and his companions continued their struggle for civil rights for blacks in the United States and they won victory after victory. On 9 September 1957 Congress approved the Civil Rights Bill which resulted in the establishment of the Commission for Civil Rights as an independent body and the establishment of a Civil Rights Department affiliated with the Ministry of Justice.

In 1959 King and his wife visited India where they spent a period studying Gandhi's methods of non-violence. After his return he moved back to the city of Atlanta where he worked with his father in the administration of the Baptist Church there. However, an arrest warrant was issued against him on charges of forging tax documents for the years 1956 and 1958. He was arrested and tried and his innocence emerged from the charges against him. He was then also accused of sitting in a public place where blacks have no right to sit and was arrested and imprisoned in 1960.

1961 saw the formation of the Free Riders group who announced their intention to take interstate buses that were covered by racial segregation laws. The Supreme Court ruled that racial discrimination on buses crossing the states was unconstitutional. Thus, the first group of free passengers used the bus that transported passengers from Washington to the state of Mississippi. However, groups of racist fanatics attacked and burned the bus in Alabama.

King was one of the leaders of the 1963 March for Jobs and Freedom on Washington where he delivered his 'I Have a Dream' speech on the steps of the Lincoln Memorial.

The following year, riots began to multiply in various parts of the country, especially with the increase in violence committed by racist members of the Ku Klux Klan organisation.

On 10 December 1964 King was awarded the Nobel Peace Prize in recognition of his tireless efforts to grant blacks their civil rights using peaceful means.

White supremacists continued the riots to terrorise blacks and discourage them from demanding their rights. They were confronting the peaceful demonstrations carried out by these people which became mixed with the participation of many white moderates in them.

The worst rioting occurred in Detroit between 23 and 30 July 1967 which killed more than 43 people and injured 324. This prompted black leaders Martin Luther King, Philip Randolph, Roy Wilkins and Whitney Young to call for an end to the violence.

In April 1968 during a meeting in the city of Memphis while he was addressing the crowds gathered in front of the hotel in which he was staying a sniper shot him in the neck. He died in the hospital a few hours later ending a life full of struggle for freedom and civil rights.

PILGRIMS alongside us

Joni Eareckson Tada

Imagine being trapped in a body that doesn't allow us to move our arms or our legs. Imagine that happening when we're 17 and have our life ahead of us. How would we find freedom?

Growing up, Joni lived an active life. She enjoyed ridinghorse, hiking, tennis and swimming. It was in 1967 she dived into the Chesapeake Bay. The water was murky and she misjudged the shallowness of the water. She found herself under water unable to move her arms or her legs.

Though she didn't know it, she had broken her back with a fracture between the fourth and fifth vertebrae. As a result she was para-lysed from the neck down. He sister dragged her from the water and she was rushed by ambulance to hospital where she underwent surgery to try to repair the injury. She woke up in the Intensive Care Unit in a frame holding her body in place.

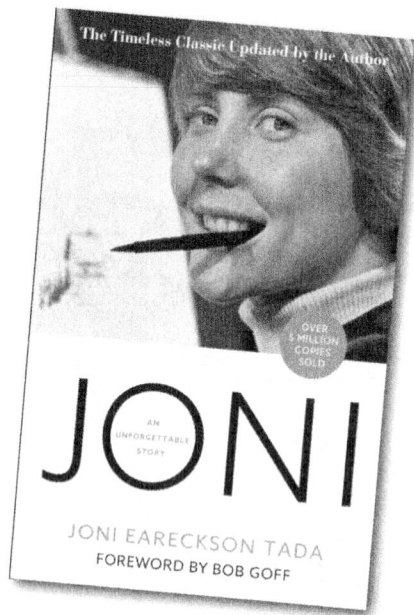

Physically she felt she was little more than a corpse. She would never walk again and sank into depression. She prayed for some accident to kill her. But though she wished for it, she couldn't commit suicide. Her arms and hands were no longer controllable to be able to achieve even that.

She had two years of rehabilitation which was far from easy. She experienced anger, depression and doubts about God. It was during this time that she learned to paint with a brush between her teeth. She began selling her paintings. In the early 1970s there wasn't the voice recognition software we have today so writing was done with a stick between her teeth tapping on a keyboard.

Joni has written over 48 books which have been translated around the world. One, 'A Step Further: Growing Closer to God through Hurt and Hardship' was translated into 30 languages including Polish and more than two million copies printed.

When she arrived in Poland she was greeted by Henryk, 'You've been a

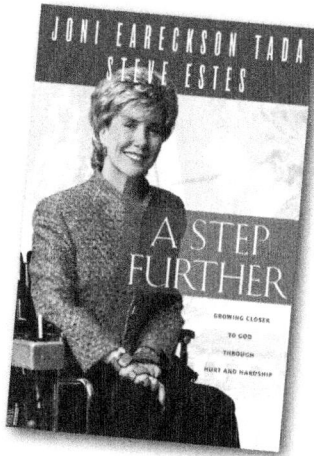

I dreamed a dream in time gone by,
When hope was high and life, worth living.
I dreamed that love would never die,
I dreamed that God would be forgiving.
Then I was young and unafraid,
And dreams were made and used and wasted.
There was no ransom to be paid,
No song unsung, no wine, untasted.

(I Dreamed a Dream from the Musical Les Misérables)

great help to many of us here. We've passed your story around to everyone in the group.' She wondered how she, as a paralysed person, could help a Polish clergyman who had spent more than thirty years under an oppressive communist regime. She had nothing in common with him. She realised that what binds the entire human family together is suffering, and the feelings of being trapped by it.

Sometimes the hope of freedom feels like a forlorn hope or dream. We know, though, that dreams don't always work out. Things don't come together as we would desire. We're disappointed and feel trapped. So is the solution to give up on dreams? A 17-year-old girl who becomes paraplegic and gave up on the dream of marriage…

God is bigger than our dreams and has bigger dreams for us. But to walk in those dreams we need to face obstacles and to follow his pilgrimage for our lives.

Joni Eareckson Tada's books, including Joni. A Step Further and Joni and Ken—the story of her falling in love with and marrying Ken Tada—are available on Amazon. They are recommended reading.

If the Son sets you free, you will be free indeed

Nader Abdel Amir

Among the famous sayings of our Lord Jesus Christ, he said:

'I am the light of the world. If you follow me, you won't have to walk in darkness, because you will have the light that leads to life.' (John 8:12-16).

Our master Jesus indicated with his words that humanity is walking in a deep spiritual darkness and that we are in dire need of the light that is in us, that is, in the Lord Christ. But the hard-line clerics, the Pharisees, were not convinced by his words and answered him, saying: *'You are making those claims about yourself! Such testimony is not valid.'* (John 8:13).

Jesus told them, "These claims are valid even though I make them about myself. For I know where I came from and where I am going, but you don't know this about me. You judge me by human standards, but I do not judge anyone. And if I did, my judgment would be correct in every respect because I am not alone. The Father who sent me is with me. Your own law says that if two people agree about something, their witness is accepted as fact. I am one witness, and my Father who sent me is the other."

"Where is your father?" they asked.

Jesus answered, "Since you don't know who I am, you don't know who my Father is. If you knew me, you would also know my Father."' (John 8:14-19)

This was a strong word. Contemporaries of Jesus needed to hear it because they had always deluded themselves that they were spiritually OK, just because they had descended from their forefathers of Abraham and Isaac. However, the warmth and sincerity of these teachings that our master Jesus spoke made many believe in them.

That is why our master Jesus also said, to those who believed in him: *'You are truly my disciples if you remain faithful to my teachings. And you will know the truth, and the truth will set you free.'* (John 8:31-32)

It was expected that all who heard these words would welcome them because they are based on the truth and because they referred to the most important topic in the world: freedom from the dominion of Satan and the bondage of sin inherent in human nature. Unfortunately, many of those who had believed in Christ believed in him only superficially. They ended up rejecting his teaching about freedom, saying: *'But we are descendants of Abraham,'* they said. *'We have never been slaves to anyone. What do you mean, "You will be set free?"'* (John 8:33)

It seems that when the Children of Israel said that they had never been

'I tell you the truth, everyone who sins is a slave of sin. A slave is not a permanent member of the family, but a son is part of the family forever. So if the Son sets you free, you are truly free. Yes, I realise that you are descendants of Abraham. And yet some of you are trying to kill me because there's no room in your hearts for my message. I am

fast in his frank and honest words. It is the liberation from the power of sin inherent in the soul of every human being.

Are we, in this materialistic age, reeling under the yoke of all kinds of calamities and sins, also ready to test the true freedom that our Master Jesus Christ spoke about?

Are we, in this materialistic age, under the yoke of all kinds of calamities... ready to try the freedom that Jesus spoke about?

enslaved, they forgot that their forefathers had been enslaved by Pharaoh, the Assyrians, the Babylonians and others, and that they were in those days under the yoke of Roman colonialism. Nevertheless, Christ was not talking about slavery in its political or geographical sense. Rather, he was talking about a type of colonisation and slavery more severe than the slavery under which the Children of Israel lived in the past. So he went on to say to them:

telling you what I saw when I was with my Father. But you are following the advice of your father.' (John 8:34-38)

The Messiah did not stop here by talking about the disease but gave the effective medicine saying: *'So if the Son sets you free, you are truly free.'* (John 8:36)

There is no freedom but in Christ. This is the true freedom experienced by all those who truly believe only in our Lord Jesus Christ and are stead-

Whoever is freed by the Lord Christ becomes truly free from the whims of the material world and the self-controlled soul. He gives his life to serve God and his fellow human beings, and works to spread the causes of freedom, righteousness and goodness.

This is exactly what we desperately need today, for individuals and peoples. And this is what it means to be on the Messianic Pilgrimage.

PROVERBS
for Freedom

Chains are chains even if made of gold. SERBIAN

The old lion is dead. Now we eat. SOUTHERN AFRICAN

You surrender your freedom where you deposit your secret. JAPANESE

Freedom is not worth having if it does not include the freedom to make mistakes INDIAN

No one can pick good fruit from the tree of oppression. ARABIC

Has anyone heard of the person who had to find a dentist in another country because he dared not open his mouth in his own? ARABIC

Cleanse your heart from greed and your feet will remain free of fetters. ARABIC

A dog barks but the elephant goes on. INDIAN

If the ear had heard, the body would have escaped. WEST AFRICAN

A person deprived of his liberty desires freedom. JAPANESE

GHANAIAN PROVERB

Holding freedom is like holding an egg. Too tight and you crush it; too loose and you drop it

The Spirit of the Lord is on me because he anointed me. he sent me to bring good news to the poor, heal the heartbroken, Announce freedom to all captives, pardon all prisoners. God sent me to announce the year of his grace — a celebration of God's destruction of our enemies — and to comfort all who mourn...

Celebrate Freedom

So let's get the party started, celebrating with a huge 'Yes' to all five of these things:

Yes, God is the great promoter of human freedom, not the great restrictor. He is proactively working his freedom restoration plan.

Yes, Christ puts his Spirit, life and power into us, deputising us as his activists, not to create the new era but to announce that he already created it by his Freedom Declaration.

Yes, I will trust Christ and his Spirit to get me through any loss of freedom I may suffer because powerful people don't want to hear the Freedom Declaration.

Yes, God's whole plan revolves around the Messiah, who issued the Freedom Declaration and sent all his followers to keep declaring it and showing what it looks like.

Yes, I will live the freedom I talk about. When people wrong me, I'm not going to say, 'You'll pay for that!' I'm going to let them go free and I'll pray that forgiveness transforms them like Christ's freedom transformed me.

Each season has a celebration where we say 'Yes' to 5 things about being a pilgrim.

Then Jesus returned to Galilee, filled with the Holy Spirit's power. Reports about him spread quickly through the whole region. He taught regularly in their synagogues and was praised by everyone.

When he came to the village of Nazareth, his boyhood home, he went as usual to the synagogue on the Sabbath and stood up to read the Scriptures. 'The scroll of Isaiah the prophet was handed to him. He unrolled the scroll and found the place where this was written:

The Spirit of the Lord is upon me, for he has anointed me to bring Good News to the poor. He has sent me to proclaim that captives will be released, that the blind will see, that the oppressed will be set free, and that the time of the Lord's favour has come.

He rolled up the scroll, handed it back to the attendant, and sat down. All eyes in the synagogue looked at him intently. Then he began to speak to them. "The Scripture you've just heard has been fulfilled this very day!"

Readings for this season

Luke 4: 14-21 The 'Freedom Declaration' of Jesus

Luke 13: 10-17 Jesus sets a woman free from being crippled

Matthew 21: 6-14 Jesus is hailed as the Liberator

John 10: 11-21 Jesus lays down his own freedom so others can be free

Acts 2: 22-32 Jesus is freed from death

Hebrews 2:14-18 Jesus frees others from the fear of death

John 8: 31-38 Obedience to the truth is liberating

5
POWER SEASON

AM I POWERLESS ?

The Power Rhythm we focus on during Power Season:

God is proactively working a strategy to bring the power of heaven to earth so people can live in the new era of freedom and power that Jesus announced. No more, 'I wish, but I can't.'

The Bible is one long coherent story. Near the beginning, God initiates a master plan to bless and heal the world by bringing heaven's power to earth through the descendants of Abraham (Genesis 12:3). Jesus takes that plan to a new level. He personally brings heaven's power to earth. It is as if the power is inside him and he is radiating it. It changes people and it does miracles.

But then the story of the Bible has a problem. What happens to the power when Jesus leaves? Does it go with him? Are humans right where they were before, doing the best they can? How are they supposed to obey Jesus and copy him if he is not around to radiate his power into them like he used to?

Power Season celebrates the answer to that question. On Pentecost Day, Jesus sent his own Spirit, his own life and power, from heaven down into his followers on earth proving that Jesus and his power were still present though he himself was not visible. Later examples in the book of Acts show that he could do it again any time and anywhere he chose. Through his Spirit, Jesus is still around. There never needs to be a spiritual power shortage again.

The other half of the big idea of Power Season:

God's strategy for our era is to channel his power to earth through all who have the Spirit of the risen Jesus living in them. We tell everybody else where the power comes from and how to get it.

When reinforcements arrive in a battle, there is always a huge sense of relief and joy. The arriving troops turn the tide, and the battle that was going to be lost is won. Afterwards the rescued ones can't thank the reinforcements enough for arriving when they did.

The arrival of the Holy Spirit of Jesus in his original followers in Jerusalem on Pentecost Day was like that. The Spirit brought the power that the followers needed in order to convince the world that their message was true—Jesus really was alive again. He was and always will be the power centre of history.

Once the Spirit of Jesus gets hold of us, the power of Jesus comes too. We can do things we could not do on

THE BIG IDEA

our own. Life gets exhilarating. How will our desires shift? Who will Jesus help through us? Is a miracle coming somewhere? Jesus is full of surprises.

Even before the surprises come, we realise that the first effect of the power of the Spirit is to lift a huge weight off our shoulders. Success doesn't depend on us anymore. Never again will we feel like losers, hopelessly trapped and powerless. We are surfing a super-wave of power that no one can stop.

Our part is simple (though not easy). All we have to do is keep letting the power of Jesus do whatever he wants it to do in us or through us.

The more his power works, the more amazed and grateful we get. And when other people notice the evidence that something unusual is going on in us or through us, we point them straight to the power source, King Jesus.

They can ask for his power just like we did. They invite Jesus to send his Spirit into them to go to work on them from the inside out, doing what- ever Jesus wants and assigning them their niche in his global campaign for an empowered world.

That is basically what the Power Season is all about. It is like calling for back-up in a situation that is getting out of our control, except that in this case we aren't merely hoping Jesus will send help quickly. We are realising he already sent it by his Spirit. So we welcome the Spirit.

Bottom line of the big idea of Power Season:

We see ourselves as walking evidence of Jesus' power for good, calling the world to embrace this power. We live in alignment with God's intentions when he sent the Spirit of Jesus down into his original followers on Pentecost Day.

Jesus made his Power Promise to his followers, *'You will receive power when the Holy Spirit comes upon you. And you will be my witnesses, telling people about me everywhere—in Jerusalem, throughout Judea, in Samaria, and to the ends of the earth.'* (Acts 1:8).

When we receive the Holy Spirit of Christ in us we become walking evidence of God's power for good, we demonstrate that Jesus' promise is coming true in us. We are participating in the new era of freedom and power that Jesus launched. We are empowered by his Spirit to play our assigned role as a member of his campaign team.

His power is meant for everybody, but not everybody knows that yet. People are living as best they can without knowing where the power of Jesus comes from, how it works, and how they can get it. If we know that power, our cause in life is to help everybody discover it.

If you don't know that power but you do want a better world, please realise that is why God sent the power through the Messiah—for the good of the world. Why not invite his power to work through you instead of contributing only what you can manage by your own power? Why not get on board with his plan instead of trying to work some other plan?

The Holy Spirit and power

A friend of mine's daughter died a few years ago. She was only middle aged, not old. It must be terrible to bury your child. My grandmother out-lived all three of her sons she had, including my father. Much of life seems really difficult.

In the 21st century we can carry a connection to almost all the knowl-edge in the world on a mobile phone in our pocket. But we cannot stop a loved one from dying.

And it isn't just the ultimate trial of death that is hard. Sometimes it can be war, sometimes it can be losing a job or a family breakup. Sometimes days seem hard when we have had a row with a friend or a member of the family.

Sometimes it could be something smaller like a tyre bursting on our car, or the computer not doing what we want it to. One way or another life seems to be difficult. People might tell us God loves us, but it certainly doesn't feel like that at times! Even praying can be difficult. I think, if we are honest, many of would admit that we fail daily.

What we lack is power. Power to save our relatives from dying, power to bring peace to the world, or to mend a broken relationship.

When the Messiah came to the earth he demonstrated the power of God in many ways. There were times when he fed 5,000 people. There were times when he healed the sick. There was even a time when he brought someone back from dead.

However, prior to being filled with the Holy Spirit we lack that power. And power is what we pray for. On the night of power, called Lailat al-Qadr, Muslims specially pray for power. But throughout the year this is something we pray for. Power to live our lives.

When the Messiah died, the disci-ples were emotionally drained. They lacked the power to go on. They met in locked rooms because they were scared what people would do to them.

Then one day the Spirit of God came on them and suddenly they became very different people. They became the people going through-out the world telling others that God loved them. Did death go away? Were they never sick? Did they always have plenty of money? No, not at all.

The friend I mentioned in the first paragraph claims to be one of those people who follow the Messiah. But when his daughter died it was still hard. Having the power of God doesn't take hardship away, but it is the power of God to continue.

This is the Season of Power. We celebrate God pouring out his Spirit on all people. Let us pray that God again pours out his power into our lives. God gives us pilgrims his spirit. In some mysterious way, his spirit dwells within us as we turn over our lives to Jesus. And the indwelling Holy Spirit is the power to live daily for the Messiah.

PROVERBS
about Power

First be a strong person. Then you can kill the hyena. UGANDAN

Not only the stout can fight; even the thin can fight. LESOTHO

True greatness knows gentleness CELTIC

A hand is but finger and finger staying together. ARABIC

People carry their superiority inside; animals outside. RUSSIAN

If young people had wits and old people had strength, everything might be well done. ITALIAN

If I had what I don't have, I could do what I can't do. SERBIAN

Following virtue is like climbing a hill. Following vice is like sailing downstream. CHINESE

One cannot learn how to swim in a field. SPANISH

No flower stays pink for ten days. KOREAN

Of what use is a lamp to a blind person? SRI LANKAN

There is no worse counselor than fear. PANAMANIAN

Talk does not cook rice. CHINESE

When force is the master, reason's house is the first to be demolished. ARABIC

If the obstacle is below you, jump over it. If it is above you, crawl under it. MALAYSIAN

The little birds have God for their caterer. CHILEAN

God gives every bird its food but never drops it in the nest. DANISH

The son of an elephant is never a dwarf

SWAHILI PROVERB

THOUGHTS
from Uncle Azis

There are times when I feel like weeping. I feel pushed around by the world and unable to make any decision. No, I'm not a Syrian refugee or a Yemeni caught up in a war not of my making... I'm a normal older adult with two children and two grandchildren, yet I often feel I have no power to control my life.

Sometimes we feel overwhelmed with what we have to do. We might be a young mother trying to look after the kids, look after the house and keep a job at the same time... We might be someone whose job is not going well and we are not sure if we will be able to provide for the family... We might be an older person unsure about our health... All of us live with stress and can feel powerless in today's world.

There is a night when Muslims seek that power, when they hope that supplications are accepted and that the mercy of God is abundant. Throughout the ages people have sought forgiveness from God and power to live our lives. This is why the Messiah said:

'These things I have spoken to you while I am still with you. But the Helper, the Holy Spirit, whom the Father will send in my name, he will teach you all things and bring to your remembrance all that I have said to you. Peace I leave with you; my peace I give to you. Not as the world gives do I give to you. Let not your hearts be troubled, neither let them be afraid. You heard me say to you, 'I am going away, and I will come to you.' If you loved me, you would have rejoiced, because I am going to the Father, for the Father is greater than I.'

John 14:25-28

'the Holy Spirit wanted to come and live inside me, not to control me, but to release me...'

More than 40 years ago I had decided to follow the Messiah. But at the same time found I was powerless to change. I was still the same person inside with all the self-centredness. Some friends told me about the Holy Spirit. I'd heard a little about the Holy Spirit, but didn't really understand. What they told me was that the Holy Spirit wanted to come and live inside me, not to control me, but to release me from some of my struggles and to make communication with God easier.

So they prayed with me that the Holy Spirit would come and fill me. It was like a deep peace suddenly descended upon me, and a joy that was not happiness, but something much deeper than that. When I next prayed I found myself using a different language, not an earthly language but a heavenly language which felt like it was communicating directly with God.

When the day of Pentecost arrived, they were all together in one place. And suddenly there came from heaven a sound like a mighty rushing wind, and it filled the entire house where they were sitting. And divided tongues as of fire appeared to them and rested on each one of them. And they were all filled with the Holy Spirit and began to speak in other tongues as the Spirit gave them utterance.

Acts 2:1-4

Pentecost was the first time that the Holy Spirit filled a group of people and gave them gifts to help them live their lives for God. Down through the ages people have rediscovered how God empowers them to live their lives for Him.

That doesn't mean that all the time I now feel on top of the world and empowered to live my life or that I only pray when God gives me a different language to talk to Him. There are still times when I cry, still times when I feel stressed but all the time, somewhere deep inside of me, I feel that the Holy Spirit of God is there helping me live my life for Him and helping me communicate with the Father who loves me.

PILGRIMS *alongside us*

Jane Fonda

In her own words: 'I had spent 60 years disembodied, trying to be perfect so I could be loved. You can't be whole if you're trying to be perfect. Now, as I entered my seventh decade and with much work, I could feel myself becoming whole and I knew: This is what God is.'

'Unfortunately, my very private, tentative step into religion became a loud public misconception. I did feel reborn, I couldn't deny that, but it had nothing to do with the perceived doctrines of fundamentalist Christianity.'

'Christianity was beginning to feel shrunken, freeze-dried. Words drowned out one of my favorite Sufi poems by Hafiz.'

> *Every*
> *Child*
> *Has known God,*
> *Not the God of names,*
> *Nor the God of don'ts,*
> *Nor the God who never does*
> *Anything weird,*
> *But the God who knows only four words*
> *And keeps repeating them, saying:*
> *'Come dance with Me.'*
> *Come*
> *Dance.*

Jane Fonda was born in New York City to American Actor Henry Fonda and Canadian socialite Frances Seymour. Her mother committed suicide and her father communicated to her that what really mattered was just her looks, leaving her with a poor self-image that she struggled with for her whole life.

She had many relationships and a number of unsuccessful marriages. It was after her divorce from Ted Turner in 2001 that she experienced God.

It was an overwhelming power of God she experienced, that she has difficulties of expressing in words:

'I began to notice that the dance was gone. I had started my journey with a powerful sense of the divine presence and I began to get scared: What had I gotten myself into?'

The words she used expressed the difference between knowing about God and actually knowing and experiencing the power of God: 'Thinking and experiencing aren't the same. One happens in the head. The other is a flash, a rush of intuition that seems to permeate our entire being. That is what Jesus meant when he said that God is within us. That is what I am seeking, and I have found that since

I have come to feel God within me, I experience less fear—of anything, including death.'

As we seek the power of God as pilgrims, it is something we experience rather than know. The risen Christ through his spirit comes to us, leads us and communicates with us at a deep spiritual level that gives us the power to follow him.

No More Leaving

At
Some point
Your relationship
With God
Will
Become like this:
Next time you meet Him in the forest
Or on a crowded city street
There won't be anymore
'Leaving.'
That is,
God will climb into
Your heart.
You will simply just take
Yourself
Along!

This poem of Hafiz'
is from 'The Gift'

REMINDER *of Power*

Remember Jesus sent his Spirit and we live with his power

Use the reminder daily to remember the theme of the season. Share it as a greeting in emails, with friends and relatives... wherever you need to focus on the pilgrimage.

PILGRIMS *before us*

Dostoevsky... the great impetus to faith

by Ahmed Atef Fathi

Fyodor Dostoevsky was born in 1822 and died in 1881. He was ill throughout his life, suffering from epileptic fits. He wrote his first novel, 'The Poor People' in 1846, with which he rose into the ranks of distinguished writers.

After some years in the military and then tourism, he settled on writing fiction. He wrote 'The Brothers Karamazov'. He also wrote the book 'Crime and Punishment'.

His stories are characterised by a tenderness that spread into our souls a sense of the presence of God. All of them are a call to goodness, love for children, enthusiasm for motherhood, the pleasure of sacrifice and rising above materialistic worldly things. In his life he was full of these emotions.

On 22 April 1849 about thirty young men, including Dostoevsky, were arrested in St Petersburg. They were accused of gathering to celebrate the birth of the French writer Fourier.

Fourier was famous for a programme proposing a changed society. When we read it these days we find almost absurd in that it provides for the formation of groups, not exceeding 1,600 people living together, as independent cooperatives. It was claimed that those thirty gathered in St Petersburg to conspire to translate this Fourier book, 'a dangerous conspiracy'!

After the defendants spent seven months in prison, they were sentenced to death and then they spent another month on death row.

Pillars were erected in the largest square in St Petersburg. Then the defendants were dressed in white robes and on the morning of December 22, with snow covering the ground they were led out. A priest arrived: He carried a silver cross and asked each of them to kiss it so that the other world will forgive them. Sixteen soldiers with rifles stood and each of them was tied to a pillar in order to be shot. The soldiers were ordered to aim their rifles, ready for the command to fire. Only at this moment they announced that the Tsar had changed the death sentence for exile to Siberia for four years!

Dostoevsky hated young men revolting against the Tsar and we often find his writings mocking and ridiculing those ideas. However his hatred for them was not based on his love for the Tsar's tyrannical regime. He was calling for a boycott of European culture at the same time as Tzar Turgenev was calling to embrace it!

When we delve into Dostovsky's writing we cannot but feel that he hated all the material sciences and the ascendant social movements based on them, and that he has a longing for people to live in faith in God, content with the words of the Gospels, which should be the foundation upon which all morals are built.

Dostoevsky was unable to reconcile the emerging European culture since the early nineteenth century replacing a human vision of progress, morals and religion from the vision of the Church.

He realised that science without religion leads to human destruction. Or, rather, we can say that he saw the tyrannical power of science in the atomic bomb in which the pilot came out drinking a glass of cognac and then killed eighty thousand people in a second and returned laughing to his airbase, as happened in Hiroshima in August of 1945.

After Dostovsky had served his sentence in Siberia and was released, he wrote to Mrs. von Wessen a letter stating:

'God sometimes gives me moments of complete calm. In these moments I find the faith in which everything is manifested to me in clarity and holiness. And my belief in this is very simple, which is that I believe that there is nothing more wonderful, more beloved, wiser, braver and more perfect, than Christ. And not only that, but I tell myself in the feeling of a jealous lover that there can be nothing.'

'More than this, which is that if someone had told me: "Christ contradicts the truth" and if this saying was true, I would have preferred staying with Christ over adhering to the truth.'

All of Dostoevsky's novels seek the faith by which a person can settle in this world, even if this faith contradicts the logic of living and the method of scientific research.

Dostovsky found it necessary to rely on faith, including the painful test when he stood before the soldiers waiting to be shot. After that he continued looking at life from the position of death, a position worthy of changing the outlook and tone of life together. It is clear that he did not forget that experience at all in all that he wrote.

From his writing we can almost conclude that religion is nothing other than looking at life from the position of death. Death is the ultimate human reality.

And when we contemplate it, we find that it changes our values and transforms them from independence to the appreciation of other humans.

In the rush of social life, we can get tired and gasp for wealth or prestige, or we can get carried away in a hideous selfishness, when we do not care about the interests of others and we do not have mercy on those we trample in order to acquire or overcome for ourselves. We are all in this situation to varying degrees but when the idea of death suddenly flashes in our minds we stand and wonder about its end.

This is the feeling of Christ, Gandhi, Tolstoy and even Voltaire, Rousseau and Schweizer. Or rather, every human being who was able to stop his social rush and contemplate the reality of death. Contemplating death can be a religious revelation.

When we contemplate people who have gone before us, we do not then ask about the person, whether they were rich or poor? Were they clever, did they have a car or a palace? Rather, I pay attention to his humanity and meditate on the person when I know that they love flowers, have affection for children, are happy to see the twilight. Rays of intelligence and a longing for freedom shine in their mind, as they feels kinship to animals and even plants. Our certainty of life after death increases our consideration of life. And that is our feeling when we read Dostoevsky. Life roars around us and almost gathers into a volcano in which emotions are trapped and then explode.

Although the reader of his stories feels, from time to time, that his faith in God is being shaken, here and there, his insistence on faith is repeated in the tone of emphasis and anger at scientific logic and the spread of European materialism. His fear of death, when he stood to face the firing squad also made him cling to faith to escape from the meanings of anxiety, doubt and fear.

This faith has made his stories full of mercy, tenderness, brotherhood and righteousness, so that when we read them, we feel these virtues run through our being, as if they were a balm and raise us above ourselves.

All power to God

Nader Abdel Amir

Translated from Arabic

It has been made clear throughout history and the succession of countries and ages that the human power that we often boast about is deceptive. For example, the forces of the human body and mind, military forces, industrial forces, urbanisation and other manifestations of power are nothing but lightning: structures that collapse and disappear, just as people disappear. Overnight they are in their grave and buried after what might have been a life of glory and honour. We do not need here to give any examples of this. Historians wrote about the rise and fall of states, the rise and collapse of city walls and the succession of dynasties, one on the ruins of another. What we are witnessing today suffices as proof of that. In terms of the ability of a virus so small that it cannot be seen with the naked eye to confound the most powerful systems in the world and threaten them with annihilation and demise.

The Holy Bible continues to teach us lesson after lesson about not being deceived by the manifestations of human strength, and trying to rely completely on them. The story of the Tower of Babel in the Bible is nothing but a reminder from God to humanity of their weakness and lack of power. The depth of the story lies in its wonderful symbolism, which applies to all people, individually and in societies, in that the tower is a symbol of proving invulnerability and strength, as well as bragging about the ability to ascend to heaven depending on human forces. In other words, a symbol of forgetting human weakness and challenging the Creator who is worthy of all glory and strength. The result is that God, the Most High, arose from his heights scorning the arrogance of humanity and with one stroke he aborted their pride and scattered them over the earth:

> They said, 'Come, let's build a great city for ourselves with a tower that reaches into the sky. This will make us famous and keep us from being scattered all over the world.' But the Lord (said) 'Come, let's go down and confuse the people with different languages. Then they won't be able to understand each other.' That is why the city was called Babel, because that is where the Lord confused the people with different languages. Genesis 11:4-9

We also have in our Master Jesus Christ a great lesson about Satan's attempt to tempt people by relying

Whenever we see a manifestation of God's power and we mention his greatness, God Almighty will bestow upon us his blessings and strength, which is the true power. Our strength is in God Almighty through our master Jesus Christ who defied the power of the world and the power of death. From God Almighty and through his Messiah, who bought us with his blood, we derive help and steadfastness in moments of weakness, fear, injustice and disease. 'Some nations boast of their chariots and horse but we boast in the name of the Lord our God'. (Psalm 20:7-8)

on human power and boasting about it. He tried in many ways to divert the attention of our master Jesus from his message that he brought to the world, by drawing his attention to the lustre of political power represented in the kingdoms of the world that he granted him to tempt him. But his endeavour failed, as we read in the Gospel of Matthew:

> Next the devil took him to the peak of a very high mountain and showed him all the kingdoms of the world and their glory. "I will give it all to you," he said, "if you will kneel down and worship me."
>
> 'Get out of here, Satan,' Jesus told him. 'For the Scriptures say, 'You must worship the Lord your God and serve only him.'' Then the devil went away and angels came and took care of Jesus.
>
> Matthew 4:8-11

Celebrate the Power of God

So let's get the party started, celebrating with a huge 'Yes' to all five of these things:

Yes, God is the ultimate power holder and He has everything under his control and on schedule. All other power holders are temporary until he decides their time is up.

Yes, God's whole plan revolves around Christ, who willingly laid aside his power and sacrificed himself in order to carry out his mission. He warned his followers they would have to do the same.

Yes, the Messiah has put His Spirit, life and power for good into me, making me a citizen of his kingdom and a member of his team of ambassadors on earth.

Yes, I keep doing the most basic thing the Spirit empowers me to do—forgiving others for everything like the Messiah has forgiven me. I will not allow vengeance to block the power flow through me.

Yes, I will trust the Messiah and His Spirit to give me power to endure whatever I may have to suffer as an ambassador of the King.

Each season has a celebration where we say 'Yes' to 5 things about being a pilgrim.

On the day of Pentecost all the believers were meeting together in one place. Suddenly, there was a sound from heaven like the roaring of a mighty windstorm, and it filled the house where they were sitting. Then, what looked like flames or tongues of fire appeared and settled on each of them. And everyone present was filled with the Holy Spirit and began speaking in other languages, as the Holy Spirit gave them this ability.

At that time there were devout Jews from every nation living in Jerusalem. When they heard the loud noise, everyone came running, and they were bewildered to hear their own languages being spoken by the believers.

They were completely amazed. 'How can this be?' they exclaimed. 'These people are all from Galilee, and yet we hear them speaking in our own native languages!'

Acts 2: 1-8

6

MERCY SEASON

WHO IS MY BROTHER?

The Mercy Rhythm we focus on during Mercy Season:

God is carrying out a campaign to show his mercy to all of us and the centre of his campaign strategy is Jesus, giving his life as a sacrifice for us. We deserved punishment, but we got a sacrifice instead. That is mercy.

The Bible is one long coherent story. The sad pattern repeated through most of this story is that humans disobey or ignore God, he punishes them, he shows mercy by giving them a second chance and they fail again. They don't learn from judgement, or if they do learn anything, it doesn't last.

Jesus breaks that pattern. His mercy is not like the old mercy, giving people a second chance after their punishment. Instead the new mercy of Jesus actually prevents the punishment from falling on us. He pays our fine. He serves our jail time. He even serves our death sentence.

Before Jesus, humanity had never seen mercy like that, not even from God. But in Jesus we get to see it. Mercy Season celebrates it. Jesus is our High Priest and he presents his own blood as the sacrificial blood that offsets our punishment and grants us a pardon.

Of course, that isn't saying we didn't do anything wrong. We did, but we aren't going to pay for it.

The other half of the big idea of Mercy Season:

God's campaign strategy for our era is to spread his mercy across the world through us who have received it from Jesus. We forgive others and point them to Christ as the source of ultimate forgiveness.

When we accept Jesus' sacrifice on our behalf, it is exhilarating. The deeper the hole we were in before, the more exhilarating it is to be lifted out of it. If we think we have done things so terrible that God could never forgive us, we have to think again. Sin is man-made. Jesus' sacrifice is God-made. The man-made problem cannot outweigh the God-made solution. No sin is too big for the mercy of Jesus.

On the other hand, we may think we have been a pretty good person with just a few sins here and there. We might be thinking of God as a scorekeeper who has told humanity the rules of the game and now is keeping a tally of our good acts

THE BIG IDEA

from https://syncx.org

and our bad ones. We may think that when our life is over, he will judge us by our total net score.

Jesus laid down his life to kill that idea and replace it with the truth. God isn't in the scorekeeping business. He is on a mercy-spreading campaign. Anyone who joins his campaign team becomes a mercy spreader, a mercy agent. That's what the team is for--to fill the world with mercy, to show the world what it looks like and feels like.

Does that mean God has become soft-hearted? Does it mean the good news of Jesus is, 'Hey, world! You can get away with anything now?' No, that is totally out of sync with Jesus' intentions when he made his sacrifice. He never intended his sacrifice as a permit to do evil. He was showing us mercy that would motivate us not to do evil any more and not to retaliate against people who do evil to us.

The grace period means punishment is postponed. We have time to get in sync with his mercy, to welcome it, to ponder it, to let it go to work on us and in us. As it does, it turns us into mercy agents. We explain the grace period so that everyone can take advantage of it before it expires. We urge everyone to say to Jesus, 'sync me with your mercy!'

Bottom line of the big idea of Mercy Season:

We see ourselves in Christ as mercy agents, showing his mercy and urging people to take advantage of the grace period. We live in sync with Christ's intentions when he presented his own blood as a sacrifice.

Our message as mercy agents is summed up in Romans 5.8: 'God put his love on the line for us by offering his Son in sacrificial death for us when we didn't deserve it at all.' (authors' paraphrase)

When we sync with the Messiah, we see ourselves as mercy agents. We realise that what Jesus intended when he sacrificed himself is coming true in us. His mercy is solving our sin problem, taking over our lives and turning us into forgiving people. We get connected, healed and blessed. This is exactly what is supposed to happen during the grace period.

It is supposed to happen for everybody, but not everybody knows that yet. People are living as best they can without knowing what the mercy of Jesus looks like, how it works and how we get it. If we know that mercy, our 'cause' in life is to help everybody discover it. We are caught up in that cause, energised by it and delighted every time we see even a small sign that the mercy is spreading.

If you don't know that mercy but you do want a better world, please realise that is why God sent the mercy—to connect, heal and bless the world. Nothing improves the world more or quicker than forgiveness, and there is no better source of transformative forgiveness than the self-sacrifice of Jesus. Why not join his campaign instead of starting your own or joining some other campaign that can't forgive like Jesus can?

THOUGHTS
from Uncle Azis

Some years back, I was on a boat heading towards Gibraltar when I heard on the boat's radio a message asking all ships to look for a wooden boat with 11 people on board. They were probably poor, illegal immigrants to Europe hoping for a better life. Unfortunately, we did not encounter them: they may have died during the crossing.

I remembered that about 1,300 years ago, Tariq Ibn Ziyad arrived with an army of 7,000 knights in what is now Gibraltar. There he burned the ships and spoke to his men, saying that the sea was behind him and the enemy in front of them, so they had no choice but victory or death. Many years more than 6 times that number have attempted to cross the Mediterranean to Europe. Many died during this and many of them were returned to their countries of origin.

But what drives people to such difficult adventures fraught with all dangers as they try to cross the sea in small boats loaded with numbers of people far beyond their capacity? They are driven by something that can be summed up in two words—poverty or death. For those of us who can choose and buy whatever food we want, wear whatever clothes we want and choose where we want to live, extreme poverty seems to us quite strange. But for many, it is a daily struggle for survival.

When God blessed Abraham and told him that his offspring would spread throughout the world, he also commanded him and his offspring to be a blessing to others. Therefore, the spiritual sons of Abraham, the people of the pilgrim band, are required to bless others through alms or tithes. Traditionally tithing is only 10% of total income but zakat can be more complicated to calculate. However, the goal is the same, to be a blessing to those who are less fortunate than we are.

Being a blessing to others

God did not command any specific form or amount of giving when he told Abraham to be a blessing. Those came later in his dealings with humanity. Many people try their best to find ways to give less. The poor are still among us, as we see every day. Many of them try to cross into the European Union or get the American green card as a passport hoping for a better life.

A friend from North Africa told me how when he was giving zakat (Islamic word for charity) to one of the poor, the latter was not only expressing his gratitude but his eyes were filled with tears with joy at the zakat he had received. This encouraged me, too, to always look for ways to be a blessing for others.

A few years ago, when I became aware of the call to be a path of grace for others I began to feel a transformation in me. Every day I prayed, 'How can I be a conduit to more grace in other people's lives?' I did not find easy answers nor did I find any formula for calculating grace.

That is grace is something related to the heart and the mind. It is a change of direction from focusing on oneself to focusing on others. This is what Christ spoke of when he asked us to repent. Repentance does not mean regret, but rather a change in the direction of our lives. It means joining the Messianic Pilgrimage instead of staying in our own little kingdoms.

The poor will always be among us. We have to be a path of grace not only for the poor, but to make our whole life a blessing and a blessing in the lives of others.

Jesus replied, 'They do not need to go away. You give them something to eat.'

Matthew 14:16

PILGRIMS *before us*

Francis of Assisi

Translated from Arabic

Although this great man of God only lived 44 years on this earth, the imprints of his love for God are still noticeable over 800 years later.

Francis was born in 1182 in the town of Assisi in Italy. His father was a wealthy textile merchant and his mother came from a noble family. His father named him Francis because he was in France on a business trip when he learned of his son's birth.

Indulged by his very wealthy parents, youthful Francis lived a privileged and high-spirited life. Around 1202, he joined a military expedition and was taken prisoner, spending a year as a captive. An illness caused him to re-evaluate his life.

He then had a vision or dream in which he felt he was called to serve people, especially the poor.

That vision was the beginning of his Messianic Pilgrimage, losing his life in order to find it. Instead of loving the world and its pleasures, he loved the creator of the world and turned to him in repentance for his life of self-indulgence.

His new life had one purpose—to convey God's love in physical acts, not with words but with love for all people. Since God's love includes everybody. Francis served other human beings regardless of their race, colour or religion.

Francis' father disliked his new lifestyle, spending so much on the needy and the poor. In an attempt to force him to change, he cut Francis off from his current support and his future inheritance. He would not even give him a job in the family business.

But Francis did not change. He worked as a daily labourer in small jobs in order to obtain his strength and sustenance for the poor whom he loved, and he insisted that he receive his wages in food and not money.

He called himself 'The Poverty Lady's Husband' as if he had married poverty. He devoted all his efforts to helping the poor. He decided to take care of neglected patients, rejected and feared by the healthy, such as lepers.

After a while, a number of others joined him, following his method of voluntary poverty, love and service to needy people. They were later called the Franciscans.

They were guided by his famous prayer, a prayer full of mercy, a great prayer for any Messianic Pilgrim. It ends, 'It is in pardoning (or showing mercy, forgiving) that we are pardoned. It's in dying (to our old lives) that we are born to eternal life.'

Francis even travelled from Italy to the Middle East to take his message of love and service and to inform all people of the love of the Lord. He arrived in Egypt and met Sultan Al-Kamel during the Fifth Crusade. He worked to mediate peace between the warring parties and negotiated a truce. Sultan Al-Kamel welcomed the truce but the Crusader army rejected it. This was a great shock to Francis, though it was reported that the Sultan decided to follow in Jesus' steps as a result.

He died in 1226, leaving his followers to keep showing God's mercy and love to the poor by deeds rather than words. There are now well over 17,000 Franscisans in about 5,000 communities worldwide. This is his legacy as a pilgrim who inspired others into the pilgrimage of mercy.

Francis of Assisi's Prayer

Lord make me an instrument of your peace
Where there is hatred let me sow love.
Where there is injury, pardon.
Where there is doubt, faith.
Where there is despair, hope.
Where there is darkness, light.
Where there is sadness joy.
O Divine master grant that I may
Not so much seek to be consoled as to console
To be understood, as to understand.
To be loved. as to love
For it's in giving that we receive
And it's in pardoning that we are pardoned
And it's in dying that we are born
To eternal life.

PILGRIMS
alongside us

Katie Davis Majors

At 18, in 2006, she disobeyed and disappointed her parents by not going to college so she could go to Uganda. 'I quit my life… I quit college; I quit cute designer clothes and my little yellow convertible; I quit my boyfriend. I no longer have all the things the world says are important.'

Katie Davis, then living in Nashville, Tennessee, quit everything she knew. She left behind her family and friends in order go to Jinja on the shores of Lake Victoria in Uganda for a year-long trip to follow God's calling on her life. That was the start of her pilgrimage, when she said 'yes' to God.

'I never meant to be a mother. I mean, I guess I did; not right now, though. Not before I was married. Not when I was nineteen. Not to

so, so many little people. Thankfully, God's plans do not seem to be affected much by my own.' Katie wrote this in the introduction to her biography 'Kisses from Katie: A Story of Relentless Love and Redemption'. That reminds me of another young girl who didn't expect to be a mother

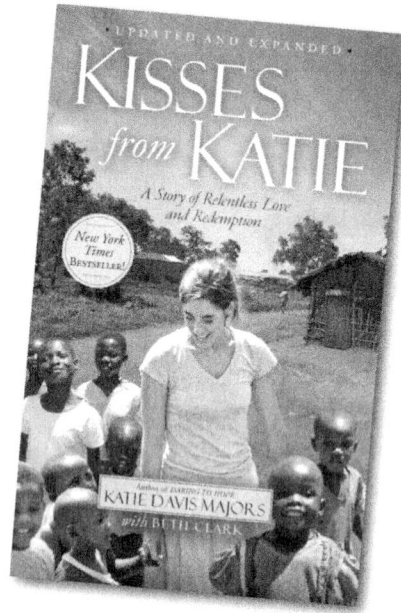

before she was married. That, too, was the result of God calling. It was to Mary to be the mother of Jesus.

Katie continued, 'Jesus wrecked my life. For as long as I could remember, I had everything this world says is important. In high school, I was class president, homecoming queen, top of my class. I dated cute boys and wore cute shoes and drove a cute sports car… But I loved Jesus.'

So Katie took a year out to go to Uganda before returning to the normal American life. But that year of following Jesus in Uganda made her realise that returning to 'normal' wasn't possible. So, in her words, she quit life, 'Jesus wrecked my life, shattered it to pieces and put it back together more beautifully.'

She is now director of Amazima Ministries. Amazima means Truth in the local language. Living on the shores of that part of Lake Victoria is not easy, with child abductions, sale of children (driven by poverty) and even child sacrifice in some traditional rituals of power.

Yet it is into this situation that God called Katie: 'As you continue reading and learning more about Amazima's work in Uganda, we hope that you continue to see the call to discipleship in what we do and how we do it. It is our belief that the Bible defines the act of caring for others in a way that is strengthened by relationships that mirror the discipleship model of Jesus Christ and that is only possible through Jesus Christ himself. There is much yet to do in service to our great God and we are well pleased to serve and work in a way that encourages others toward the way and the truth and the life.'

'The answer to everything is relationship,' is one of Katie's phrases. Her home is like others in that part of Africa and centres around the kitchen. She sometimes felt she spent the majority of the day there… washing dishes and making dinner and singing worship songs to the Lord. The children trailed in and out with endless questions, laughter and muddy footprints filling her home with joy. This might sound magical and sometimes it is. But, 'sometimes it isn't. Children bicker and this mama loses her temper and the bread burns in the oven and things can unravel very quickly.'

Amid all this was pain. Pain of seeing friends die, beating her hands on the bathroom floor begging the Lord that she would not have to bury yet another friend. 'He didn't make the pain easy. But he made it beautiful. He held me close and whispered secrets to me and revealed things about himself that I had not yet known.'

One of her favourite Bible verses is Psalm 37:4 *'Take delight in the LORD and he will give you your heart's desires.'* She says that her understanding of it was that if she followed his commandments and was a 'good girl' He'd make her dreams come true. But she came to realise that it's not about God making her dreams come true, but about God changing her dreams into his dreams for her life.

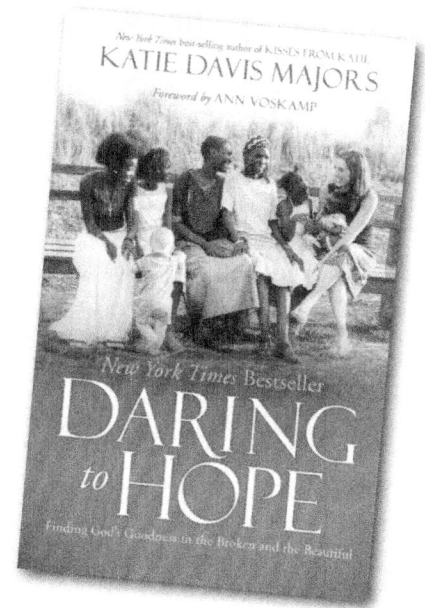

The books 'Kisses from Katie' and 'Daring to Hope' are both available on Amazon. They will encourage you to see how God leads us on out pilgrimage if we only say 'Yes'.

'I am I AM, the merciful and gracious God,'

Nader Abdel Amir

Translated from Arabic

Mercy is a central attribute of God, as it is written in the book of Exodus: *The Lord passed in front of Moses, calling out, "Yahweh! The Lord! The God of compassion and mercy! I am slow to anger and filled with unfailing love and faithfulness."* (Exodus 34:6) It is also written in the book of Psalms, *'The Lord gives righteousness and justice to all who are treated unfairly… The Lord is compassionate and merciful, slow to get angry and filled with unfailing love… He does not punish us for all our sins; he does not deal harshly with us, as we deserve. For his unfailing love toward those who fear him is as great as the height of the heavens above the earth… The Lord is like a father to his children, tender and compassionate to those who fear him.'* (Psalm 103:6-13)

In Islam, two of the Most Beautiful Names of God are derived from mercy. God is described as 'merciful and merciful' in an attempt to capture the vastness of his mercy. And 'the Most Merciful, the Most Merciful' is one of the seven repetitions without which no prayer is considered valid.

Mercy on the part of Almighty God is not repaying us with what we deserve. On the part of humanity, it is showing compassion in our dealings with others, especially during their periods of distress. But despite what we see of the cruelty of the hearts of the people around us, we know that God did not create them cruel, but rather created them merciful in his image. We wonder where people came from with all this cruelty, before which we often stand astonished.

The answer is in the Bible, which says, *'Since they thought it foolish to acknowledge God, he abandoned them to their foolish thinking and let them do things that should never be done.'* (Romans 1:28)

God is compassion and a source of mercy and when people walked away with him the result was that they became *'full of every kind of wickedness, sin, greed, hate, envy, murder, quarreling, deception, malicious behaviour and gossip.'* (Romans 1:29) We know that Jesus did not only teach his disciples and his followers mercy, but made their hearts a source of mercy and compassion for others.

This is clear in many different forms, including:

- Empathise with the person who suffers and show mercy. As we read in the story of the Samaritan who showed mercy to the wounded man who was who was lying on the road about to die.

We read how he tenderly bandaged his wounds, carried him on his horse, took him to a hotel and then paid the hotel fee. And then Christ admonished his listener, *'now go and do the same.'* (Luke 10:33-37).

- Have compassion for parents and watch over their comfort and happiness, because blessed are the children who are merciful to their fathers and mothers, as we read in the Book of Exodus, *'Honour your father and mother. Then you will live a long, full life in the land the Lord your God is giving you.'* (Exodus 20:12).

Faithful children, merciful toward their parents, make it easier for them to be faithful to God. God has used the human relationship as a symbol of our relationship with him, whether in terms of his creation for us, or in terms of his bounty and grace.

- Compassion for animals: We read in the Book of Proverbs this verse: *'The godly care for their animals but the wicked are always cruel.'* (Proverbs 12:10).

We read in the book the story of Balaam, the evil, cruel-hearted man, who kept beating his donkey fiercely and harshly and even wished that he had a sword to kill it. With the bitter irony of the blindness and cruelty of the human heart.

The Bible also tells us that those who lack mercy have bitter consequences. Jesus told a story about a slave whose master forgave him ten thousand coins, which is the equivalent of millions today but this evil slave refused to forgive a fellow slave with only one hundred coins and had him put in prison.

So the king brought that servant to him again and said, *'You evil servant! I forgave you that tremendous debt because you pleaded with me. Shouldn't you have mercy on your fellow servant, just as I had mercy on you?'* (see Matthew 18: 21-35)

His master was angry and handed him over to the torturers until he paid all that he owed.

Then the Messiah concluded the lesson from this parable, saying: *'That's what my heavenly Father will do to you if you refuse to forgive your brothers and sisters from your heart.'* (Matthew 18:33).

So whoever forgives and is merciful and has compassion on his brothers, God will treat him in the same way. Let us be merciful!

THOUGHTS
from Uncle Azis

In the late 20th century a Muslim family moved from Bangladesh to the UK. The family lived Bethnal Green in London 5 miles from the British Houses of Parliament. Their first daughter Renu was born and then around the turn of the century another daughter Shamima was born, appropriate as their family name is Begum which means 'a woman of high rank'.

Early in 2015 Shamima stole a passport and left the country together with two friends. She went to the Daesh controlled areas of Syria. She said she was inspired to join Daesh by videos of fighters beheading hostages and also what she had been told was 'the good life' under the group. There she married a Dutch Muslim and had three daughters herself, all of whom, sadly, died. Peace loving Muslims do not associate with the actions of Daesh.

Her father subsequently moved back to Bangladesh. He said 'If she at least admitted she made a mistake then I would feel sorry for her and other people would feel sorry for her, but she does not accept her wrong.' And he later asked for forgiveness on her behalf, 'She has done wrong, I apologise to everyone as her father, to the British people. I am sorry for Shamima's doing. I request to the British people, please forgive her.'

What if Shamima were my daughter? Could I forgive her? If she refused to admit she did wrong? How much wrong is enough to make me forgive or not forgive?

All of us have done some wrong. God doesn't weigh up the good and the bad and say, 'your good outweighs the bad'. None of us are faultless and none of us are in the place God wants us to be. *For all have sinned and fall short of the glory of God*. (Romans 3:23)

Shamima's father Ali has things to teach us 'If she at least admitted she made a mistake then I would feel sorry for her'. Yes, we all need to admit our mistakes. That is the first step. The second is where he takes on himself some of her shame 'She has done wrong… I am sorry for Shamima's doing.'

We read in Isaiah 53 a prophecy about the Messiah telling us how he will deal with our wrongdoing. He would take on himself our misconduct and shame: *'it was our weaknesses he carried; it was our sorrows that weighed him down. And we thought his troubles were a punishment from God, a punishment for his own sins! But he was pierced for our rebellion, crushed for our sins. He was beaten so we could be whole. He was whipped so we could be healed.'* (Isaiah 53: 4-5) He went through death so we could be made whole.

So, if Jesus gave his life for our forgiveness; we admit our sin and ask for his forgiveness, how should we then deal with other people who sin against us?

Then Peter came to him and asked, 'Lord, how often should I forgive someone who sins against me? Seven times?'

'No, not seven times,' Jesus replied, 'but seventy times seven! Therefore, the Kingdom of Heaven can be compared to a king who decided to bring his accounts up to date with servants who had borrowed money from him. In the process, one of his debtors was brought in who owed him millions of dollars. He couldn't pay, so his master ordered that he be sold—along with his wife, his children, and everything he owned—to pay the debt.'

'But the man fell down before his master and begged him, "Please, be patient with me, and I will pay it all." Then his master was filled with pity for him, and he released him and forgave his debt.'

'But when the man left the king, he went to a fellow servant who owed him a few thousand dollars. He grabbed him by the throat and demanded instant payment.'

'His fellow servant fell down before him and begged for a little more time. "Be patient with me, and I will pay it," he pleaded. But his creditor wouldn't wait. He had the man arrested and put in prison until the debt could be paid in full.'

'When some of the other servants saw this, they were very upset. They went to the king and told him everything that had happened. Then the king called in the man he had forgiven and said, "You evil servant! I forgave you that tremendous debt because you pleaded with me. Shouldn't you have mercy on your fellow servant, just as I had mercy on you?" Then the angry king sent the man to prison to be tortured until he had paid his entire debt. That's what my heavenly Father will do to you if you refuse to forgive your brothers and sisters from your heart.'

Matthew 18:21-35

REMINDER *for Mercy*

Remember Jesus' sacrifice and we share his mercy

Use the reminder daily to remember the theme of the season. Share it as a greeting in emails, with friends and relatives... wherever you need to focus on the pilgrimage.

PROVERBS for Mercy

The strong forgive. The weak remember. ECUADORIAN

When your eye reveals to you the immoral deeds of others, say, 'Oh, eye, they have eyes too.' SWAHILI

No revenge is more honourable than the one not taken. SPANISH

We are bound to forgive an enemy. We are not bound to trust him. VENEZUELAN

It is easier to catch a tiger on a mountain than to beg for help. CHINESE

The remedy for injuries is not to remember them. GERMAN

Good people, like clouds, receive only to give away. INDIAN

The voice of the poor has no echo

INDIAN PROVERB

A thread from everyone will make a shirt for the needy. RUSSIAN

The bird who has eaten cannot fly with the bird that is hungry. NATIVE AMERICAN

Those who have the same illness sympathise with each other. CHINESE

If God gives you sickness, God gives you its cure. GHANIAN

Oh Coeur ne connait pas l'inimitié.

Et avec toi, suivre le chemin d'amour.

Je t'ai connu un cœur tendre, qui pardonne.

Comme la rosee doucement embrassée
un bourgeon.

Et toute ta beauté s'est manifestée.

Aussi largement que la mer illimité .

Et seullement l'amour qui embellit.

Cette vie de misère et d'amertume.

Et illumine par ses rayons éclatants.

L'obscurité de la nuit de notre haine noire.

Pardonne mon ami, sans rancunne.

Peu importe combien, pardonne.

Ne pense jamais que la rancune,

Sera un jour la qualité du vertueux.

Quant au pardon c'est une force,

C'est la noblesse et la dignité.

My heart does not know enmity.

And with you, follow the path of love.

I have known you with a tender,
forgiving heart.

Like the rose that gently kissed a bud.

And all your beauty has manifested
itself.

As wide as the unbounded sea.

And only love that embellishes.

This life of misery and bitterness.

And illuminates with its dazzling rays.

Our black hatred of the darkness
of the night.

Forgive my friend, retain no animosity.

No matter how much, forgive.

Never hold a grudge.

One day will be the quality of the
virtuous.

As for forgiveness, it is a strength,

It is nobility and dignity.

Author Unknown

Celebrate Mercy

So let's get the party started, celebrating with a huge 'Yes' to all five of these things:

Yes, God is proactively rescuing the human race. He isn't angrily keeping score and reacting to what we do.

Yes, Christ has put his Spirit, life, and power into me, connecting me to his sspiritual family that goes all the way back to Abraham.

Yes, I will trust the Messiah and his Spirit to get me through any suffering that comes from those who set themselves up against his message of mercy.

Yes, God's whole plan revolves around the Messiah, the Rescuer who shows us what mercy looks like and what it costs.

Yes, I am doing what other pilgrims do—showing mercy to others whether they deserve it or not. I can afford to do that now that Christ has shown mercy to me.

Each season has a celebration where we say 'Yes' to 5 things about being a pilgrim.

from https://syncx.org

That first covenant between God and Israel had regulations for worship and a place of worship here on earth. There were two rooms in that Tabernacle. In the first room were a lamp-stand, a table, and sacred loaves of bread on the table. This room was called the Holy Place. Then there was a curtain, and behind the curtain was the second room called the Most Holy Place. In that room were a gold incense altar and a wooden chest called the Ark of the Covenant, which was covered with gold on all sides. Inside the Ark were a gold jar containing manna, Aaron's staff that sprouted leaves, and the stone tablets of the covenant. Above the Ark were the cherubim of divine glory, whose wings stretched out over the Ark's cover, the place of atonement. But we cannot explain these things in detail now.

Readings for this season

Hebrews 9.1-15. The last 'Day of
    Atonement'
Romans 5.1-11. How mercy changes us
Isaiah 53.3-12. Jesus suffered what
    we deserved
Matthew 6.7-15. The 'Mercy Prayer'

When these things were all in place, the priests regularly entered the first room as they performed their religious duties. But only the high priest ever entered the Most Holy Place, and only once a year. And he always offered blood for his own sins and for the sins the people had committed in ignorance. By these regulations the Holy Spirit revealed that the entrance to the Most Holy Place was not freely open as long as the Tabernacle and the system it represented were still in use.

This is an illustration pointing to the present time. For the gifts and sacrifices that the priests offer are not able to cleanse the consciences of the people who bring them. For that old system deals only with food and drink and various cleansing ceremonies—physical regulations that were in effect only until a better system could be established.

So Christ has now become the High Priest over all the good things that have come. He has entered that greater, more perfect Tabernacle in heaven, which was not made by human hands and is not part of this created world.

With his own blood—not the blood of goats and calves—he entered the Most Holy Place once for all time and secured our redemption forever.

Under the old system, the blood of goats and bulls and the ashes of a heifer could cleanse people's bodies from ceremonial impurity. Just think how much more the blood of Christ will purify our consciences from sinful deeds so that we can worship the living God. For by the power of the eternal Spirit, Christ offered himself to God as a perfect sacrifice for our sins. That is why he is the one who mediates a new covenant between God and people, so that all who are called can receive the eternal inheritance God has promised them. For Christ died to set them free from the penalty of the sins they had committed under that first covenant.

Hebrews 9:1-15

Luke 24. 36-49. Spreading the
    message of mercy
Psalm 103.1-12. The Lord's amazing
    mercy
Isaiah 54.6-15. God's merciful
    restoration of his people

7

REST STOP SEASON

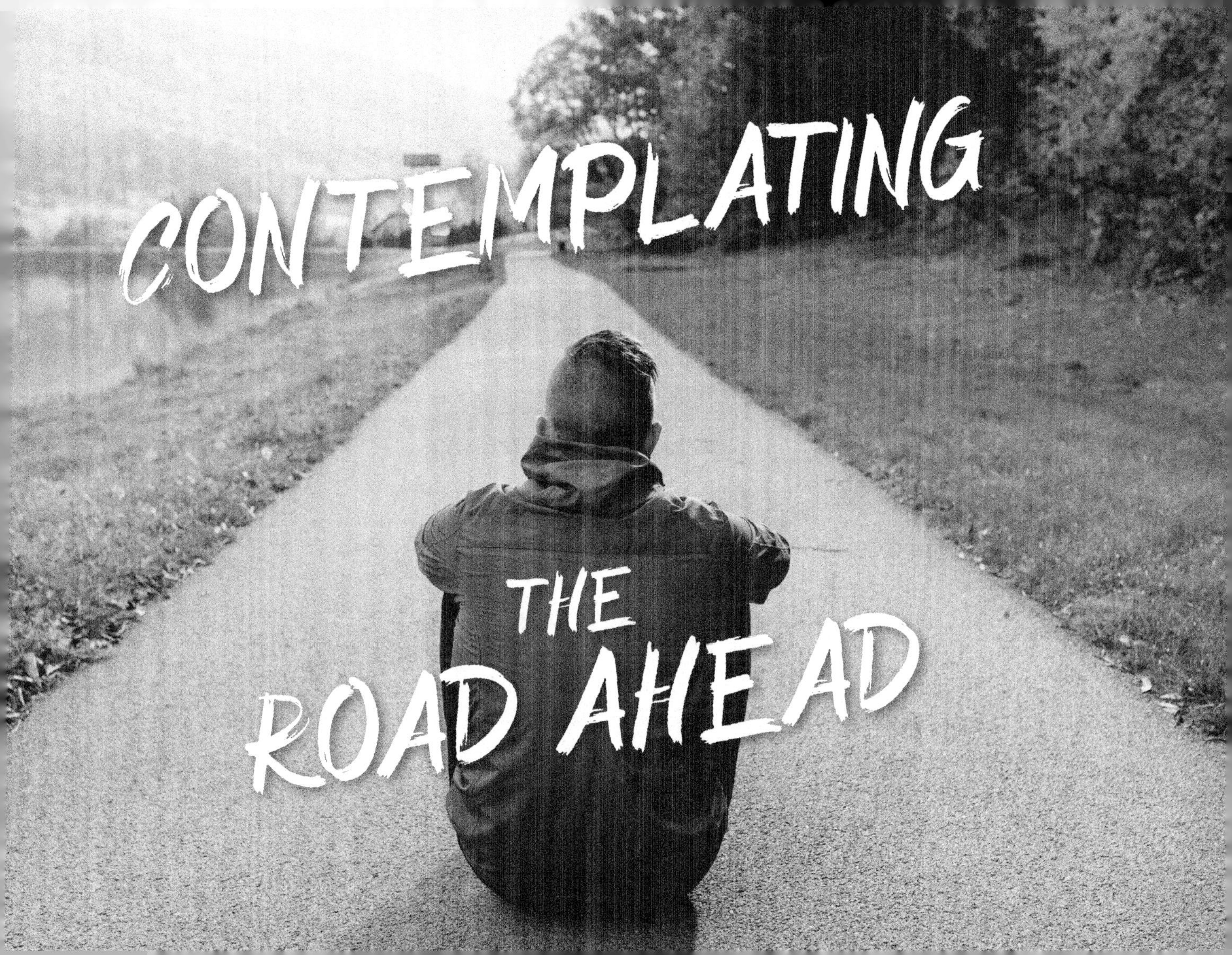
CONTEMPLATING
THE
ROAD AHEAD

Here is the big idea, the Rest Rhythm we focus on at our Rest Stop before continuing

The Messianic Pilgrimage includes a Rest Stop, a chance to look back at the whole journey in celebration and look forward towards the final vision.

The Messiah is no slave driver. He has our well-being in mind as he leads us on our pilgrimage. He does not push any of us to our breaking point. If we ever do hit our breaking point, we missed his guidance somewhere. We either pushed ourselves too far, or we let other voices drown out his.

If we stay alert for his voice during the Rest Stop we get genuine relaxation because he tells us that success does not depend on pushing ourselves to our limits. We just stick with the Messiah and his timetable. When he says, 'Rest,' we rest and that is that.

During our rest we hear him telling us to look back at the phases of the pilgrimage he has already brought us through. That is energising and can be fun. We get reminded of how amazing he is as a guide. We laugh about things that seemed scary at the time. We get overwhelmed with gratitude that we made it this far and full of confidence for the next part of the journey.

Here is the other half of the big idea of the Rest Stop:

An enemy keeps trying to prevent or disturb our rest, whispering lies in our ears.

What lies? 'The great life is the full life lived 24/7, never bored, never missing out on anything.'

24/7 only works for machines and convenience stores; it ruins human beings. None of us are built for it. God knew that if left to self-manage our lives, many of us would try to live 24/7. We would work ourselves into a death spiral driven by greed, financial anxiety, desire to prove our worth, or escapism from other parts of life and we would pull others down with us.

Like work, the all-pervasive fear of missing out can consume us night and day so that we never get to savour anything. We grab a bite before rushing over to the next table to see what we might be missing there. In the process, we miss even the little joy of the bite we took.

THE BIG IDEA

from https://syncx.org

But if we let the Messiah direct us, we find ourselves free from 24/7 and all its life-sucking consequences. In fact, it's our job to be free of them. The pilgrimage is supposed to enrich the lives of the people who join it wholeheartedly. One of the ways it does this is to give our lives a rhythm, including the pauses.

If we don't get the benefit of those pauses, if we are part of the Messiah's pilgrim band but remain half-dead, stressed out, worn out, who will join the band? They will take one look at us and shut their ears to the Messiah's call to join him.

That's why God doesn't just allow us to rest from the pilgrimage; he commands it. So be a good pilgrim. Sit down and rest. Savour it!

Bottom line of the big idea:

We 'see ourselves in Christ' as blessed with a satisfying rest, not driven to ceaseless activity laced with strands of inadequacy and guilt.

In sync with Jesus, we are connected to rest and peace. Like all the other phases of the pilgrimage, the Rest Stop is a gift, an unearned blessing from God's grace.

When we sync with the Messiah as people who get to rest, we realise *we already have what the whole world is looking for!* They will ask how we got it. The glow of our inner peace as we rest will attract people to the Messiah as powerfully as anything else we will ever do.

So rest with all your might, and enjoy it with all your heart. And by the way, don't over zealously think, 'How can I use this rest to attract more people to the Messiah?' That spoils it. It turns your rest into a work project. The truly attractive thing is just to rest while you are resting. If you can do that, the Messiah has you right where he wants you.

REMINDER *for Rest*

Remember God rested from labour and we too take time for rest

Use the reminder daily to remember the theme of the season. Share it as a greeting in emails, with friends and relatives... wherever you need to focus on the pilgrimage.

Contemplating...
the story of
Hayy Ibn Yokdhan

I love stories, especially when the story communicates something deeper. A story I have just read and loved was that of Hayy Ibn Yokdhan by Ibn Tufail. In this story Ibn Tufail tells us of the secret birth of Hayy and how his mother gave him to the protection of God who took him to another island. There he was nurtured by a roe deer and grew to a young child living in relationship with other animals though no humans.

As he grows he controls his environment attacking the wild animals and using the skin of an eagle as clothing. Sadly, the roe deer who nurtured him dies, and he learns of the pain of death. He learns to create weapons and to ride a wild horse. As he grows, he contemplates and thinks on the different types of things he discovers: Solid, liquid and gas, animal, vegetable and mineral.

He learns of hot and cold, of fire and of how things change from hot to cold and cold to hot. As he grows to adulthood, he contemplates wider still his island world with its water boundary and the wider heavenly bodies he sees at night. In that he thinks of how the finite and infinite are different, pondering the motion of the sun, moon and stars. He perceives that their motion is spherical and how the whole heavens are interconnected.

Having thus assembled in his mind his world he then contemplates its creation.

Now, whereas it appeared to him that the whole world was only one Substance which stood in need of a voluntary Agent and that its various parts seemed to him but one thing, in like manner as the bodies of the lower world which is subject to generation and corruption, he took a broad view of the whole world and debated within himself whether it existed in time after it had been and came to be out of nothing; or whether it was a thing that had existed from eternity and never wanted a beginning.

In respect to this matter, he had many and grave doubts within himself, so that neither of these opinions prevailed over the other. *For when he proposed to himself the belief of eternity, there arose many objections in his mind with regard to the impossibility of an infinite being, just as the existence of an infinite body had seemed impossible to him.*

His conclusion to his contemplation is that there must be a creator without bodily substance. This creator had to be all powerful…

So all this world is created and caused by this Agent out of time, whose command is, when he would have anything done: Let it be and it is.

Hayy admires the work of the Creator and in his contemplation thinks how Creation points to the Creator. This encourages him to examine the senses: Hearing, sight, smell, taste and feeling. All of which he recognises to be physical, yet the Creator to be other. The Creator must therefore be infinite rather than finite.

So if we can find out anything which has an unlimited perfection, infinite beauty, brightness and splendour, that does not proceed from it, then he who is deprived of the sight and knowledge of that thing, after having once known it, must necessarily suffer inexpressible anguish, so long as he remains destitute thereof; whereas he that has it continually present before him, must needs enjoy uninterrupted delight, perpetual felicity, boundless joy and gladness.

This is like a journey into heaven for Hayy but in returning to the temporal and physical world it is not long before another human called Asal arrives on the scene. Asal teaches Hayy to speak. In communication, both realise they are given to contemplation considering the meaning of life and of the universe in which we find ourselves.

Now, here the story develops as Hayy and Asal are rescued from the island and return to what we might call civilisation. How, we might wonder, are they received since both have now learned much of the world and its Creator. We won't reveal that… you need to read the book for yourself!

The story of Hayy ibn Yaqdhan, along with three poems, is all that remains of the writings of Ibn Tufail who served Sultan Abu Yaqub Yusuf. The book was influential among medieval Jewish scholars at the Toledo School of Translators run by Raymond de Sauvetst and its impact can be seen in The Guide for the Perplexed of Maimonides. Edward Pococke of Oxford, while visiting a market in Damascus, found a manuscript of Hayy ibn Yaqdhan made in Alexandria in 1303 containing commentary in Hebrew. George Keith, a Quaker, translated it into English in 1674.

Daniel Defoe, author of Robinson Crusoe, was heavily influenced by the work as well as by the memoir of the Scottish castaway Alexander Selkirk. In the Muslim world, the book is an honoured Sufi text.

Some people believe that the best rest comes when we try to empty our minds of all conscious thought. This may include keeping the body very still, isolating oneself, repeating a sound that blocks out other sounds, etc. The goal is to enter a state of complete relaxation.

The Messiah teaches his pilgrims a very different way to find true rest. It involves their minds and their bodies, and they never do it alone. The Messiah tells them that rest comes not in extreme detachment but from deep connection. Our goal is not to empty our minds but to fill them with the Messiah!

Resting with the Messiah

Connection to what?

Picture a group of tourists visiting a famous site. Can you tell who the guide is? Sure! He or she is usually carrying a flag or tall placard so everyone in the group can stay close by and stay safe. Bad things can happen if they get separated from their guide.

The Messiah is like a tour guide for the pilgrims who join him. He taught his first followers a memorial ritual that works like a flag. They can relax or rest as long as they stay close to this flag. If they ever lose sight of it, they will panic because they have got separated from the Messiah.

Pilgrims never want to empty their minds of him. They cannot rest at all unless they know where he is every minute. And that is why he taught the memorial ritual, the only ritual he ever taught. Every time pilgrims participate in it, it engages their minds, their bodies, their souls, and their relationship to the whole band of pilgrims. And it brings them true rest.

7

This is how the Messiah established the memorial ritual

The memorial reminds them of the way Jesus gave his body, his blood, his life in order to connect, heal, and bless the world. It was the complete opposite of our human desires to manage our own lives, avoid pain, an enjoy what we want to enjoy.

The memorial calls to us, 'This way! This way! This is what I did and it is what I call you to do--leave your old self-managed life behind and come with me on the pilgrimage.' (authors' paraphrase)

The memorial includes physical activities--chewing the bread and swallowing the wine that represent Jesus' body and blood. It also intensely focuses our minds on the Messiah giving his life to establish a new link or covenant between heaven and earth, signing it with his blood. And it overwhelms our hearts and souls with gratitude since the whole thing is a gift. We do not qualify to get an invitation to this 'meal'. God just invites us. All we do is agree to share in the meal and to let the food do its work to change us.

How can food change us?

Alcohol certainly can! And different foods have different effects on various parts of our bodies.

The food is a symbol of the Messiah. When in this ritual we symbolically take his 'body and blood' into our bodies, we are as closely attached to the Messiah as we can ever get. We realise that God himself has accepted us because of the Messiah and now we are connected through him.

His life gets into us by spiritual means that are beyond explanation, like getting infected in a good way. His strength comes. So do his peace, his love and his willingness to sacrifice.

All of that adds up to a kind of relaxation the world does not know. All we can say is, 'Thank you Jesus!'

Since we are so closely attached to the Messiah, we are also closely attached to all the other pilgrims who follow him. Eating and drinking together are two of the most basic ways of building a relationship, and that is what we do in this memorial--build solidarity within the band of pilgrims.

We enjoy this kind of rest when we are together, not when we are isolated from each other. The Messiah gives us peace with each other.

We are not a tour group. We are fellow pilgrims, looking out for each other, encouraging each other, and sticking together close to the Messiah for our whole lives.

The memorial brilliantly achieves all this by focusing us on the Messiah.

But there is one exception, one way that the ritual can become poisonous instead of invigorating and restful. The same chapter we quoted above says that people had been poisoned (many got sick and some had died) because they participated in the memorial ritual 'unworthily' (1 Corinthians 11.27-30).

In other words participation in this ritual does not automatically or magically have a good effect. If people do it without realising that it is supposed to change them into sacrificial people, they are rejecting the Messiah's self-sacrifice. They are saying, 'I want the benefit of the Messiah's death for me but I will not make any sacrifices for anyone else.'

They are still living their old lives, their self-managed lives. They are fake pilgrims, and they do not become genuine pilgrims by participating in the memorial ritual. They become genuine by a change of heart, a realisation of what the Messiah did for them and how it turns them into different people.

PILGRIMS *before us?*

Rabia of Basra

Translated from Arabic

Rabia was the fourth daughter of her family hence named Rabia which is the Arabic word for 'fourth'. She was born in the city of Basra between 714 and 718 CE.

According to legend, when Rabia was born, her parents were so poor that there was no oil in the house to light a lamp, nor even a cloth to wrap her with. Her mother asked her husband to borrow some oil from a neighbour but he had resolved in his life never to ask for anything from anyone except God. He pretended to go to the neighbour's door and returned home empty-handed.

The beginning of her adult life was one of wine and self-indulgence and spent a period of her life as a beloved slave to a master whom she loved and adored. After his death, which was a shock to her, she began to think about the reality of life and death. She started to think about the Creator and his care for his creation. She gradually began to melt in love with the Creator, being freed from her previous life to a new life, singing of love for God and talking to others about that beloved.

It is said that one of the rich people of Basra, whose name was Muhammad bin Suleiman al-Hashemi, once searched for a wife and those who knew him referred to him to Rabia al-Adawiya. So he sent her a love letter with an explanation of his wealth and that he would put all that money under her feet. But her reply was a rejection: 'As for me, even if offered double what you offer, I would rather work for God.'

She is one of the founders of the idea of divine love within Islam, a Sufi mystic. She built on longing, passion and sympathy in the relationship between people and their Lord.

Because of her intense love for God, she wove many illusory stories around her but they all focus on the idea of love and adoration between the human soul and its Creator.

After the death of her father, famine overtook Basra. She left her sisters and went into the desert to pray, living a life of semi-seclusion. She is a model of mutual love between God and his creation; her example is one in which the loving devotee on earth becomes one with the Beloved.

God blessed Rabia with the talent of poetry and this talent was fuelled by a strong passion that owned her life, so the words came out from her lips, expressing what she felt from finding and loving God and presenting that poetry as a message to those around her to love that great beloved.

We don't know if Rabia ever knew the Messiah and whether her pilgrimage was the same as ours or alongside ours. Regardless, she expressed intimacy and rest in her relationship with God, but never really moved on from that resting stage to re-engage with the world.

Prayer of Rabia of Basra

O Lord, if I worship You because of fear of Hell,
then burn me in Hell;
If I worship You because I desire Paradise,
then exclude me from Paradise;
But if I worship you for yourself alone,
then deny me not your Eternal Beauty

My joy
by Rabia al-Basra
English version by Charles Upton

My joy —
My Hunger —
My Shelter —
My Friend —
My Food for the journey —
My journey's End —
You are my breath,
My hope,
My companion,
My craving,
My abundant wealth.
Without You — my Life, my Love —
I would never have wandered across these
endless countries.
You have poured out so much grace for me,
Done me so many favours, given me so
many gifts —
I look everywhere for Your love
Then suddenly I am filled with it.
O Captain of my Heart
Radiant Eye of Yearning in my breast,
I will never be free from You
As long as I live.
Be satisfied with me, Love,
And I am satisfied.

PILGRIMS
alongside us

Henri Nouwen

Henri Nouwen was born in Nijkerk, the Netherlands on January 24, 1932. He was the oldest of four children born to Laurent and Maria Nouwen. His father was a tax lawyer and his mother worked as a bookkeeper for her family's business in Amersfoort.

Nouwen studied at the Jesuit Aloysius College in The Hague before spending a year at the minor seminary in Apeldoorn. His spent six years of study for the priesthood, consisting of training in philosophy and theology, at the major seminary in Rijsenburg.

As an academic, Nouwen was a professor of pastoral theology at Yale Divinity School between 1971 and 1981, where he began to establish a broad readership. While a professor at Yale, Nouwen also spent consid-

erable time at the Abbey of the Genesee. The journal of his first seven month visit was published as 'Genesee Diary: Report from a Trappist Monastery'. After his mother died he returned again and resulted in the book 'A Cry For Mercy: Prayers from the Genesee'.

After nearly two decades of teaching at academic institutions including the University of Notre Dame, Yale Divinity School and Harvard Divinity School, Nouwen went on to work with individuals with intellectual and developmental disabilities at the L'Arche Daybreak community in Richmond Hill, Ontario.

Although he had a significant impact on the lives of those at the L'Arche Daybreak community he will be remembered more for his writing. Nouwen published 39 books and authored hundreds of articles many on the subject of contemplation.

Some of Nouwen's writing may make more sense to the introverted pilgrim than the extroverted one when he reflects on 'our desire for solitude' contrasted with the 'demands of contemporary life'. He reminds us that it was in his times of solitude that Jesus found the courage to follow God's will.

In his book 'Reaching Out/Beyond the Mirror' Nouwen echoes two thoughts that are pertinent to the Messianic Pilgrimage: 'reaching out from our arid independence to self-giving' and to God who 'calls us from darkness of our illusions into the light of his glory.'

A chance encounter with a reproduction of Rembrandt's 'The Return of the Prodigal Son' catapulted Henri Nouwen on an unforgettable spiritual adventure.

He then wrote a book with the same title as the painting: The themes of homecoming, affirmation, and reconciliation will be newly discovered by all who have known loneliness, dejection, jealousy, or anger. The book challenges us to love as God loves, and to be loved as God's beloved. As he put it, 'unlike a fairy tale, the parable provides no happy ending. Instead, it leaves us face to face with one of life's hardest spiritual choices: to trust or not to trust in God's all-forgiving love.'

For Nouwen it was intensely personal: 'For most of my life I have struggled to find God, to know God, to love God. I have tried hard to follow the guidelines of the spiritual life—pray always, work for others, read the Scriptures—and to avoid the many temptations to dissipate myself. I have failed many times but always tried again, even when I was close to despair.'

'Now I wonder whether I have sufficiently realised that during all this time God has been trying to find me, to know me, and to love me. The question is not "How am I to find God?" but "How am I to let myself be found by him?" God is looking into the distance for me, trying to find me, and longing to bring me home.'

Nouwen's last book 'Can you drink the cup?' explores the deep spiritual impact of the question Jesus asked his friends James and John based on the time the mother of James and John came to him to ask a favour:

'In your Kingdom, please let my two sons sit in places of honour next to you, one on your right and the other on your left.'

But Jesus answered by saying to them, 'You don't know what you are asking! Are you able to drink from the bitter cup of suffering I am about to drink?'

'Oh yes,' they replied, 'we are able!'

Jesus told them, 'You will indeed drink from my bitter cup. But I have no right to say who will sit on my right or my left. My Father has prepared those places for the ones he has chosen.' (Matthew 20:20-23)

Pondering contemplation

Nader Abdel Amir

Translated from Arabic

Contemplation means to reflect on the matter or ponder the matter in the sense of meditating and reflecting on it slowly. For philosophers and mystics it is often the preoccupation of the mind on a subject to an extent that makes one neglect other things.

Contemplation has many forms. We find some of the most important of them in the ancient eastern religions, philosophies and spiritualities, in India and China in particular. Almost all of them agree that meditation is emptying the mind of every thought so that we can see things as they are. Likewise, the Bible greatly raises the importance of contemplation or meditation but it differs from the ancient eastern religions and spirituality in that it does not invite us to repeat mantras—any specific phrases or formulas, or to empty the mind of every thought but rather invites us to think about topics of high and deep meaning such as the divine I AM, the attributes of the Creator and the question of creation and universes. In the Book of Psalms we read: *'I remember the days of old. I ponder all your great works and think about what you have done.'* (Psalm 143:5) and also: *'I lie awake thinking of you, meditating on you through the night.'* (Psalm 6:63)

We can divide our thoughts into sections, the most important of which are:

- Mental reflection, which is the deepening of consideration of the things around us and an attempt to contemplate what they are.

- Spiritual contemplation, which goes beyond the level of mental contemplation to the level of interaction between the mind and spirit. It then elevates the latter to the level of interaction with the Spirit of God dwelling in us, where the Holy Spirit raises us to high levels and enters us into horizons that did not occur to us before, and inspires us with spiritual ideas. From the gateway of this form of contemplation, we can enter the place of thanksgiving, praise and praise: *'I will praise you, Lord, with all my heart; I will tell of all the marvelous things you have done.'* (Psalm 9:1).

- Practical contemplation, which is the practical application of God's commandments in his book. From this daily application comes the spiritual experience that the believer accumulates through his contemplation of his worship, faith practices and his journey with God *Taste and see that the Lord is* good. *Oh, the joys of those who take refuge in him!'* (Psalm 34:8). Practical contemplation, in other words, reading God's book which is alive today.

Practical steps

We must always bear in mind that our master Jesus Christ is the role model and example in the matter of reflection. He used to spend a long time in seclusion, prayer and contemplation, apart in the wilderness, away from the noise of the world: *'Jesus often withdrew to the wilderness for prayer.'* (Luke 5:16).

Hence we emphasise the issue of solitude as one of the important practical steps in practising contemplation, in addition to other steps that Jesus taught us, such as contemplating nature and the universe *'Look at the lilies and how they grow. They don't work or make their clothing, yet Solomon in all his glory was not dressed as beautifully as they are.'* (Luke 12:27) and also *'Look at the ravens. They don't plant or harvest or store food in barns, for God feeds them. And you are far more valuable to him than any birds!'* (Luke 12:24).

Moreover, the life of the Lord Christ remains the greatest field for contemplation and contemplation: his birth, fasting, signs, teachings, sacrifice of his body in order for us to live, his death and his resurrection from the dead. That is why Augustine famously said, 'There is nothing more useful than to reflect each day on what Christ has endured for us.'

PROVERBS
about Resting

Be relaxed and cool to regain strength. BOTSWANA

Yam thrives well when its mound is cool. TOGOLESE

A fertile field, if it does not rest, becomes sterile. ARGENTINIAN

The heart at rest sees a feast in everything. INDIAN

An interval of sleep is paradise. JAPANESE

Better linger than hurry. SERBIAN

No work is worse than overwork. RUSSIAN

Bad sItting is preferable to good walking. RUSSIAN

Whom God favours, to him it is given in sleep; whom God does not favour, it falls from the spoon. SERBIAN

The peaceful person always has good light. BOTSWANA

The fruit of silence is tranquility. ARABIC

Your restlessness got you. UGANDAN

The rusher has to eat goat; the patient one gets to eat beef. LESOTHO

Quietude is superior to activity

CHINESE PROVERB

Peace

Sara Teasdale

Peace flows into me
As the tide to the pool by the shore;
It is mine forevermore,
It ebbs not back like the sea.

I am the pool of blue
 That worships the vivid sky;
  My hopes were heaven-high,
   They are all fulfilled in you.

I am the pool of gold
When sunset burns and dies, —
You are my deepening skies,
Give me your stars to hold.

MUSIC
to my ears

Fayrouz is a well-known Lebanese artist, who gained fame in all Arab countries thanks to her very distinctive voice, and also thanks to the great revolution she brought about in Arab music with the Rahbani brothers. Although she is better known by the name Fairouz, her real name is Nohad Haddad.

Nouhad Haddad was born in 1935 in Jabal al-Arz in Lebanon to a Syriac Orthodox Christian family and grew up in the Zkak al-Blat neighborhood of Beirut. There she entered Saint Joseph's School in Beirut before her father had to transfer her to a public school during World War II. Since her childhood, she has been fond of the songs of Asmahan and Laila Mourad.

The first to discover her talent when she was no more than fourteen was the composer Mohamed Fleifel, founder of the National Conservatory of Music. He accepted her into the institute. Then, while working on the Lebanese radio as a member of the choir, she was discovered again by the composer Halim Al-Roumi who was also working there. But the big turning point in her life and artistic path was her meeting with the two brothers Assi and Mansour Al Rahbani who worked hard to bring her great singing and artistic potential into fruition through their words and melodies. Around the world, she became more and more famous.

Fayrouz cooperated with Philemon Wehbe, Muhammad Abdel Wahab, Elias Rahbani, Muhammad Mohsen and Zaki Nassif and was awarded the Medal of Honour in 1963 and the Gold Medal in 1975 by King Hussein of Jordan. In March 1994 she gave a huge concert in London that attracted more than 6,000 fans which made Western critics compare it to Billie Holiday and nicknamed her 'Callas of Arabia'.

But all the glory that Fayrouz has achieved over the years is not equal to the joy we feel when she sings and then notice that someone is deeply

listening to her because singing for her is not just an artistic practice, it is a way of life.

Today, though Fairuz no longer sings, she continues to attend the mass of the village church in Antelias. There the simple villagers chant every year during Holy Week with devotion equalled, perhaps, only by their simple piety. This dedication is what constantly refines the talent of the artist Fayrouz and distinguishes her art from all other forms of singing and music spread across the Arab countries.

Translated from Arabic

Celebrate Rest

So let's get the party started, celebrating with a huge 'Yes' to all five of these things:

Yes, God is proactively bringing heaven's restfulness to earth. Nothing will pick us up like that does.

Yes, Christ has put his Spirit and his peace into me, plugging me into the campaign for rest that goes all the way back to Abraham.

Yes, I realise my life may get very hard because some people don't want Christ or the rest he brings but I am trusting him and his Spirit to get me through the pain.

Yes, God's whole plan to restore rest and peace to the world revolves around the Messiah, the Rest-bringer.

Yes, I am taking my first step in peace-spreading now by the Spirit's power — forgiving everybody for everything like the Messiah has forgiven me.

Each season has a celebration where we say 'Yes' to 5 things about being a pilgrim.

'That is why I tell you not to worry about everyday life—whether you have enough food and drink, or enough clothes to wear. Isn't life more than food, and your body more than clothing? Look at the birds. They don't plant or harvest or store food in barns, for your heavenly Father feeds them. And aren't you far more valuable to him than they are? Can all your worries add a single moment to your life?'

'And why worry about your clothing? Look at the lilies of the field and how they grow. They don't work or make their clothing, yet Solomon in all his glory was not dressed as beautifully as they are. And if God cares so wonderfully for wildflowers that are here today and thrown into the fire tomorrow, he will certainly care for you. Why do you have so little faith?'

'So don't worry about these things, saying, "What will we eat? What will we drink? What will we wear?" These things dominate the thoughts of unbelievers, but your heavenly Father already knows all your needs. Seek the Kingdom of God above all else, and live righteously, and he will give you everything you need.

'So don't worry about tomorrow, for tomorrow will bring its own worries. Today's trouble is enough for today.'

Matthew 6: 25-34

8
VISION SEASON

TOGETHER FOREVER!

The Vision Rhythm we focus on during Vision Season

God has promised that Jesus will come back, take charge as King of the world, and create a permanently perfect world.

That is God's vision for the future, shared with us through the Bible. The campaign to connect, heal, and bless the world will be a magnificent success. All the way through the biblical story, God has made promises through his prophets, and he has been keeping them. There is a 100% chance that he will keep this final promise that Jesus, the Spearhead of the campaign, will come back and take the campaign to total, final victory.

The other half of the big idea of Vision Season

Living under Christ's rule, we are 'beings from the future.'

Wild as it sounds, Jesus has taken part of the future and put it into us already by his Holy Spirit. We are not just waiting for his future; we are living the future already! In the future, he will reign over all territories, all political powers, and all ethnic groups. But he already reigns over us who honour him as Messiah and leader of our pilgrimage. He is already gradually changing us the way he will finally change the whole world when he rules it all.

Bottom line of the big idea

We 'see ourselves in Christ' as actors in trailers for a movie about the coming world of peace and joy.

In sync with Jesus, we are never behind the times. We are ahead of the game! That's our focus for Vision Season.

When we sync with the Messiah it is as if we are actors in a trailer for God's movie about the future, we see the direct life-changing connection between our lives and the destiny of the world. It's not like we are helpless, unworthy, stuck with all kinds of weaknesses now, but everything will magically be perfect later.

In Christ some of that future perfection is already arriving, and it's working. Those who are not in Christ can see it working on us, and some of them ask, 'What's that? What's got into you?' The future has got into us! We are living the dream!

THE BIG IDEA

He who risks nothing can gain nothing

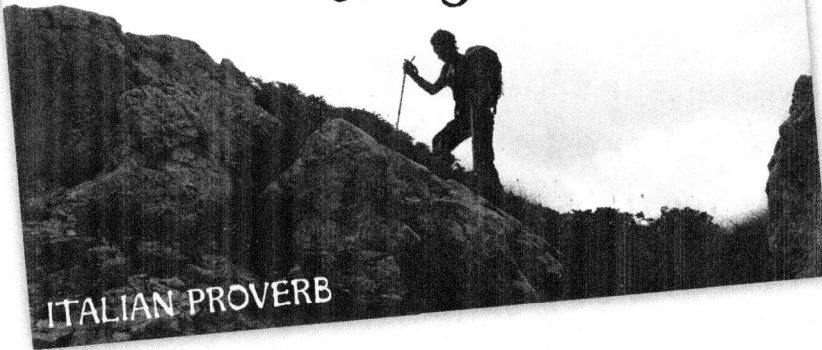

ITALIAN PROVERB

We need to risk the climb with the Messiah. When he risked his life, his friends… everything, it was to show us the way. When he died it looked like the end. It looked like he fell. But three days later he was alive again, to show us that falling, that death, is not the end. So we keep our eyes on the summit. We climb with the Lord who gives us the power and shows us the way.

REMINDER *for the Vision*

Remember the coming King and we see his glory dawning

Use the reminder daily to remember the theme of the season. Share it as a greeting in emails, with friends and relatives… wherever you need to focus on the pilgrimage.

There are a few days when I really struggle. There are some days when I merely survive. There are days when I look around the world and say 'enough is enough'. Like days when I see children arrested for trying to protect their home. Or days when I look at Syria or Ukraine and see people killing people. Or days when I hear a friend has cancer and will die. Sometimes it feels like hell on earth.

Do you think you will go to hell when you die? Or are you, like me, hoping for paradise? Often, when I meet with Muslims, Jews or Christians, the subject of paradise and hell comes up. Frequently this is because a lot of Muslims, Jews and Christians believe the other religions are going to hell but their religion is going to paradise! It is what we all want to believe… 'I am right and you are wrong!'

There is a time when we will find out. That is when time will cease to exist. When God says 'enough is enough…' and time as we know it, the earth as we know it, indeed everything as we know it ceases.

On that day 'He will wipe every tear from their eyes. There will be no more death or mourning or crying or pain, for the old order of things has passed away.'

Then everyone will be judged. some will go to paradise and some will go to hell.

What will paradise be like? What will hell be like? There is a saying 'five arabs, six opinions' and I have certainly found this to be true when discussing paradise or heaven and hell.

Muslims, Christians and Jews all agree that God is great. So when God says, 'enough is enough…' what will he do? How will he judge? If as a Muslim I have missed one call to prayer will I go to hell? That doesn't seem fair, if I am compared to someone who has killed many people. But Surah 57:30 says, *'grace is in the hands of Allah. He gives it to whomsoever he pleases'*. So is it more like tossing a coin and not knowing whether it will land on one side or the other?

God's grace though, truly leads the way to salvation. *'He forgives whom he pleases and punishes whom he pleases'* (Surah 5:19) So what is important therefore is to try to let God look on us favourably.

This season is one where we think about the final day. The day God says 'enough is enough…' the day he will judge us and send some to paradise and some to hell. Yet Surah 2:63 says *'Surely, the Believers and the Jews and the Christians and the Sabians—whichever party believes in God and the last day and does good deeds—shall have their reward with their Lord and no fear shall come upon them, nor shall they grieve.'*

And the Bible says in Matthew 25:31-32, *When the Son of Man comes in his glory, and all the angels with him, he will sit on his glorious throne. All the nations will be gathered before him, and he will separate the people one from another as a shepherd separates the sheep from the goats.*

So we should not fear but look to God in his glory. The question then is: how should we prepare for that final day? Yes, God is great but also God is love. Nobody better demonstrated that God is Love than the Messiah. Throughout his life he healed and cared for people. Then he said, *'Follow me'*. Followers of the Messiah believe he will return on the day that God says 'Enough is enough…' because that is what is written in the Bible.

But is paradise dependent on our good deeds? The good news is that God *'gave his one and only Son, so that everyone who believes in him will not perish but have eternal life.'* (John 3:16) So though connecting, healing and blessing is what we are called to, eternal life with the Messiah is dependent on following him rather than our deeds.

On that day *'He will wipe every tear from their eyes, and there will be no more death or sorrow or crying or pain. All these things are gone forever.'* (Revelation 21:4)

If that is what it means for God to be coming in Glory, my cry is 'please come quickly, Lord'.

PILGRIMS *before us*

CS Lewis

'We do not truly see light, we only see slower things lit by it, so that for us light is on the edge.'

So wrote Lewis, not in a theological treatise but in his science fiction trilogy dealing with the near and distant future. When we think of a vision for the future it's easy to get caught up in trying to interpret prophetic writing. But Lewis lifts us to realise we never actually see light, but only what is lit by it.

CS Lewis was born in Belfast before the partition of Ireland into two countries. As a teenager he rejected the faith of his parents, declaring himself an atheist, but paradoxically describing himself as, 'very angry with God for not existing' and 'equally angry with him for creating a world'!

Lewis quoted Lucretius as having one of the strongest arguments for atheism which he translated poetically as follows:

Had God designed the world,
* it would not be*
A world so frail and faulty
* as we see.*

He went to university at Oxford, joining the Officers Training Corps and then as part of the army was sent to France to fight in the First World War. He was wounded by a British shell falling short of his target, suffered depression and after being demobilised returned to his studies at Oxford where he became friends with another writer, JRR Tolkien.

But God sought him out, calling him to this pilgrimage... 'kicking, struggling, resentful, and darting his eyes in every direction for a chance to escape'.

He later moved to Cambridge University as Professor of English Literature. In 1956, Lewis married American writer Joy Grisham, who was 17 years younger than him, and who died four years later of cancer at the age of 45.

Converted from a non-believer to fullness of faith in God, he wrote many books in which he communicated his experiences and thoughts. Frequently he communicated his ideas about this pilgrimage through life in the fiction stories he wrote, giving the characters in them thoughts that leave us understanding more about the vision before us:

'There are a dozen views about everything until you know the answer. Then there's never more than one.' and 'Good is always getting better and bad is always getting worse: the possibilities of even apparent neutrality are always diminishing.' (That Hideous Strength). Of Lewis' books perhaps the best known books are the Chronicles of Narnia, starting with 'The Lion, the Witch and the Wardrobe'.

As we think about our pilgrimage we may wonder: is it safe? That was the question Lewis answered in respect of Aslan, the Lion… 'Safe? Don't you hear what Mrs. Beaver tells you? Who said anything about safe? 'Course he isn't safe. But he's good. He's the King, I tell you.'

And in that book it proves unsafe for Aslan as he is tied to the stone table and killed by the White Witch. She thinks that is the end. But it is not. In in the metaphor of that story, Lewis points us to the vision ahead…

'Though the Witch knew the Deep Magic, there is a magic deeper still which she did not know. Her knowledge goes back only to the dawn of time. But if she could have looked a little further back, into the stillness and the darkness before Time dawned, she would have read there a different incantation. She would have known that when a willing victim who had committed no treachery was killed in a traitor's stead, the Table would crack and Death itself would start working backward.'

The landscape which inspired Lewis to write The Chronicles of Narnia. He wrote 'I have seen landscapes ... which, under a particular light, make me feel that at any moment a giant might raise his head over the next ridge.'

PILGRIMS
alongside us

Tom Hanks

Most of us have seen Tom Hanks in one of his many movies. Some, like Forrest Gump, challenge us to see life differently. The story starts in 1981, at a bus stop in Georgia, where a man named Forrest Gump, recounts his life story to strangers who sit next to him on a bench. Gump a slow-witted and kind hearted man from Alabama, who witnesses and unwittingly influences several defining historical events in the 20th-century United States, illustrates how it isn't just the rich and powerful that can be important in our lives.

More recently he starred in 'The Da Vinci Code' a fictional conspiracy theory about the Catholic Church. Tom Hanks himself was raised Catholic and Mormon, and one journalist described Hanks as a 'Bible-toting Evangelical' in his teenage years. But this is only part of his pilgrimage and is not what he would call himself today.

At school he was unpopular, both with other students and with teachers. He describes himself as 'horribly, painfully, terribly shy' as a teenager while 'yelling out funny captions during filmstrips in class'! Hanks said he originally wanted to be an astronaut but the closest he ever got was being a supporter of NASA's crewed space programme, and he advocates for space exploration.

After high school he went to and then dropped out of college, after finding he enjoyed being in theatre more than studying it. His career went from theatre to TV and then to movies, which is where most of us know of him.

Hanks' personal life has been complex, like many in the movie business, marrying and then divorcing Samantha Lewes. He then met Rita Wilson while doing a TV comedy called

Bosom Buddies. She is of Greek and Bulgarian descent and a member of the Greek Orthodox Church. Hanks became a member of that church before marrying her.

They have two children and as a family actively attend church. 'I must say that when I go to church—and I do go to church—I ponder the mystery. I meditate on the "why?" of "why people are as they are", and "why bad things happen to good people," and "why good things happen to bad people".'

Hanks also starred in the movie 'Angels and Demons' but stressed that he isn't a believer when it comes to conspiracy theories. This is the second movie about the unorthodox visions of novelist Dan Brown who seems to go out of his way creating Vatican conspiracies.

Hanks stays on solid ground: 'Conspiracy theories, I think, are ... conjured up by people who can then sell their books about conspiracy theories,' said Hanks, with a shrug. 'Anytime someone says, "You know how they did that? You know what that's about? You know what the conspiracy is?" I automatically tune that person out.'

The Messiah described himself as 'The way, the truth and the life'. So being aware of conspiracy theories and rejecting them is something we, as pilgrims, need to do,

Even though he plays the part of a conspiracy theorist in the films, Hanks prefers to quote the Swiss Guard commander, 'My church feeds the hungry and takes care of the needs of the poor. What has your church done? Oh, that's right, Mr. Langdon, you don't have one.'

'This is true,' noted Hanks, 'the church does feed the poor. It does take care of the hungry. It heals the sick. I think that the grace of God seems to be not only in the eye of the believer, but also in the hands of the believer.'

After contracting and recovering from a COVID-19 infection early in the pandemic, Hanks and his wife donated their blood antibodies for virus research.

Hanks' questions of 'why?' cannot be easily answered but we keep our focus on the vision before us, the vision of a new heaven and a new earth where the questions he asks will be no more. And, in the meantime, we don't let our questions stop us from doing what the Messiah has made clear to us.

THOUGHTS
from Uncle Azis

I watch the news: War in Ukraine… in Yemen… in Syria… recent wars in Iraq, Libya… rumours of upcoming war with Iran… countries fighting countries… A man goes into the Saudi Embassy in Turkey and is killed there… refugee children from Syria are water-boarded by other school children in the UK… the list seems to go on and on.

The Messiah told us what to expect and it's surprisingly similar to what we see today. And he said it 2,000 years ago.

'And you will hear of wars and threats of wars, but don't panic. Yes, these things must take place, but the end won't follow immediately. Nation will go to war against nation, and kingdom against kingdom. There will be famines and earthquakes in many parts of the world. But all this is only the first of the birth pains, with more to come.' (Matthew 28:6-8)

Both Christians and Muslims believe in the second coming of the Messiah. Is this something we're looking forward to or something we're dreading? What Jesus describes is distressing for people who follow the Messiah:

'Then you will be handed over to be persecuted and put to death, and you will be hated by all nations because of me. At that time many will turn away from the faith and will betray and hate each other, and many false prophets will appear and deceive many people.' (Matthew 24:6-13)

This doesn't sound at all pleasant.

So how do we prepare for the end time? 15 years ago I visited Syria. It was a beautiful country. The people were welcoming and friendly. How could the people of Syria prepare for the destruction we now see in their country? I visited Iraq after the invasion and I saw then the destruction of that beautiful country.

The Messiah again *'Let no one on the housetop go down to take anything out of the house. Let no one in the field go back to get their cloak. How dreadful it will be in those days for pregnant women and nursing mothers!'* (Matthew 24:17-19)

And when we see streams of refugees, mother and babies, we do think how dreadful it is. But be prepared:

'Now learn this lesson from the fig tree: As soon as its twigs get tender and its leaves come out, you know that summer is near. Even so, when you see all these things, you know that it is near, right at the door.' (Matthew 24:32-33)

So I struggle. I do not want any more war anywhere. I long for peace. Yet I long, too, to see the Messiah. Waiting for his return to earth, we read the story of his life and try to follow his calling on our lives. Then one day we will see him in glory.

MUSIC to my ears

The Book of Revelation and the Angels' Dance

I'm just an ordinary music artist. I am no good at dancing, nor am I the kind of person who deals with mystical or quasi-religious feelings; which made what happened to me at night while I was composing this music so wonderful.

I have travelled a lot all over the world. Because of my work, I have lived in many countries, so that I have friends of all faiths, races and colours. So when I listened to the words of that passage from the Book of Revelation of the apostle John (Revelation chapter 7), and put it to music to accompany it, a great crowd of people from all the countries of the earth appeared to me with the eyes of my imagination.

They were praising God while the trumpet of God blared over them. Then with the announcement of the hour at midnight, I saw myself surrounded by a great crowd of angels dancing around me. I realised that the music I was writing for that passage had taken the form of a great dance, so I bowed there with tears streaming from my eyes in reverence for the greatness of the glory of God.

In the music room I have a slogan written in Romanian on the wall that says:

Dacă viaţa te lasă fără cuvinte, cântă!

Which means 'If life leaves you without words, sing!'

For me, music is as natural a means of expression as speech. So when I was invited to compose music for Nizar Qabbani's poem 'Will You Allow Me?', I read the poem once and put it aside. Then I began to imagine how I would feel if my life were subjected to the same challenges that the poem describes, if I lived in a

blown force that now pushes me forward and pulls me back, pushes me forward and pulls me back? And I spontaneously tried to translate that feeling into music: the rhythm was the same as in the video: three steps in one direction, two steps in the other... alarmingly.

Earthly glory and heavenly glory

Nader Abdel Amir

Translated from Arabic

Many talked about glory, and many were fascinated by it, and many sought after it, but few of them realised that all glory comes from God and not from the earth, humanity, or man's creations. Glory is the supreme kind of beauty, splendour or glow that settles on things and gives them a powerful attraction that draws people's hearts.

From here, we understand the Bible's warning to us in more than one location not to be tempted by the glory of earthly things, whether they are majestic beauty in nature or worldly authority or some creativity, because these things are destined to vanish. We will inevitably feel great disappointment if we link glory to them organically.

This is the idea contained in Psalm 49 saying: *'Do not be over-awed when a person becomes rich, if the glory of his house increases'*. (Psalm 49: 17)

The idea is that glory is not erased from existence upon the death of any person who has lived glorified,

The heavenly glory, ie emanating from God Almighty, is the origin of the idea that we hear many believers say about death: that a person is 'promoted to glory', and it is the phrase taken from Psalm 73, 'But I am always with you'.

Every glory, wherever it appears, is nothing but the glory of God

because the source of glory is heavenly, not earthly, and is not conditioned by what is earthly.

Every glory, wherever it is manifested is nothing but the glory of God, whether in a natural scene, music, painting, person, human face, or elsewhere.

That is because when a believer dies, he is taken to the presence of God. There he finds himself surrounded on every side by the glory of God, without the need for a material medium to show him that glory as it is on earth.

This is what the Apostle Paul said in 1 Corinthians 13:12: *'Now we see things imperfectly, like puzzling reflections in a mirror, but then we will see everything with perfect clarity. All that I know now is partial and incomplete, but then I will know everything completely, just as God now knows me completely.'*

The bottom line of the foregoing is that the glory of God is fixed and does not pass away. We see it many times, perhaps in one day, during our stay on earth, through the scenes suggestive of beauty and greatness that we see around us, whether in a person or a piece of art or just a wonderful idea that comes to our mind.

But in the end, we have to penetrate from the material membrane of glory embodied in things to the essence of glory that all belong to God. And our only way to God, as the book says, is through our master Jesus Christ, his word that he told about himself embodied in him, because the greatest expression in truth about the glory of God is the person of our master Jesus Christ.

The greatest expression in truth about the glory of God is the person of our master Jesus Christ

He lived on earth in a state of absolute perfection as described by John when he said: *'So the Word became human and made his home among us. He was full of unfailing love and faithfulness. And we have seen his glory, the glory of the Father's one and only Son.'* (John 1:14).

He also said at his crucifixion, *"Now my soul is deeply troubled. Should I pray, 'Father, save me from this hour'? But this is the very reason I came! Father, bring glory to your name." Then a voice spoke from heaven, saying, "I have already brought glory to my name, and I will do so again."'* (John 12:28)

PROVERBS
about the Vision

The longest night will have an end. RUSSIAN

The tablet is well preserved on which God wrote destiny. SWAHILI

What heaven ordains must be fulfilled on earth. COLOMBIAN

God permits but not forever. CHILEAN

Think on the end before you begin. RUSSIAN

The musician begins to play and a thousand ailments heal. SERBIAN

Hope is a comrade: if it doesn't bring you up to your journey's end, it will yet entertain you on the road. ARABIC

Hope is the dream of the waking. DANISH

Hope is the pillar of the world. WEST AFRICAN

The cart will find its way around the hill when it gets there. CHINESE

If the old is not gone the new will not come. CHINESE

If you do not sow in the spring, you will not reap in the autumn. CELTIC

He who has no care for the far future will have sorrow in the near future. KOREAN

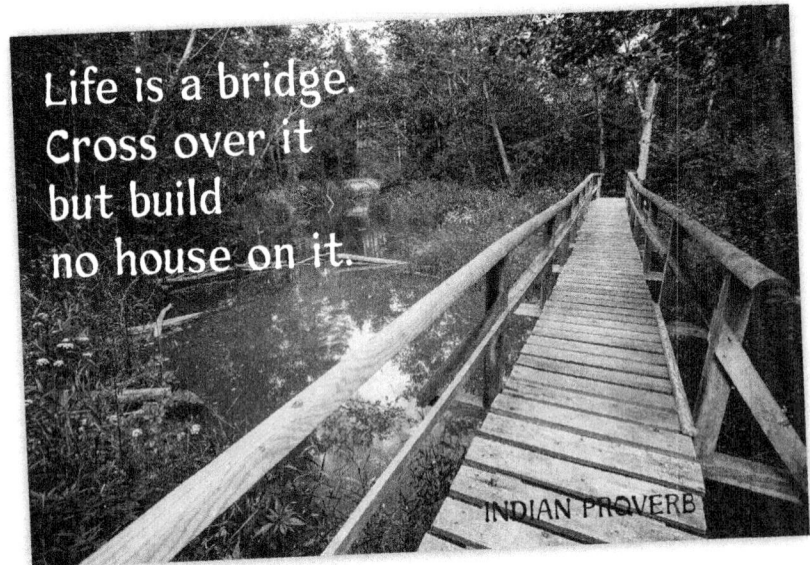

Life is a bridge. Cross over it but build no house on it.

INDIAN PROVERB

THOUGHTS
from Uncle Azis

What really worries me ...is the pain of death

What really worries me is the pain of death. I don't usually tolerate pain very well, and the thought of the pain of death frightens me a lot. Also, the older I got, the more I thought about the pain of death. We have all witnessed the death of elderly relatives, the death of which is sometimes quiet, but often very painful. Who among us awaits a painful death?

But what when we die? What after death? We know that we will remain in our graves until the Day of Resurrection, when we will all rise from our graves and stand before God to judge us for what we have done in our worldly lives, unless God has already declared us righteous.

But before that there will be a day when Christ will return, and that day will be the day when justice will be restored to the earth and the Antichrist will be defeated. You may be, like me, looking around and wondering if we have a false Christ among us today, We also know that the period of the true Christ's return will be a very glorious period.

That day will be the beginning of a new heaven and a new earth. Long ago, God created this earth, and created the human race in the midst of a lush paradise. The whole earth was a garden which we spoiled, unfortunately, and our spoiling continues in it. And God revealed in his revelation to the Apostle John the shape of this new heaven and new earth. However, the strange thing this time is that it will not be a paradise, but a city.

Our idea of cities through human experience is that they are dirty, foul-smelling, noisy places: the exact opposite of our idea of heaven, where there is no disease, no pain, no sorrow.

So why, when God speaks in the book of the visions of the Apostle John about heaven, does he talk of a city? The answer is that the Almighty thinks of the issue of connection and relationships, not of worldly goods and possessions, although God will provide us abundantly there with everything we need.

He is the Almighty, trying to tell us that the idea of heaven has more to do with how we relate to each other and our connection with him, more than the issue of acquisitions and possessions of gold or jewellery and more than the issue of pleasures.

So when we think about the Vision Season, let's remember that the core of everything is connection. The relationship between God and humanity, and between one person and another person. And if the ties with each other and with him, the Most High, have been cut off, then let us heal them during this Vision Season and give thanks to God.

Celebrate the Vision before us

So let's get the party started, celebrating with a huge 'Yes' to all five of these things:

Yes, the vision that will save the world is not any human vision but God's vision that he has been proactively and patiently working since the time of Abraham.

Yes, Christ has put his Spirit, life, and power into me, turning me into a different person and putting me onto the team that is working for this vision of a healed, blessed, and connected world.

Yes, I will trust Christ and his Spirit to get me through any opposition that comes from people who are pushing other visions for the world.

Yes, God's whole vision for the world revolves around the Messiah, the king he sent to lead the campaign for this vision.

Yes, I agree not to force the vision on anyone, but to spread it by living it out. I will start now by forgiving others like the Messiah has forgiven me.

Each season has a celebration where we say 'Yes' to 5 things about being a pilgrim.

from https://syncx.org

The twenty-four elders sitting on their thrones before God fell with their faces to the ground and worshiped him. 17 And they said, "We give thanks to you, Lord God, the Almighty, the one who is and who always was, for now you have assumed your great power and have begun to reign. The nations were filled with wrath, but now the time of your wrath has come. It is time to judge the dead and reward your servants the prophets, as well as your holy people, and all who fear your name, from the least to the greatest. It is time to destroy all who have caused destruction on the earth."

Then, in heaven, the Temple of God was opened and the Ark of his covenant could be seen inside the Temple. Lightning flashed, thunder crashed and roared, and there was an earthquake and a terrible hailstorm.

Revelation 11: 15-19

Then the seventh angel blew his trumpet, and there were loud voices shouting in heaven:

"The world has now become the Kingdom of our Lord and of his Christ, and he will reign forever and ever."

PART TWO

The Messianic Pilgrimage
seen in a North American context

The Messianic Pilgrimage is designed to include and bring together people from all cultures. It can be understood better when it is viewed from more than one cultural perspective.

Part Two uses a North American perspective to view the same basic ideas presented in Part One from a Middle Eastern perspective. In places Part Two also goes into more detail about the Scriptural and theological background of the pilgrimage.

The material for this part comes mainly from the syncx.org website.

MOVING WITH THE RHYTHM

of the story of the world

The Messianic Pilgrimage and SYNC

Whereas Part One of this book used mainly the Messianic Pilgrimage language, the second part uses mainly SYNC language. This can be confusing at first, but they are really just two sides of the same coin. What they both illustrate is that the core idea of living in connection with Jesus can be expressed and understood in whatever way is appropriate to the culture that we find ourselves in.

The language of the Messianic Pilgrimage works better in North Africa and the Middle East and the language of SYNC works better in North America. As coaches or guides we need to be in tune with the culture we find ourselves in and adapt the language without changing the core ideas.

So what is SYNC?

SYNC is one tiny component of God's ancient and ongoing campaign to save the world from itself. SYNC is our chance to get a fresh take on what it means to 'See Yourself iN Christ'. That involves everything about us—who we are, what we are part of, what we are worth, and what our purpose is.

We get that fresh take on life as we explore God's agenda and strategy for the world. And it is not a set of rules. It is a beautiful, ancient, complex story that God is still unfolding. It is the story of his grace working through his people to change his world.

Jesus Christ is the centre, holding the whole story together, and we gradually discover our true identity as we see ourselves in Christ. We call that 'SYNCing with Jesus.' We can start the process with two words, 'sync me.' To finish the process may take a lifetime, but we will love the ride.

How we see ourselves

If you See Yourself iN Christ (SYNC), what will you see? A new you who has received some new gifts that give you a new identity and purpose.

Each gift is a result of what SYNC calls a 'game-changer' or called a 'ground-breaking event' in this book, a specific act of God at some point in the story of our world. That act makes a specific gift available in a new way from then on in the story.

Once we get that idea and embrace the gifts, we see ourselves as participants in this story. And it's a great story to be part of! It is the story of the Messiah connecting, healing and blessing the world.

S<small>EE</small> Y<small>OURSELF</small> i<small>N</small> C<small>HRIST</small>

Three pillars of SYNC

1. ### The big idea — the huge thing God is doing

   SYNC is built on one main idea—something huge and ancient is going on in our world today, though most people are clueless about it. God is orchestrating a campaign to connect, heal and bless the world. Jesus Christ is the leader of that campaign.

2. ### The whole SYNC process in two words — 'sync me!'

   Once we get the big idea of God's campaign, we go with it. We sign up for the campaign team by saying to Jesus, 'sync me'. The SYNCx.org site helps us unpack those two words.

3. ### Two questions for all campaign team members

   What general things does every team member need to know about the campaign's story, goals and methods? We read the Bible bit by bit to find out.

   What specific things are my niche role and my daily assignments in the campaign? We stay alert for thoughts that Jesus puts into our minds through his Spirit, especially while we are reading or discussing the Bible.

Trying to evade God's campaign to transform this world into the world of our dreams is like trying to ignore the elephant in the room. People say, 'I don't see anything. What God? What campaign?'

Or they assume they know God's campaign strategy already—tell people the rules, tell them to be more loving, bless them when they do it, punish them when they don't. That strategy is so simplistic, boring and ineffective that many people can't stand it. They have no motivation at all to join a campaign with such a lame strategy.

'Sync me'

But when people see what God's campaign is really about—connecting, healing and blessing the world—and when they start appreciating how complex, surprising and brilliant his actual campaign strategy is, many want to get on board. They say, 'Sync me.' 'Sync me' means, 'OK, King Jesus. I trust you. Sync me with the rhythm you put into the story of the world. Sync me with what you intended when you did those game-changing events long ago. Include me in your campaign team and give me my campaign assignment.' (authors' paraphrase)

'Sync me' is simply a 21st century way of saying exactly what Jesus said in the middle of the pattern prayer he gave to his followers in the 1st century—*'As in heaven, so on earth.'* (Matthew 6:10) Or, 'sync earth with heaven.' He was starting a campaign, always calling people to 'follow him' as the campaign leader. That prayer was one of his tools for recruiting new people for the campaign team and equipping them for campaign work.

The entire SYNC project is about helping people to open up to God by praying that prayer authentically and often. When we do that we welcome heaven to earth and discover a new identity in the process. We are members of a campaign team, caught up in Jesus' mission to connect, heal and bless the world.

As a campaign team member, we say 'sync me!' to Jesus Christ every chance we get—first thing in the morning, last thing at night, going out the door to work, before any other SYNC activity we may do, with family, friends, team, etc. We take it as our new 'mantra', and discover what it means and how it feels to be part of a campaign that is so ancient, so futuristic, and so good.

Why we will like where this is going

If we see ourselves in Christ, we will like ourselves. We will sleep a lot better because in sync with him, we are good for ourselves and for everybody else.

Jesus has everyone's good in mind, and when we are in him, so do we. If there are any parts of us that we don't like, they are usually the parts that are out of sync with him. We are destined to be in sync with him, and getting in sync will feel like coming home even if we have never been at this place before.

Seven things we will see in the mirror

- A life-bringer who enjoys and respects all creation
- A fruitful branch on an ancient family tree
- An activist for a new era of freedom
- A walking piece of evidence of God's power for good
- An agent of forgiveness
- An honourable finisher inspired by Jesus carrying his cross
- An actor in a movie trailer for the coming world of peace

from https://syncx.org

Our identity, security, and significance

All kinds of good things happen when we realise that our basic identity will never be secure if we think it can be based on:

- expressing ourselves
- achieving goals
- righting some wrong we have suffered
- being liked, or
- obeying rules

What gives us a secure identity is syncing with something beyond ourselves, something that is already going on with its own life and energy. Syncing with something huge, ancient and good is not a chore or a challenge. It's a privilege. It is our response to God's grace.

God's grace makes these seven gifts available to those who sync with him.

Each gift harks back to a particular ground-breaking act of God. As we explore these gifts and the specific ground-breaker that brought each gift within our reach, our view of ourselves in Christ will grow. God had certain intentions in every game-changer, and we sync with those intentions. A few examples:

- 'Lord, whatever you intended when you breathed life into the first human, fulfil those intentions in us.'
- 'Lord, whatever you intended when you sent the Holy Spirit at Pentecost, fulfil those intentions in us today.'
- 'Lord, whatever you intend to do in the world when you return in glory, please do some of that in us already.'

The common thread running through all seven gifts is that we are people who welcome the gifts, are changed by them, and share them. That's who we are. That's what we are here for. When we realise we are in SYNC with God's ancient, brilliant, grace-soaked strategy and purpose, we know we are in a good place.

We find terrific security in this identity in Christ, plus a great sense of significance, without any desire to boast about it or look down on anybody. It's like Christ is picking us up and carrying us along with him, and it starts happening long before we truly get our minds around it all.

Getting started on seven new ways of seeing ourselves in Christ

1. Life-bringers who enjoy and respect all creation

Relevant Scripture

- Key verse: Genesis 1.1, God creates the universe
- Key story: The creation story: Genesis 1:1–2:3
- How we see Christ: the Creator: John 1:1–4

Why do we get to be life-bringers?

God wants his life to fill everything and everyone, but he does not just zap that into everyone. He puts it into some people to carry to other people. We are the carriers, the life-bringers. We see what God is doing and why, and this is it:

We are part of a world God created. Beauty, music, children, food, colours; everything was designed so that human life would be good and joyful. When Jesus came to earth, he took that to a new level: even better and more joyful. When we act like life-bringers, we are in sync with God's plan. When we hurt or tear down other people, we are out of stnc. That is not who we are.

We are life-bringers because we realise where life comes from. Since God created everything, he owns everything, just like we own whatever we make. That means that all the things we call 'ours'—our clothes, our food, our toys—actually belong to him because we ourselves belong to him. We just get to use 'our' things for a while. So we should not get too grabby.

Messianic Pilgrimage notes:

Originally the Life Season was called the Creation Season in the Messianic Pilgrimage. It was the first season, since the series of seasons goes from Jesus' action in creation through to his coming again in glory. We are not just reciting a story in the proper sequence though. At each stage we are learning more about the core values of being a follower of Jesus. We let those values soak into us more and more deeply.

2. Fruitful branches on an ancient family tree

Relevant Scripture

- Key verse: Genesis 12:3, all families blessed through Abraham's family
- Key story: God's promises to Abraham: Genesis 12:1–3
- How we see Christ: the one who grafts us into the family tree: Galations 3:29

Why do we get to be fruitful branches on the Abraham family tree?

God wants his blessing to go to every family in the world, but he does not give it to every family directly. He created a special family through Abraham, and he used that family to bless all the rest. Because of Jesus, we get to be members of Abraham's family, fruitful branches on Abraham's family tree. We see what God is doing and why, and this is it:

He is keeping his ancient promise to Abraham. He promised that Abraham's family would grow to become millions of descendants, and God would bless every family on earth through that huge family. Jesus was one of those descendants of Abraham. He expanded the family to include spiritual descendants, not just Abraham's relatives by birth.

from https://syncx.org

That means we can be grafted into the Abraham family tree like branches being grafted onto a fruit tree.

Once we are attached, we have Abraham's faith and Jesus' life flowing into us by his Holy Spirit. Then we can produce lots of fruit like love and joy that can bless many people. We are part of the fulfilment of God's ancient promise to bless every family through Abraham's family.

Messianic Pilgrimage notes:

This season is called the Identity Season in the Messianic Pilgrimage. At one stage it was called the Connection Season indicating God's connection to his people. Later we called it Tribes Season, to indicate our connection to both the 'Tribe of Jesus' and our earthly community. We finalised on Identity because all of the above is about our Identity as a follower in the footsteps of the Messiah.

3. Freedom activists

Relevant Scripture

- Key verse: Luke 4.18–19, Jesus' proclamation of the dawn of an era of freedom
- Key story: The resurrection story: Matthew 28:1–20
- How we see Christ: the King who issues a proclamation: Luke 4:43

Why do we get to be 'freedom activists'?

God wants everyone on earth to be free of everything that is ruining their lives, but he does not just break all their chains magically. He sends out 'activists,' official messengers to take the freedom message to the whole world. Jesus sent us to carry on what he started.

He was an activist, proclaiming a new era of freedom and calling people to follow him into it. His enemies in the establishment executed him to show the world that Jesus' proclamation was bogus, but God brought him back to life to show the world it was true. That's why the resurrection of Jesus is so important. It validates his proclamation.

Jesus did not Tweet his proclamation. He put the message into people, all of us who welcomed the proclamation when we heard it. We get to show the world what it feels like and looks like to live free. Nobody has to live any more like they are tied in knots by their desires, their habits, their traumas, or their fears. They can be free if they live 'in Jesus,' that is, if they welcome him as their King.

That's who we are—'freedom activists,' authorised representatives who declare that Jesus is alive and are ready to do anything it takes to draw others to join us in his Freedom Era. That is our cause, and we are not going to shut up about it.

4. Walking evidence

Relevant Scripture

- Key verse: Acts 1:8, power to show that Jesus is alive
- Key story: The story of Jesus sending the Holy Spirit into his followers: Acts 2:1–21, especially v. 1–4
- How we see Christ: the holder of all power and authority: Matthew 28:18–20

Why do we get to be walking evidence of God's power for good?

God does not want the world to have to wait to see his power until Jesus comes back to earth in person. He wants the whole world to be glad right now that Jesus brought heaven's power to earth, and that it is still here. That is where we come in. We are walking evidence of his power for good. We see what God is doing and why, and this is it:

He is continuing the work Jesus did on earth. Jesus did many miracles. When he left, he took all that power to heaven with him, but not for long. Ten days later, he sent his power back down into his followers. He sent his Holy Spirit to live in them.

The Spirit changed them inside. They became new people, more and more like Jesus every day. They were able to do things that were not humanly possible so that people would know the power of Jesus himself was still working on earth. On the day this started, they all spoke languages they had never learned! They were praising God in these languages, pointing to Jesus as the one who had released the power for this.

The Holy Spirit is still pointing to Jesus by doing things in us and through us that we could never do on our own. The Spirit reaches the parts of us that we can't reach, and he changes the parts of us we can't change. And the Spirit still works miracles sometimes, not every time we snap our fingers, but every time God decides to do something special to point to the Messiah. Watch for it.

5. Forgiveness agents

Relevant Scripture

- Key verse: Romans 5:8, Christ died for us out of sheer mercy
- Key story: The story of Christ's one-time sacrifice on God's altar: Hebrews 9:1–14
- How we see Christ: the sacrifice whose wounds heal us: Isaiah 53:4–12, especially v. 5–6

Why do we get to be forgiveness agents?

God wants people to be living guilt-free lives. He does not want them kicking themselves for the bad things they did, nor does he want them faking it, pretending they were never guilty of anything. But God does not just give everyone a free pass and tell them they do not have to feel guilty. He sends his representatives to show and tell how genuine guilt removal works. That is who we are, God's forgiveness agents, God's guilt-busters.

Forgiving does not come naturally. When someone hits us, the natural reaction is to hit back. They are guilty. They deserve it. If we forgive them, we think they will hit us again because we let them get away with it the first time.

Jesus shows us that life is not like that. He let people hit him, torture him, and kill him, but it did not mean they could do it again. It meant he was letting it happen because he realised he was an innocent, willing sacrifice. He took the punishment we deserved. His death killed our guilt.

When we see that and accept Christ's mercy and sacrifice, we are changed inside. We never really get over it. We start showing mercy even to the 'bad' people, and that is how evil loses its control of the world. The 'good' people accept God's mercy and become merciful people, so that even the 'bad' people can change.

Messianic Pilgrimage notes:

The Mercy Season was originally the Mercy and Forgiveness Season, but was shortened down to just Mercy. Even though we dropped it from the Messianic Pilgrimage name it's important not to lose forgiveness within this season.

6. Honourable finishers

Relevant Scripture

- Key verse: Hebrews 12:2, Jesus heroically endured the cross and despised the shame

- Key story: Jesus being flogged and mocked by the soldiers, then being too weak to carry the cross all the way to his execution Mark 14:15–21

- How we see Christ: our commander and example, carrying the cross: Luke 14:27

Why do we get to be finishers, never giving up?

God knows how unfair the world is. Even when his messengers do everything right and are good to everyone, the world will still attack them and try to shame them.

Jesus never told his followers that following him would be easy. In fact, he said the opposite. They would need the endurance of a long-distance runner plus the courage of a person facing a dangerous attack. In a word, they would need grit: toughness, determination, and loyalty.

Where do we get that? Jesus showed us what it looks like to endure shame and torture, and we get strength from his heroic example. Since his Spirit lives in us, we can finish like he did: fearless, with our heads held high. And we also have God's promise to honour those who overcome what they suffer for his name (Revelation 3.21).

We are finishers not quitters because we keep looking at Jesus, letting his Spirit give us courage, and trusting his promise. We can even inspire others, passing on some of Christ's inspiration. That is what we pray for. 'Lead us on, Jesus, until we hear you say, 'It is finished!''

Messianic Pilgrimage notes:

The Honour Season was also known as the Courage Season in the Messianic Pilgrimage, because the Messiah showed courage when going to the cross, which was his honourable finishing event. We often need courage too when persecuted or challenged about following Jesus. But this is wider than just courage, it's about living honourably and loyally to Jesus, courage is only part.

7. 'Movie trailers' for the coming world of peace

Relevant Scripture

- Key verse: Revelation 11.15, Christ takes power on earth
- Key story: The seventh trumpet heralding the beginning of Christ's reign on earth: Revelation 11:15–19
- How we see Christ: the Messiah, the perfect King of the whole world: Daniel 7:14

Why do we get to be trailers for a movie about the coming world of peace?

God wants people's lives to be full of hope about how the world will turn out in the end. He knows they have plenty of reasons to be afraid it will be awful. That's why he puts out some signs of things to come, so people can have a good reason to trust him about the future. As we trust Jesus today, he puts some of the good things of the future world of peace into us. We are from the future! And we can tell people what we know is coming when Jesus takes charge.

Jesus' plan is for us to work like movie trailers, showing people enough of what is coming that they want to get in on it. When Jesus returns to earth, he will rule everywhere and there will be peace and life everywhere. Right now he rules inside us. That means he is already doing in us what he will do everywhere later. So when people see us, they see the future.

We don't show it perfectly or show it all. Movie trailers never show us the whole movie. But they show us enough that we know what kind of a movie it will be. And this 'movie' is going to be great!

Messianic Pilgrimage notes:

The final Vision Season celebrates the Messiah returning in glory, and was thus originally called the Glory Season but is actually the vision set before us. As 'movie trailers' we let other people start seeing the vision too so we call it the Vision Season.

The Rest Stop is not in the original SYNC cycle but it is in this section of the book. It was added for the Messianic Pilgrimage version, just before the Vision Season, to make the seasons fit better with the lunar calendar.

It was originally called the Contemplation Season—a season when we took time out to think about the journey ahead. Time out from the busyness of everyday life is something that Jesus did and calls us to do. It is rest and time to contemplate, time to See Yourself iN Christ.

His pilgrimage...
The Messiah is both our model and our companion

As we take our pilgrimage with the Messiah, it is a good idea to look at his pilgrimage on earth and how that relates to ours. Since he never sinned, he did not have to take a pilgrimage from an old life to a new life like we do. But he still had a pilgrimage through life, and we can learn much from it that will help us listen to his voice as we take our pilgrimage.

His birth

Before the Messiah was born the Holy Spirit of God was preparing the way. Firstly with Elisabeth and then with Mary. I cannot imagine what it must have been like for Mary, a young girl engaged to be married but hadn't had sex with her fiancé. Then an angel comes and tells her the Holy Spirit will make her pregnant. Though she responds that she is a servant of the Lord, so it should be according what to the angel said, I'm pretty sure she might have had doubts until she visited her cousin Elisabeth.[1]

Scripture records that when Mary arrived at Elisabeth's house and greeted her, Elisabeth's baby leapt in her womb.[2] Something about that movement inspired Elisabeth through the Holy Spirit to confirm to Mary what the angel had said, that the baby inside Mary was indeed the Lord.[3]

As we think about our pilgrimage with the Lord, it is with the Lord walking alongside. It is often the words of another person that confirms the voice of the Holy Spirit within us. We are called to travel together so that we can encourage each other as we each hear from the Holy Spirit. And even then we may still be filled with doubt.

As it grew close to the time for Jesus' birth the Roman authorities wanted to take a census.[4] Unlike today where they come to our door to ask questions, in those days they had to travel to their family home town. So Mary and Joseph had to travel from Galilee where they lived, to Bethlehem—a distance of about 130 km or 80 miles—which would have taken about a week walking or on a donkey. Being heavily pregnant, it would not have been surprising if Mary had wondered if she had heard correctly from the Lord. This would have been especially true since when they arrived there wasn't any place for them to stay except a barn with the animals.

However, the pendulum of doubt might have swung when a group of shepherds appeared at the barn telling her that they had been told by an

They found him in the Temple discussing with teachers there

angel that indeed the little baby she had just given birth to was the Messiah. Again, we see others confirming the initial words of the Holy Spirit before even the Messiah had formally started his pilgrimage.[5]

His childhood

We know little of the childhood of the Messiah other than one episode when the family and friends from his community went to Jerusalem for the annual festival of the Passover. Jerusalem was slightly closer than Bethle-

hem and would have been only four one-day hikes of between 12 and 20 kilometres (8-12 miles).

After the festival, the extended family and friends set off back to Nazareth. His parents assumed the 12-year-old Jesus to be among this group. So when they stopped for the night, they were shocked to be unable to find him and returned to Jerusalem to look for him.

They found him in the Temple discussing with teachers there. Surprised, they reprimanded him, expressing their distress. Because the time was not yet right for him to start his own pilgrimage, he returned with them and the Scriptures record that the Messiah submitted to his parents.[6]

Ritual washing

Elisabeth's son John was called to a very different path. He was called to encourage people to prepare for their pilgrimage through a form of ritual washing. He wasn't a gentle encourager either, using strong words to say that in order to go on the

Messianic Pilgrimage one needs to change direction.[7]

The Messiah, too, came to start his pilgrimage this way. In part to demonstrate his humanity and association with us on this pilgrimage, he too undertook a ritual washing. When he did so there was a voice from heaven and a physical manifestation of the Holy Spirit saying, *'You are my beloved Son; I am very pleased with you'*. Now although those words had special meaning for the Messiah, as fellow pilgrims God accepts us as adopted sons and daughters. So those words apply equally to us: We are children with whom God as our Father is very pleased when we accept the Messiah as our guide for life.[8]

Giving life in creation

Because we tend to think of the Messiah from his birth, his involvement in creation seems a bit of an anathema. In one sense, because God is three persons in one Godhead, it's implicit that all three were present at creation. But there are various Scriptures that point to the Messiah's direct involvement. And that is kind of mind-blowing because we're thinking of this human being – the incarnation of God on earth – being involved with creating the earth, the universe, everything long before he was born.

Here are two verses of Scripture that explicitly indicate the Messiah's involvement: *'God created everything through him, and nothing was created except through him.'*[9] and *'He came into the very world he created, but the world didn't recognise him.'*[10]

'You are my beloved Son; I am very pleased with you.'

But let's put that on one side for the moment and just accept that God created everything so Jesus, as part of the Godhead, was therefore involved. Taking it that way the pilgrimage starts at the beginning, from creation, and finishes at the end, to his second coming in Glory.

However, there is more to creation than the initiation of the universe. Three of the stories the Messiah recorded in the Gospels were about stewardship and therefore encourage us to care about creation.

One of the stories of stewardship is about three servants each being given different amounts of money to look after. Each one dealt with it in different ways, two of the three giving back more and the third just returning what they were given. The first two are commended while the third is dealt with in a manner reminiscent of how some people describe Hell.[11] Frequently we hear this parable being used as an example of why we need to be wise with what we are entrusted. Whereas it's true we should be wise with the creation we have been entrusted with, does this paint a picture of a loving God or of a harsh and vengeful God?

The Messiah goes on to explain this story: The good servants are those who, seeing someone hungry feeds them and who welcomes strangers. He separates those on the pilgrimage from those on a different path.[12] This demonstrates how we should deal with creation – both the physical world and human beings created in the image of God.

So what about another of these stories: The story of the dishonest manager? Here we have a story that appears to be both unethical and approving of dishonesty. The manager hears the company owner is about to return and so goes round revising the invoices down so that the creditors settle quickly before the owner returns. The owner apparently commends the dishonest manager for his shrewdness. But… and there's a but… the Messiah goes on to say that only those faithful in small things will be trusted with large things and that those dishonest in small things will also end up being dishonest in larger things. So if we cannot manage honestly someone else's wealth how can we expect God to entrust us with wealth of our own? Nobody serves both God and money. The same can be true for how we care for the earth.[13]

His honour and his courage

There is one big difference between our pilgrimage and that of the Messiah: We don't know how ours will end, but he did; he knew his would involve him sacrificing his life. Sometimes he hints at things but they are hidden from us till later. Sometimes we're thankful that they are.

Take, for example, the time when with his closest followers he went up a mountain to pray. While they were praying there was some kind of vision of the spiritual reality. And his followers didn't understand it and suggested all kinds of rather inappropriate ideas.[14]

This is courage: Knowing what will happenand still facing it.

Following that, Jesus healed a boy who had seizures of some kind, possibly spiritually initiated, which left them all marvelling at what he had done. In the middle of this Jesus said to them, 'You need to let this sink in: I'm about to be handed over to a bunch of evil men.' (authors' paraphrase) He was indicating that these evil men would kill him.[15]

It was then that he set his face to Jerusalem where he was to be killed. This is courage. Knowing what will happen and yet still facing it, still continuing on the pilgrimage.

When things are going well we don't need courage, but often in life things are not going well and it's a struggle. We need to realise that this pilgrimage is not without cost. Jesus' followers were walking with him and two brothers, James and John, came and asked if they can sit either side of him when he was in his glory. His response was to question whether they really understood what they were asking and whether they could follow in his footsteps. They believed they could, and Jesus foretold that they too would die a martyr's death. Not all of us are called to martyrdom, but in the Messianic Pilgrimage we are all called to courage.

Rejection at home

Having started his pilgrimage the Messiah went to his home town to share the vision. He went to the synagogue, as was his custom, and read from the book of Isaiah where it talks about the Holy Spirit anointing him for this journey.[16] It's good news for the poor; sight for the blind; liberty for the oppressed and so on.

But the people in his home town were not impressed and wanted to kill him by throwing him off a cliff outside the town. He walked away from all this.[17] There was no attempt to change them, he just walked away. We too may face rejection when we start the Messianic Pilgrimage. We too need to just walk away, but at the same time not be deterred from our pilgrimage or our destination.

Identity as a member of the People of God

The rejection by his home town is shocking because Jesus lived his whole life as a respectful descendant of Abraham, Isaac and Jacob. The first chapter of the New Testament traces his ancestors back 42 generations to Abraham, almost 2,000 years.[18]

For all those centuries the Jews had had a very hard time staying on God's pilgrim path because their leaders were so unreliable. When God finally sent the Messiah as the true Leader they needed, the Jewish leaders refused to believe God sent

him. They called him a fake and a blasphemer.[19] They said that anyone who followed him would be kicked out of the synagogue, that is, cut off from the community of the descendants of Abraham.[20]

But Jesus knew he was the true son of Abraham and they were the fakes. *'Our father is Abraham!' they declared. 'No,' Jesus replied, 'for if you were really the children of Abraham, you would follow his example. Instead, you are trying to kill me because I told you the truth, which I heard*

'The Spirit of the Lord is upon me, for he has anointed me to bring Good News to the poor'

from God. Abraham never did such a thing. No, you are imitating your real father… the devil. [21] They got so furious about this that they picked up stones to kill him, but he slipped away. [22]

Jesus escaped all their attacks until the hour that God had set for him to give his life. Then the official leaders of the descendants of Abraham, Isaac, and Jacob arrested him and asked him in court whether he was the Messiah. If he had said no, he could have walked away as a free man. He said yes, and they condemned him to death for blasphemy.

Of course, they were the real blasphemers. God sent Jesus as the Messiah and they said he was not the Messiah! Let none of us make that horrific mistake.

We honour Jesus as the Messiah, the leader of the true descendants of Abraham. That is how we get to join the pilgrimage of the same 'tribe' that Jesus belonged to, the true People of God.

His freedom

God sent Jesus to earth on a freedom mission. As the Messiah his work was to proclaim a new era in the history of the world, an era of freedom from darkness, corruption and death.

This freedom is what he announced in his home town that almost got him killed. [23] This is what he proclaimed all the time and also sent his followers to proclaim to the whole nation. This is what the crowds in Jerusalem celebrated when he triumphantly entered Jerusalem for the national freedom celebration (Passover). [24] And this is what brought the death sentence on him. [25] The authorities said he was a dangerous rebel not a liberator.

Jesus knew that the earthly authorities were not the real authorities over him. Long before his trial he told the crowds, *'No one can take my life from me. I sacrifice it voluntarily. For I have the authority to lay it down when I want to and also to take it up again. For this is what my Father has commanded.* [26] During his trial by the Roman governor, Pilate, he

It is power and authority from the Holy Spirit that help us on our journey

repeated this. *"Why don't you talk to me?"* Pilate demanded. *"Don't you realize that I have the power to release you or crucify you?"*

Then Jesus said, "You would have no power over me at all unless it were given to you from above." [27] Jesus knew the freedom of a person obeying God's will for him.

His power

One of my favourite stories about the Messiah is how he dealt with a foreigner: an officer in an oppressing and occupying military force in his country. This officer had sent a message to the Messiah asking him to come and heal his servant. Unsure how Jesus would respond, the officer sent local community leaders to Jesus to plead on his behalf. They explained that he had been extremely good to the local people, even helping to build a community hall.

So Jesus set out for the home of the foreigner. But even before he arrived the army officer sent his friends asking Jesus to heal his servant without actually visiting, because he was unworthy to receive him. The occupying army officer claimed to be unworthy to entertain a teacher from the country he was occupying. This understanding of true power and authority was something that the Messiah had not seen among his own people.[28]

It is this power and authority that we receive through the gifts of the Holy Spirit and which help us on our journey.[29]

His mercy

God set the agenda for mercy when he promised to bless Abraham and all his descendants, so that all the people on earth would be blessed through him.[30] The Messiah in a much greater way was following in Abraham's steps. He was bringing blessing through mercy.

Like us, the Messiah met many hurting people; some physically, some emotionally and some hurting in their spirit. One of the occasions that was

Seeing hungry... we feed them, thirsty... we give them drink

most memorable is when people brought someone who was paralysed to Jesus to heal him. Because they couldn't get into the house they took the person on a bed onto the roof, removed part of the roof and lowered him into the middle of the crowd in the room.[31]

That was a clear example of needing mercy both physically and spiritually. To start with, Jesus spoke words of healing spiritually. The religious people were unimpressed and challenged him on this. I suspect he knew this was coming, which is why he did it in this order, to demonstrate the veracity of the spiritual healing. He then went on to physically heal the man, thus proving he had the authority to spiritually heal too.

Now we, on our pilgrimage, may not find we are always physically healing people by our prayers. However, we are called to offer mercy—physically, emotionally and spiritually—to those we meet on the journey. And we can expect to come into conflict with unmerciful religious leaders while doing so.

The Messiah also commanded us to show mercy in ways that seem counter to what we experience normally: *'Love your enemies and do good to those that hate you, bless those who curse you and pray for your abusers'*.[32] He said that if we just do the normal thing of loving only those who love us, we're not in the pilgrimage, we're only doing what normal people do. In that case we're like one blind person trying to guide another.[33]

But mercy is more than just being kind to others. Receiving mercy is not getting the punishment we deserved. And *'everyone has sinned; we all fall short of God's glorious standard'*.[34] Jesus going to the cross is where God showed us mercy. God only expects us to do what he has already done for us.

This God-inspired mercy leads us not to judge others,[35] not to condemn, but to forgive.[36] We overflow with this mercy and God is pleased with us as his children. Then we keep receiving overflowing grace and mercy ourselves.

We need to listen to the Holy Spirit guiding our direction

Rest stop

Before the start of the pilgrimage the Messiah took time out for contemplation. It was a time of preparation for the journey ahead. It was a time of challenge: How important are the physical parts of life compared to the spiritual? How much do we trust God for the journey ahead?[37]

Contemplation takes us further than just looking inward. We are physical beings living in a physical world and so we are body, mind and spirit all integrated. It's easy to get these out of balance. But if we are open to and listening to the Holy Spirit, then he can lead us on the journey ahead.

Jesus demonstrated this clearly as an example to follow in his time of contemplation. Throughout his pilgrimage the Messiah took time out to pray and rest.[38] Thus the Messiah is both our companion on the journey and also the model pilgrim to follow.

Final vision

As spiritual descendants of Abraham, we inherit his call to pilgrimage. He was told, *'Leave your country, your people and your father's household and go to the land I show you'*[39]. God was telling Abraham to trust him about this new vision of his future. God would make it come true for Abraham without the protection or help of his family or clan. That is the same trust we have to have as we join the Messianic Pilgrimage.

The pilgrimage is both the spiritual journey from our old selves to our new selves, and also from the world as we know it to the world we can envision: a beautiful world under the control of God and his Messiah free from all the conflict and tragedy we see in the news every day.

But what does this vision lead us to do until the day the Messiah comes back in glory to take control and change our world into this new world? Do we do nothing except wait? Do we try to create that world ourselves as if we are representatives of God, authorised to use force against people who do evil?

Either of those approaches to life might seem logical ways to go along with the vision. But the Messiah did not use either of them. Neither did he teach his followers to use them.

The true Messiah did not do a lot of things that people expect messiahs to do. He did not claim any city or any territory and govern it. He did not give his followers any military training or organisation. He did not instruct them to conquer some territory and then use it as a base to conquer more. He did not impose his vision of the world on anyone, or punish anyone who refused it.

Only once in his life did he use force against humans doing evil. He threw the merchants out of the Temple where they were overcharging people for sacrificial animals.[40]

If the Messiah did not use force to impose God's vision for the world, what was his main strategy for living with the vision in mind? He set up a kingdom of the willing and he called people to join it.

But is a kingdom of the willing really a kingdom at all? Isn't it just a vision, a hope that a lot of people will join it and the world will get a little better? Don't bad people have to be forced to go along with a good vision? If they can reject it won't they stay bad forever?

They may, but, according to the Messiah, that is not our problem. Our job is to be good citizens of the kingdom of the willing. That means we keep listening to the voice of the Messiah through the Spirit he has put into us.

The Spirit makes the vision come true in us one step at a time, one day at a time. There is peace wherever the Messiah rules. So, as we accept his rule in us, we experience his peace. The future vision starts coming true already in us.

Don't bad people have to be forced to go along with a good vision?

And what about the bad people? We do not force them to comply with the Messiah's vision for the world. We endure their opposition like Jesus did. We do not retaliate. We even ask God to forgive them. And we trust the Messiah himself to impose the new world on the bad people on the day that God has set for that to happen.

If he someday assigns us to start imposing the vision, we will start then, but he has not said one word about it yet. Until he does, we just keep submitting to his Spirit one day at a time—living the vision, calling others to join it but never imposing it.

Bible References from previous section

1	Luke 1: 5-57		24	Luke 19:28-44
2	Luke1:41		25	Matthew 26:57-68
3	Luke 1:42-45		26	John 10:18
4	Luke 2:1-5		27	John 19:10-11
5	Luke 2:8-21		28	Luke 7:1–10
6	Luke 2:41-52			Matthew 8:5-13
7	Luke 3:1-20		29	1 Corinthians 12:7-11
8	Luke 3:21-22		30	Genesis 12:1-3
9	John 1:3		31	Luke 5:17-39
10	John 1:10		32	Luke 6:27-36
11	Matthew 25:14–30		33	Matthew 15:14
12	Matthew 25:31-46		34	Romans 3:23
13	Luke 16:1-13		35	Matthew 7: 1-6
14	Matthew 17:1-8		36	Matthew 18: 21-22
15	Matthew 17:14-23		37	Matthew 4:1-11
16	Isaiah 61		38	Matthew 14:23
	Luke 4:14-30			Mark 6:46
17	Luke 4:28-30			Luke 6:12
18	Matthew 1:1-16			Mark 1:35
19	Matthew 9:1-8			Luke 5:16
20	John 16:2			Matthew 26:36
21	John 8:39-41,44		39	Genesis 12:1-8
22	John 8:59		40	Matthew 21:12-17
23	Luke 4:14-30			

Dates of the seasons in solar and lunar calendars

Solar Calendar Seasons

Note that in the Solar year the seasons vary slightly, depending on dates like Easter. The following shows the dates from 2021. Current year season dates can be found on the SYNCx website.

Life Season - 1 January (New Year's Day) to 16 February (Mardi Gras/Carnival)

Identity Season - 17 February (Ash Wednesday) to 27 March

Freedom Season - 28 March (Palm Sunday) to 12 May

Power Season - 13 May (Ascension Day) to 6 August (Feast of Transfiguration)

Mercy Season - 7 August to 16 September (Day of Atonement)

Honour Season - 17 September to 20 November

Vision Season - 21 November (Feast of Christ the King) to 31 December (New Year's Eve)

Lunar Calendar Seasons

Life Season - Muharram & Safar

Honour Season - Rabi Al-Awwal & Rabi Al-Thani

Identity Season - Jamada Al-Awwal & Jamada Al-Thani

Freedom Season - Rajab & Sha'ban

Power Season - Ramadan

Mercy Season - Shawwal

Rest Stop Season - Dhul Qadah

Vision Season - Dhul Hijjah

Online English

English material for SYNC can be found on the SYNCx website **https://syncx.org**

That material follows the Solar Calendar (ie starts 1 January and ends 31 December each year).

Material directly linked to this book can be found at **https://messianicpilgrims.org**

Online Arabic

Arabic material for the Messianic Pilgrimage can be found on the Ushaaqallah website (Ushaaqallah means 'passionate about God') **https://ushaaqallah.com**

That material follows the Lunar Calendar (also known as the Hijri calendar) used in the Middle East and North Africa.

There is also a Facebook page **https://www.facebook.com/ushaaqallah** and Facebook group **https://www.facebook.com/groups/202185213163525/**

SEASON 1

GOD SAW EVERYTHING THAT HE HAD MADE AND IT WAS VERY GOOD....-

The 5G flow during Life Season

Ground-breaker
There was nothing. Then there was something. Everything changed.

Each Messianic Pilgrimage season starts with a claim that God did some specific thing that changed the story of the world, affecting everything right down to today. The ground-breaking event for Life Season is the creation of the universe. In fact, there was nothing at all before this ground-breaker! Then God pronounced the universe into being just like a minister pronounces two people to be married. This is the origin of all life.

'In the beginning God created the heavens and the earth' (Genesis 1:1). If this ground-breaking event, this first verse of the Bible, is fake news, then we are all on our own to make a better world, however we define better.

But if the ground-breaker happened as the Bible sketches it for us, if the God of the Bible created a good world and a good human race, we can all agree that better would mean 'better aligned with what the world was like when God created it'. The better world would also be freer of all the evil that came about later as people turned their backs on God (Genesis 3-11).

Humans turned God's good world into the not-so-good world we see today. Humans disconnected from him, inflicted all kinds of wounds, and filled the world with curses. That's why God launched his campaign to connect, heal, and bless the world. It was his strategy to undo the damage humans did to his good creation. The other seven Messianic Pilgrimage seasons will describe that strategy one step at a time. But for now, we go back to the beginning.

Gift
All life and all of the physical universe is a gift from God.

An engagement ring has a much greater meaning to a woman than a ring she finds on the street. If the world is a gift to humanity we should appreciatively find the meaning that the giver put into it. If the world just happened, there is no giver to thank for it, and it has no built-in meaning.

Each of God's ground-breakers brings us a new gift. The gift we get from the first ground-breaker is our bodies, our planet, our universe. The earth and sky were not there until he said so, and then they were.

As humans, we can imagine many things. With a few lines of code (our creative words) we can create them from nothing in a virtual world, but that doesn't work in the real world. We have a hard time defining life in the real world, much less creating it. We stand in awe of a God who has that power.

As gifts, our lives and our universe have meaning. They are not just atoms and accidents. Someone deliberately put them there, made them beautiful and did it from a good motive and for a good reason.

Get it
We recognise the built-in meaning of life.

As the whole planet is a gift, so our individual lives are each a gift. We didn't create ourselves. We didn't earn the right to be born. Life was given to us. If we understand that, we should seek what the giver meant for each and every one of us.

If we truly appreciate that, we realise how amazing a gift this groundbreaker was and is. Nobody asked God to create the world. We didn't ask him to be born, and we didn't do anything to deserve it. God gave life to us out of his own goodness. When that hits us it is the 'aha' moment when something inside us changes. The world we live in will never look the same to us again.

If we don't get it, we assume either that the world just happened or that the god who made it is more like a business person than a giver. If God treats the world as a business he owns, we have to do transactions with him. We make up different religions trying to guess which transactions to make and what is the right way to make them.

The world is more like a garden God landscaped, or a work of art he produced than it is like a business he runs for profit. He made the world to be enjoyed. Entry is free but permission to stay is not guaranteed to people who trample the garden or put graffiti on the work of art. Those people don't get it. They insult the owner by acting as if they can treat the gift any way they want. They wear out their welcome.

The world is like a garden God landscaped or a work of art he produced

Go with it

Once we get that our life is a gift, we embrace life and share it.

Once we see the big picture that the world is a gift and we see the personal detail that our own life is a gift, we pay attention to the Giver's intentions for the gift. We live gratefully and joyfully. We know who we are and why we are here, and that feels great!

We explore, we discover, we make the most of the opportunity. We do not do what I once saw a young boy do in a buffet restaurant. With hundreds of delicious options before him, he ate three plates full of the same two items--macaroni and cheese with red jello on the side!

He left the buffet happy about his choices, but he had not made the most of his opportunity. He let his own familiar desires decide things for him and he missed out on most of what the buffet owners had made available to him.

How do we actually go with the gift of life? We pay attention to the Creator's campaign to restore life on earth to its original glory and joy. We explore and discover. We get familiar with the Bible, which sets the rhythm for the whole campaign for people to have enriched and fulfilled lives. We also listen constantly for updates to our personal assignments in the campaign. The Spirit of Jesus lets us know what they are. We go with what we hear from the Bible and the Spirit.

Genuineness

As we go with it, we become a fountain of life for those around us.

We realise we are connected to an infinite source of life, we discover we have plenty to share. We don't have to grab for as much life as we can get, or work so hard to defend what life we have. We can afford to help others. We become generous.

If we are guests in the world and we act like guests, everything is as it should be. We are authentic human beings, grateful to the good God for his open-door policy and not wanting to dishonour our gracious Host. We are fully alive, in sync with God's magnificent intentions when he spoke that first creative word.

This means we are good to everybody. Life overflows from us or even gushes out, blessing those around us. When we see our effect on them, we are happy because we have the privilege of contributing to a better world. We don't have the burden of trying to force anything on anyone. We just share life so their lives can be better.

We don't get arrogant about it though. What makes us genuinely happy is that good things happen for other people, not that we will get any praise for doing them. We realise that we didn't really do them. Our motivation and our strength or skill all come from God, so he gets all the credit for whatever he does through us.

The view from here

God, the real God, creates a beautiful world with life everywhere, but people are tricked into thinking he is still withholding something from them. So they take and try for themselves the one thing he warned was poisonous. Sure enough, death gets loose and the world gets ugly with shame, violence, abuse and funerals.

But God does not give up. He takes things to a new level. Through Abraham, he creates a whole God-tribe to show all the other tribes the key to life and this is the key—when our life depends on it, we do what God is telling us, even if that does not look like what is best for us.

Down through the centuries we see how this works out in a whole string of rescue stories for Abraham and his descendants like Joseph, Moses, David, Elijah and Esther. We also see the tragic end for people like King Ahab and Queen Jezebel, who trusted their own judgment more than God's guidance.

During the ups and downs of Abraham's descendants, God keeps sending messengers with an astonishing prediction—sometime, somehow, the real God will send the ultimate life-bringer, the most important descendant of Abraham ever.

Forty-two generations after Abraham the prediction comes true. You can read the list in Matthew 1. The Messiah, the one-of-a-kind God-person, is born. They name him Jesus, which means, 'The real God rescues'.

He tells the whole nation descended from Abraham, 'This is it! God is bringing heaven's life to earth now. Follow me and see what I mean.' Many are thrilled to follow him but the leaders think he is a fake and His life is threatened. He sees death coming and he has to decide whether he will trust God's strategy and accept death, or trust his own judgment and look for a way out.

He trusts God, gets arrested and gets executed on a cross. But here is the best part of the story—God the

Down through the centuries, we see how this works out in a whole string of rescue stories for Abraham and his descendants

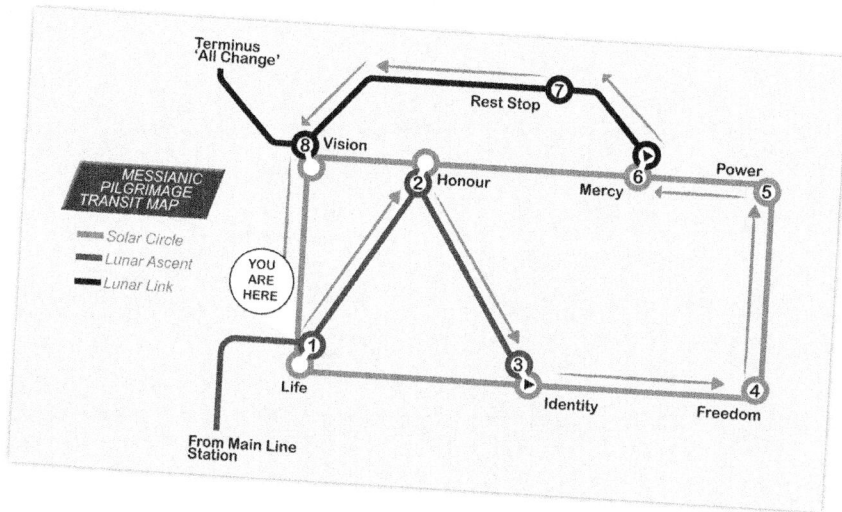

MESSIANIC PILGRIMAGE TRANSIT MAP

Terminus 'All Change'

Rest Stop

Vision

Solar Circle
Lunar Ascent
Lunar Link

YOU ARE HERE

Honour

Mercy

Power

Life

Identity

Freedom

From Main Line Station

Father puts new life, un-killable life, back into him and he walks out of His grave more alive than ever! For 40 days Jesus keeps visiting his followers and explaining what is going on. Then the Father takes him to heaven and installs him as King of Life.

Jesus then gives his followers a super-injection of his life. He sends his Spirit, life and power down into them so they know he is way more than a memory. He is alive and he is with them. Out they go, radiating his life, showing and telling that he really is the Messiah, the key to forgiveness and life for everybody everywhere including right here right now.

Not all these messengers are physical descendants of Abraham but they all become his spiritual descendants.

It is as if they have been born all over again but this time with the 'Abraham gene'. Now they can trust God more than their own judgment, like their forefather did.

Some people eagerly join the spiritual family. Others can't bring themselves to trust God quite that far. Some see Jesus as a threat to life as they know it. They try to shut the messengers up but it doesn't work. The messengers are able to show the same mercy and courage Jesus showed when he was tortured. His life keeps bubbling up inside them no matter what.

That's how things stand for the time being, but when the set time comes, the King of Life will come back to earth in person to destroy death and reconnect the whole world to God's life, once and for all.

So that's our story. That's why we live the way we live and make life better for everybody we can. Who are we? We are life-bringers, with the life of the Creator flowing through us to all who will welcome it.

A BATTLE BETWEEN LIGHT AND DARK

SEASON 2

The 5G flow during Honour Season

Ground-breaker
Jesus went to the cross and inspires us to finish honourably too

Jesus' people thought that God's prophets had predicted that the Messiah would establish the reign of God on earth by crushing all evil by force. When Jesus carried his cross he showed us that the Messiah would have to suffer (Luke 24:25-27). And so would his followers.

Before Jesus' execution, he taught his followers that he and they would all have to suffer but they didn't get it. They still assumed he was going to set up a kingdom and exercise power to rule. Two members of his inner circle even asked him if they could be his right-hand men when he did. (Mark 10:35-37)

When Jesus carried his cross to his place of execution, everything changed. His followers had to face the truth that had been unimaginable to them before. The reign of God that Jesus announced was not going to be brought in by power holders, but by the victims of power holders. And the victims would bring it in not by revolt but by accepting their victimisation.

How could that happen? Who 'takes power' by accepting victimisation? Jesus did and we as his followers are still doing it. We look at our victimisation like Christ looked at carrying his cross—it is our role in the process of bringing God's mercy to earth. When we accept it, we create the opportunity for everyone, even our victimisers, to welcome God's amazing grace.

That's what God wants—for everyone to have a chance to be awestruck by his mercy, even those who do not deserve a chance. He does not want people to have his kingdom rammed down their throats.

Gift
Now that Jesus changed everything, we have what it takes to handle rejection and pain

The gift we get from Jesus is the courage to endure whatever hardship or opposition we meet as we carry his message of mercy and look forward to his glorious return.

Our courage rises when we realise that as Jesus carries his cross God's strategy is not getting blocked or frustrated. With that cross beam on his shoulders Jesus looks for all the world like a loser, but he is not going to lose.

The cross is not the end of God's mission or of Jesus' work. It is the path to the resurrection and to Jesus taking the throne in heaven. *'Because of the joy awaiting him, he endured the cross, disregarding its shame. Now he is seated in the place of honour beside God's throne.'*
(Hebrews 12:2)

God has set it all up so that Jesus, by loyally playing his painful role, will inspire the courage of billions of human beings for many centuries to come. We are part of the same strategy God is using. The courage we get from Jesus is not courage to overthrow governments and seize positions of power. It is the courage to trust God when we suffer for calling people to welcome Jesus as the Messiah, the rightful ruler of us and of every system of power.

Get it
The gift helps us if we get it that loyalty to our mission won't be easy.

Jesus is not just our substitute; he is also our example and our hero. Anyone who supposes that Jesus suffered so we don't have to doesn't get it yet. The Honour Season is a wake-up call. It is true that Jesus paid the penalty for our sin so that we would not have to pay it. There is zero sin debt remaining for us to have to pay by our own suffering. That is done.

But our suffering is not done. There is a different kind of suffering that starts for us after Jesus has done all the suffering for our sin. It is the suffering that carries on God's strategy for ridding the world of sin.

This is the idea we have to get. This is how it works. Jesus sends us out as messengers of his resurrection, that is, witnesses that he is the resurrected King, not the loser he looked like when he carried his cross. Sinful people and oppressive governments don't want to hear this. They can make life difficult for us. But when they see our courage under fire it gives them a second chance to realise that we are telling the truth--God really is at work in us.

Christ's willingness to suffer and die for his cause is not our ticket to an easy life. It is our example for dealing honourably with the shame and suffering that will get added to our lives if we represent him in this world. Our honourability testifies to his resurrection.

Go with it
Once we get it, we stick to whatever assignment God has given us.

Our resilience is evidence that Jesus is alive, helping us endure the unendurable and even to rejoice in the middle of it.

This is not hard to explain. It is hard to do. It goes against every bit of self-preservation in our DNA. But our re-birth in Christ helps us overcome that DNA so that loyalty to the mission he has given us is more important than self-preservation.

The mission is to point to him as the King who changes the world and to show how he is already changing us. And one of the key changes he makes is that he turns weaklings into heroes. When we say, 'sync me' to Christ, we are saying, 'sync me with your courage'. Then he empowers us to go with his heroic example, trusting him to work it all out in the end.

This is a great way to live. As honourable finishers, we convince people that there is hope for the world. They thought they couldn't trust anybody but they see they can trust us. They thought everybody was trying to take advantage of them, but they see we are laying down our preferences and comforts for their good. We are living the authentic lives they thought nobody was living.

On the other hand, we dare not claim the benefits of Christ's death on the cross if we don't step up to carry our own cross, loyally enduring opposition to the mission God has given us. If we don't step up, we are not going with Christ's honour and his plan. We are out of sync with his purpose and strategy. We are dishonourably trying to work the system hoping he will go with our desires even if we don't go with his heroic example.

Genuineness
As we go with it, we become honourable finishers

We find our authentic identity in Christ because of the way he accepted and endured the hard part of his mission. Hard times reveal the genuine followers of Jesus and expose the fake ones, those who are in it for their own gain.

We find our authentic identity in Christ because of his honour. We are purified by enduring opposition to our mission like he endured opposition to his. Sharing his experience of suffering is the fire that refines us like gold. In the Mercy Season we will see that during the fire we have to bite our tongues, stop our urge to retaliate and turn to God with our tears.

But nothing is more genuine evidence of God's secret power at work than the way we handle the wrongs people do to us when we represent Jesus to them. The deeper people scratch us, the more they reveal that we are gold all the way to the core.

There is no human explanation for our good will toward their enemies, our joy that bubbles up no matter what and our trust in the King who will make everything right in the end. The only explanation is that Jesus is alive, that he really has sent us to represent him and he really is with us when we do.

His gift to us is his presence which explains our courage and our ability to finish honourably. He syncs us with his intentions when he carried his cross: that billions of his followers would join him in God's sacrificial strategy for bringing his mercy and power to earth. That is what it takes to undermine the power of sin. Thanks to Jesus, we have what it takes.

The view from here

If the Bible is right, we humans didn't start as uncivilised cave men and women. We started with more honour than we have now. Look at the picture the Bible paints in Genesis 1 and 2. God honours the first human beings by giving them control over the rest of his creatures. He honours them by preparing a garden spot fit for a king and queen to live in and it is virus-free. He even honours them with daily visits.

How do they respond? They disgrace themselves by eating from the one and only tree that God declared off limits. God expels them from the garden and they live under his curse. Over the centuries, life deteriorates into a shameful mess of corruption, violence, drunkenness, arrogance and racism. Human technology evolves, but human honourability doesn't.

But that curse is not God's last word to humans. He takes a blessing to an old man called Abraham who is suffering one of the biggest disgraces of ancient times—a barren wife. He promises the couple that their descendants will be enough to bless every family on earth. And it comes true. Miraculously, they have a son, and that son has a son who has twelve sons, each the patriarch of a clan in a whole tribe.

Later when God makes his link with Abraham's tribe official through Moses, his top demand is that they honour him and only him. Sometimes they do, but they keep disgracing themselves, worshipping other gods in spite of God's warnings through his prophets. Finally God lets their enemies take them away to live in shame as a captive people for 70 years.

When they return, they try to recover their honour, rebuild their capital and their Temple. They keep hoping that God will send a special ruler to restore the nation's honour as the prophets predicted, but 400 years go by with no sign of him.

Then Jesus arrives and it sounds like he might be the one. He proclaims that God's reign on earth is beginning and he says what every would-be messiah says, 'Trust me! Follow me!' He heals people, he trains his followers and he treats even despised people honourably, but he also exposes the shameful hypocrisy of the powerful leaders of his tribe.

Finally in the Garden of Gethsemane, he faces the crisis of his life. He prays that he will not be killed by his enemies who want to put a stop to all his work. But, in the end, he says to God his Father, 'I am going to honour you by doing this your way,

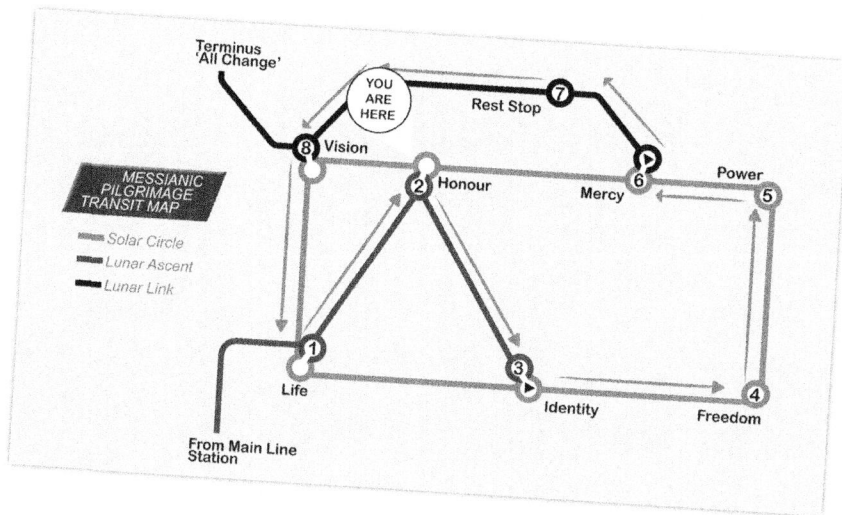

MESSIANIC PILGRIMAGE TRANSIT MAP

Terminus 'All Change'

YOU ARE HERE

Rest Stop

Solar Circle
Lunar Ascent
Lunar Link

7

8 Vision

2 Honour

6 Mercy

5 Power

1 Life

3 Identity

4 Freedom

From Main Line Station

not mine.'

What happens next is awful. Jesus is betrayed, abandoned, condemned, beaten savagely then nailed naked to a stake and left to die slowly in public as his enemies taunt him. But as he accepts the disgrace he shows us what it means to finish life honourably. As a willing human sacrifice he regains for the whole human race the honour that we lost in the beginning.

Two days after his burial God the Father honours the trust of his dis-graced Son by bringing him back to life. Jesus secretly meets his stunned followers but he does not shame them. Instead he tells them that they will carry his mission on as soon as one more thing happens. They are to wait for it.

Then God the Father takes Jesus up to heaven to take his throne and they wait. Ten days later he sends his Holy Spirit down to live in them empowering them to tell the world of his resurrection and his mercy. They face the shame of arrest, beating, jail and even execution but nothing can stop them. To them, being shamed for Jesus' sake is not shame. It's a badge of honour!

Jesus empowers his movement to keep growing. It is still growing today in spite of the fierce opposition that Jesus predicted and it will keep growing until the set day when he comes back to bestow honours on his ambassadors. The persecutors will be ashamed that they ever lifted a finger against them.

Who are we? We are honourable finishers. Jesus' Spirit in us gives us Jesus' strength. Shame does not slow us down. Disruption of our plans does not stop our witness.

And that's why we live the way we live and tell this story no matter whether people love it or hate it. It's our story. We live by it and we are prepared to be 'shamed' and to die by it. Jesus did and look how that turned out!

CONNECTED EVERYWHERE

SEASON 3

The 5G flow during Identity Season

Ground-breaker
God creates his own campaign team to bless the world

With one promise to Abraham, God solved the identity problem of every human being and every ethnic group. God announced that through Abraham he would create a new sub-group of the human race, connect it tightly to himself and give it an identity as the group that exists to bless all the others.

Why are so many people 4,000 years behind the times?

Many people have the idea that God is like a cosmic head teacher, trying to help his human students toward maturity by making the rules, blessing them when they do well and punishing them when they don't. That actually was God's strategy at the dawn of human history but he only used it long enough for us all to see that it was not going to work.

That approach does not get any-where. It spins its wheels in an ugly cycle that goes like this: God's command, human failure, God's judg-ment, God granting another chance, and humans failing again, as if we learned nothing from the last cycle. This cycle is repeated over and over in Genesis 2-11, the first 1% of the Bible.

Lots of people think that human identity is still the identity of losers who keep making the same mistakes. They don't get it that a ground-breaking event happened almost 4,000 years ago making a new identity possible. God had been using a head teacher strategy (punish losers) but he launched a different, more effective strategy that creates winners.

So what is this other strategy?

It's more pro-active. Instead of just laying down the law and then reacting to humans as they do well or badly, God takes the initiative. He launches his campaign. And the way he does it is to start his own group of people, his 'campaign team', and assign them to bless all human beings and groups whether they are part of the team or not.

God, the campaign team and other humans/groups are the three 'main characters' of the biblical story. The rest of the Bible (99%, from Genesis 12 onward) is the story of the ways that God's campaign progressed and is still playing out.

The strategy is two-pronged. God gives some of his blessing and heal-ing to all humans directly but he gives the lion's share to his campaign team. Their assignment is to pass it on to everyone and every group.

Gift

New identity in the campaign team was a gift to Abraham, and it gives us security and significance

God's ground-breaking promise went beyond Abraham's wildest dreams. Abraham did not see it coming and had done nothing to earn it. God just said, in effect, 'You are the one. You will have millions of descendants and they will bless every family on the planet.' (authors' paraphrase) This whole campaign started as a gift and it comes to us today as a gift. We have the privilege of belonging to something so huge, so ancient, and so good—God's campaign team! What identity could be more secure and significant?

In other words, we have roots and we're part of God's family! We get to be fruitful branches on an ancient family tree, the Abraham tree. Even if some other group excludes us, our identity is secure. We know we are included in the one group that really matters—the campaign team. We never again feel lost or aimless in life because we share in the team's special assignment to bless the world. We never get bored because there is so much campaign work left to do—connecting, healing, blessing.

Our new identity is not just a new label on the outside of us. We become different people.

Get it

A gift this huge and undeserved obligates the recipient to the giver

If we win the lottery we can do whatever we want with the money. But when we receive a personal gift we always consider who gave it to us and why. Abraham got that. He realised that because of the gift, he owed God a debt of gratitude and trust. And if we are privileged to be adopted into the team we owe the same debt.

If we get it, we realise how amazing a gift this ground-breaking event was and is. Humans were failing time after time to learn the lessons God was teaching them through commands and punishment (Genesis 3-11). So in Genesis 12, God starts his campaign team and he starts it from nothing. He goes to a childless old couple and tells them they are his choice as the parents of the team.

All they have to do is trust him, and they do not have to make the first move. God selects them first; they trust him later. They respond by trusting the promises he gives them and obeying the things he tells them, even when those things do not make sense from a human point of view.

That trust is in the attitude of the campaign team, the true physical or spiritual descendants of Abraham. It is exactly what the first humans did not have. People who have not joined the team still do not have it. But the team does.

When that hits us, it is the 'aha' moment. Our new identity is not just a new label on the outside of us. We are different people. It is like we have been born for a second time and had some of our DNA altered.

We were not on the team before. Perhaps we did not even know it existed. But now we are included in the team because God gave us that trust of Abraham. The world we live in will never look the same to us again.

Go with it
Once we get it we participate as members of the campaign team

When we realise our new identity, when we get it that Jesus has put his Spirit into us to turn us into campaign team members, the natural response is to 'Go with it', to live like a part of the team that Jesus is leading.

Our roots give us tremendous security. This campaign can't fail because it is not a human idea. It was all God's idea set in motion in the ancient time of Abraham and Sarah and brought into our lives now by the Spirit of the Messiah.

The Spirit of Jesus gives us our personal niche assignments in the campaign one day or one minute at a time. If we have not experienced that kind of guidance, think of it as being similar to our conscience. The conscience tells us what not to do. The Spirit tells us what to do.

For example, 'Give this gift.' 'Talk to that person.' 'Ponder this idea.' 'Watch for such-and-such today.'

'Make some time for this new habit.' This specific guidance is for us at that moment, not for anyone else, or at any other time. When we are on the team we get this guidance and we go with it.

That is half of the story of going with the campaign. The other half is the Bible, which gives us the big picture of the connect-heal-bless campaign. That's basically what the whole Bible is—the step by step story of the campaign and the instructions that apply to all team members at all times. Our forerunners in the campaign have shown us many things about how to do it and how not to do it. That is why reading the Bible is so important to going with the campaign.

The Bible gives campaign guidance that is the same for all team members in all places and all times. Our mission in the campaign is to connect, heal and bless. This gives us a deep sense of significance though it is also an awesome responsibility. If we are on a campaign team, we had better

Let us do what the Spirit moves us to do, then our gratitude will never end.

Genuineness
As we go with it, we become fulfillments of God's promise to bless the world through Abraham's descendants, fruitful branches on the Abraham family tree

throw ourselves into the campaign work with the same passion the campaign director has. We can't just show up for the team photo!

But passionate good intentions can lead to foolish tragic mistakes if we do not stick with what the Bible tells us about our mission of blessing. For example, if the Crusaders had read their Bibles well, they would have known that God's campaign is about connecting, healing and blessing. What did they do? The exact opposite—dominate, attack, and seize. In their passion they forgot the Bible and disgraced the Messiah.

Let us not make their mistake. Let us rather hear what the Bible and the Spirit are really saying, and let us do what the Spirit moves us to do. Then our gratitude will never end because we are living the dream, thrilled to have a share in knocking death out of the world and pouring life in. We get to be in on healing old wounds and preventing new ones, bringing blessings of all kinds and calling others to connect with the Messiah. What an identity! Thank God for his gift!

We find our authentic identity in the campaign team led by Jesus the Messiah. We are 100% genuine people, following Jesus who died for the campaign and who lives to keep leading it. We are not pretending that we are the saviours of the world but we are genuinely participating in saving the world as the power of Jesus flows through us.

When we live as part of the campaign team we are fulfilments of God's ancient promise to bless the world and everything is as it should be. We are authentic human beings, grateful to the good God for making us spiritual descendants of Abraham and assigning us to carry his goodness to the whole human race not just our fellow team members. We are fully alive, in sync with God's intentions when he made that original promise to bless the world through Abraham. This is our new identity.

More about the team and what Jesus has to do with it

God's campaign team is not a SWAT team of angels that instantly kills all the agents of death and magically fills the world with God's life. God's team is a team of human beings that keeps developing and working over the centuries and the millennia.

Almost everything Jesus did while on earth was done with and for this team. He was leading the team to a new identity, a new level of understanding its special assignment and a new power to carry out the connect-heal-bless campaign.

There is much to learn about this team as we go along, but let's not get lost in the details. We must never forget that God's strategy is a team strategy. Our individual relationship with Jesus is important but it was never meant to exist apart from God's team. Jesus means us all to connect.

With one promise to Abraham, God solved the identity problem of every human being and every ethnic group

The view from here

God, the Real God, creates a beautiful world, perfectly inter-connected and peaceful. He walks and talks with the first humans, Adam and Eve. He puts everything at their fingertips. They just pick and eat.

But wouldn't you know it, they sneakily try the fruit of the only tree he said not to eat from. They do not trust God enough to know what is good for them. Shamed and uprooted from their paradise they discover labour, pain and fear.

Centuries go by and things keep falling apart. Humans cannot re-root themselves in God or recover the kind of life they had. So God steps in. He chooses a man named Abraham to be the new root of a new nation.

The first thing God does to Abraham is to uproot him! He tells him to leave his homeland and go to a land that will be the inheritance of the nation that will come from him and Abraham does it even though he is already old and has no children. He believes God's promise that he will have descendants as uncountable as 'sand on the seashore', and they will be the key to bringing God's blessing to the whole world.

Over the centuries it gradually comes true. Abraham's grandson Jacob has twelve sons and each becomes the father of an entire tribe. God roots the new nation in the region he had promised Abraham and he gives them one command above all others:

'No false gods. I am the Real God, the God of Abraham, and you are mine.' (Exodus 20:3-5)

They promise to stay true to their roots in Abraham, but it doesn't last. They start worshipping the false gods along with the Real God. He warns them through his messengers but they don't listen. Without his protection, they get uprooted again and transplanted into a foreign land called Babylon.

But this is not the end. Besides warning the nation, the messengers had also predicted that some day a Rescuer would be born, a descendant of Abraham and of King David. Like them he would never worship the false gods. He would perfectly and permanently re-root the nation and the world in God.

Centuries later that prophecy comes true. Jesus is born, a descendant of Abraham. He does not directly declare that he is the long-awaited king or messiah, but he keeps talking like it—'This is it! God is reconnecting with earth, setting up his kingdom to

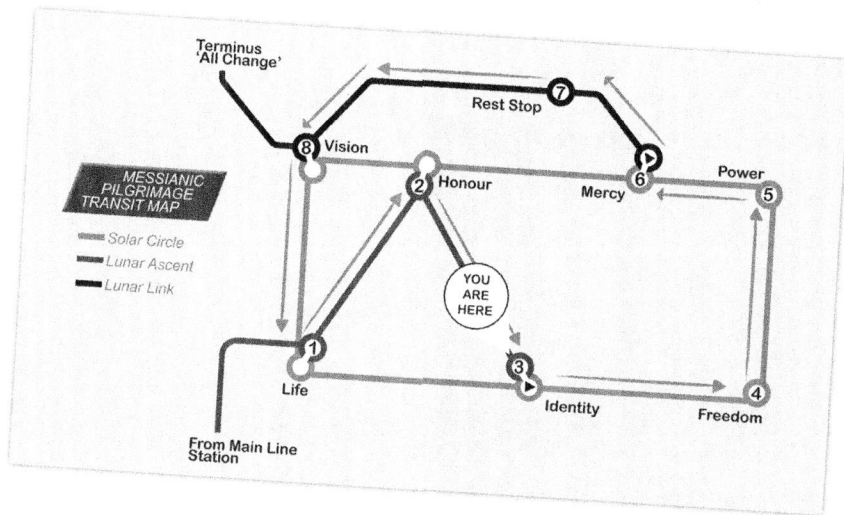

MESSIANIC PILGRIMAGE TRANSIT MAP

Terminus 'All Change'

Rest Stop

7

8 Vision

Power

2 Honour

Mercy

6

5

Solar Circle
Lunar Ascent
Lunar Link

YOU ARE HERE

1

Life

3

Identity

4

Freedom

From Main Line Station

deliver his blessings. Follow me and see what I mean.'

The authorities of the nation, also descendants of Abraham, decide that Jesus is a false messiah and they get the Roman governor to execute him. But the Real God proves Jesus is the real Messiah by bringing him back to life.

Here is the shocker: Jesus' death changes the line of descent from Abraham. From then on, people who are blood descendants of Abraham lose their connection with the promises God gave Abraham for as long as they think Jesus is a fake. All those who accept Jesus as the genuine king are grafted into Abraham's heritage. It does not matter whether they are blood descendants of Abraham or not. All is forgiven. They receive the Spirit of Jesus, like a new DNA, a new bloodline.

These spiritual descendants of Abraham keep getting attacked by people who are furious about what they say Jesus is doing and how he is doing it. Nevertheless, they show mercy to their attackers following Jesus' instructions and example at any price. They know their mission is to bless the world.

Why are they so confident? Roots! Through Jesus they are connected all the way back to their spiritual fore-father Abraham. Jesus also connects them forward, all the way to the end of the world, when he will come back to earth in person to uproot all evil and throw it away forever.

So that's our story. That's why we live the way we live and tell this story so gladly. Who are we? We are fruit-ful branches on the Abraham family tree. We are spiritual descendants of Abraham who are recruiting others to become descendants of Abraham and to participate in God's 4,000 year old strategy to bless the world.

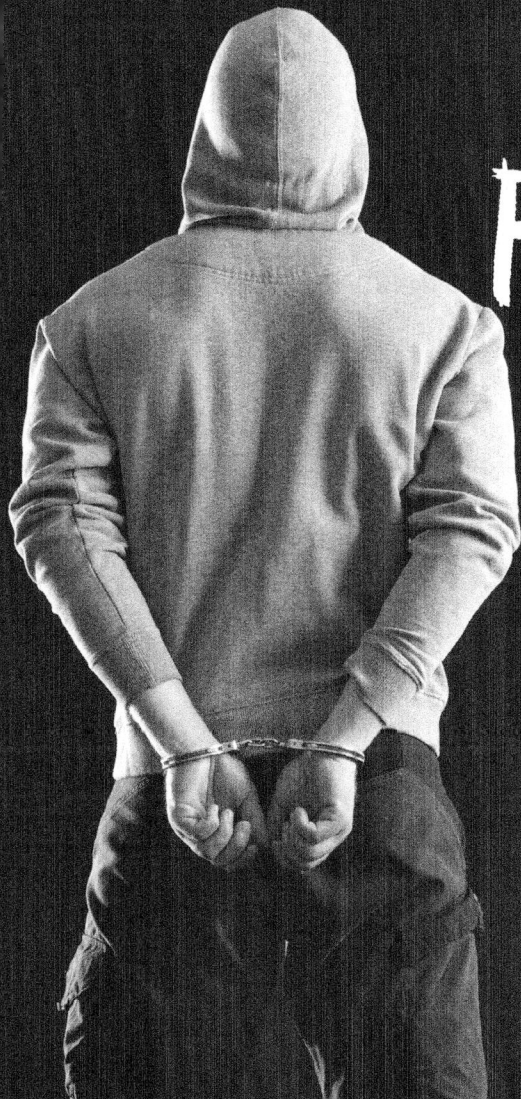
FREE AT LAST?

SEASON 4

The 5G flow during Freedom Season

Ground-breaker

How Jesus launched a new era of freedom in the world

What happened?

Before Jesus arrived, people already knew they should love God, be kind, etc. When Jesus taught about those things he was not changing the game. He was affirming the familiar rules, but that was not his main mission.

He was sent to earth not to raise the standard set by familiar truths about love, but to issue the Freedom Declaration, announcing a new era in the history of the world *'He has sent me to proclaim that captives will be released, that the blind will see, that the oppressed will be set free, and that the time of the Lord's favor has come.'* (Luke 4:18-19). His teaching was all about this new era. He was hailed by massive crowds in Jerusalem as their potential liberator. His main enemy was the religious establishment of the old era. And in God's timing he was executed on the National Freedom Day or independence day, Passover, when the nation celebrated God's deliverance from slavery in Egypt. Everything about him was soaked with the smell of freedom.

So what is this new era? What changed?

The new era is Freedom Time. Because of many prophets God had sent, Jesus' nation had believed for centuries that at some point God would send a Liberator. He would be the 'Messiah' or 'Anointed one', that is, the person specially appointed by God to lead the nation to freedom. As God's chosen king, he would go on to rule the whole world the way it should be ruled--with justice and fairness for the good of all--and his rule would never end. Under his rule, the world would be healed, blessed and connected. The campaign that God started through Abraham would be completed through him.

Jesus' assignment was to say to his nation, 'Time's up! This is it! This is the day you have been waiting for. God is taking over now.' (authors' paraphrase)

When he talked that way, he put burning questions into people's minds.

'When does the new era start, and how?'

'What will it look like?'

'Are you the Messiah?'

'If not, do you know who he is and where he is?'

People must have been asking questions in the market places and wherever they met together.

Most of Jesus' teaching related to these questions, but he did not give the expected answers. For example, people expected that the new era would come like a bolt of lightning,

from https://syncx.org

and he talked about it coming like a seed or a bit of yeast. They thought they could declare him king, but he turned that down. Still, he kept teaching about the new era from many angles, typically starting his parables with the phrase, 'The kingdom of God [that is, the new era under God's reign] is like…'

Jesus was careful to dodge the question about whether he was the Messiah. If he had admitted that in public he would have been arrested for trying to launch a revolution. So he strategically avoided the question until he knew the time was right. But meanwhile people were beginning to work it out for themselves. They heard him keep talking like a liberator, saying, 'God is taking over now'. Just like campaigners everywhere, he kept saying, 'Follow me!' People also noticed that he never said something that all the other prophets had always said loudly and clearly, 'Someone greater is coming'.

But Jesus died young. How did he launch his freedom era without taking power?

He forced a clash between the old era and his new era. Jesus sent out groups of followers in an awareness campaign covering the nation with news of his Freedom Declaration. His following swelled. The authorities of the old era got more and more nervous. They tried to discredit him by asking several loaded questions in public but he used their own words to challenge them. Finally, in desperation, they arrested and executed him for saying, during his trial, that he was the Messiah: the person God sent to lead his nation and the world into a new era.

The authorities killed Jesus in order to prove that they were in charge, that the old era was still in place, and that all his talk of a new era was just talk. His death would make his Freedom Declaration null and void, or so they thought. The resurrection of Jesus validated the Declaration and that is why the resurrection is the main theme of every record we have of every sermon Jesus' followers preached (all through the book of Acts). The resurrection amplifies the message, 'This is it! The new era of freedom is here through Jesus the King!'

And the cross, supposedly the end of Jesus' freedom, turns out to be the ransom payment that sets us free from the kidnapper's hold. Jesus heroically gave up his freedom to win ours, to give us the right to become free citizens of his kingdom, members of his campaign team. That is a lot more helpful than just telling us we should be more loving. Jesus changed the whole game.

Gift

The gift of living free in Christ is available now because of the ground-breaking event
Each of the Messianic Pilgrimage eight ground-breaking events comes with a new gift for us. The gift we get from Jesus as Liberator is the privilege of becoming free citizens of his kingdom.

The way the gift works for each of us depends on what we need to get free from. Jesus freed people from blindness, disease, demon possession--even death. He freed them from wrong ideas about the era of freedom and how it would arrive. He freed up space in the Temple so that foreigners could worship in their designated area without being disrupted by people changing money and selling sacrificial animals. By his resurrection he freed his followers from the despair of thinking that all was lost, that not even God could turn things around.

As we discover the gift of freedom, the story of our lives gets more and more interesting. That leads us to the other half of the gift, the gift of being sent out as freedom activists, members of his freedom campaign team. People around us are in all kinds of chains that they do not need to be in, and we have the bolt-cutter that can cut those chains. We can set them free to enjoy all the privileges of the citizens of Jesus' kingdom.

We don't coerce them in. Jesus wants people to join his kingdom freely and he leaves them free to walk away if they choose. But that is so sad. As activists we want to do whatever we can do to encourage people to join. The best thing we can do is live free and tell our personal freedom story.

Get it

The gift helps us if we get it that our old idea of freedom is now outdated

If we get it we realise that we had the wrong idea of freedom when we were thinking it means 'no restrictions, no controls, free to do whatever I want'.

We lived in Colorado for a while. One of the things we learned as we were starting to ski was that a beginning skier who gets out of control on a steep part of the slope never yells, 'I'm free! I'm free!' Freedom and control are partners not opposites. When our skis get out of control the first and only thing we think about is getting them back under control. Then we are free to enjoy the mountain. If we don't get them under control our freedom may turn out to be a free ride off the mountain, horizontal on a ski patrol sledge.

Similarly, professional football players do not complain that they are not free to skip a game when they want to. They are glad they get the privilege of playing on the team. Astronauts do not complain about any loss of freedom when they are strapped in for a launch or confined to a very small space for a long time. They are giving up some freedom of movement in order to gain the freedom to walk on the moon.

Christ's Freedom Declaration works like that. It's doesn't give us freedom to do whatever we want. It gives us freedom to enjoy life under the liberating control of Jesus. Yes there are restrictions in the kingdom of Jesus, but they are all there in order to open up a whole new life for us.

Another amazing thing we realise when we get the meaning of Christ's freedom is that he, with his authority as the Son of God, established the freedom era. We humans had nothing to do with the announcement or the timing. We didn't earn it by keeping God's commands better than people in previous centuries. We didn't fight for it. We barely saw it coming and as it arrived in Jesus, we didn't get it.

He had to do it all and explain it all. It took a lot of explaining because he launched the freedom era in the most unlikely way--with no loyal followers, his own execution and his resurrection. When we get that, when we realise what he did and what it means for our freedom, it is like a bomb goes off inside us. It blasts our old idea of freedom into a thousand pieces, and we don't even care. The new idea of freedom is a thousand times better.

Go with it
Once we get it, we enjoy the gift and work so others can enjoy it

After that, the natural response is to Go with it, living like free people. Our old chains start dropping off--old addictions, old wounds, old attitudes, old fixations. Things we thought would never change start to change and we may not even know how. God's Spirit, who is turning us into freedom activists, works at some levels deeper inside us than we can consciously reach.

As that happens, we discover one kind of freedom that we thought was impossible--freedom from the inner conflict of our desires. In our old lives, without Christ's freedom, it was often necessary to suppress desire A in order to satisfy desire B or C. We suppressed our desire to get drunk all the time because we wanted to fulfill our desire to keep our job. Or we indulged our desire to get drunk all the time and we realised we had to give up our desire to have a happy stable family. Either way, we were only partly happy and we did not think it could be any other way. It is just not possible to satisfy all our desires at the same time because they contradict each other.

But in Christ this problem gets solved. Christ does not have any internal conflict in his desires. His are all positive and all aligned in harmony. When we Go with it, when we enter willingly into his new era of freedom, we submit our desires A, B, C and all the way down to Z to come under one desire, which is the desire to please him. That integrates everything inside us. Jesus will not feed two desires in us that conflict with each other.

Yes, the old desires will still pop up but we don't have to listen to them any more. When the voice in our head says we have no choice but to do what our desires are urging us to do, we remind the voice that there is a new city mayor and he has created a new era for all the citizens. The old desires tried to stop him when he arrived. They threw everything at him but they lost and they know it. He created the era that he came to create and if any voice inside us tells us that he didn't, we call that voice a liar.

This is Freedom Time. That's our story and we are sticking to it.

Genuineness

As we go with it, we become genuinely free citizens of the kingdom of Jesus the Messiah

When we go with the new era of freedom, we become freedom activists. The world is living under a colossal hoax that the old era of bondage is still in force and that Jesus' death and resurrection didn't change that. We are calling everybody to wake up to the new era we are living in. We are authentic human beings, grateful to our Messiah and Liberator for letting us become his citizens and his activists.

We know what true freedom is because of Christ and in him we get to live the truth. We are in sync with Jesus' intentions when he first announced the Freedom Declaration in the synagogue in his home town (Luke 4.18-20). We never forget that he laid down his life for our freedom and how could any authentic human being walk away from a sacrifice like that?

FAQs

1. Wasn't Jesus' teaching mostly about love? Where does all this freedom talk come from?

Many people, including some Christians, have the idea that Jesus was a good teacher who emphasised the same things that people already knew (loving God and loving neighbour). They admire him for being so committed to love and non-violence that he died as a martyr. But they don't think he fundamentally changed everything. All he did was stand up strong and tall for things that people already knew were good.

That view, common as it is, misses the whole point of Jesus coming to earth. His God-given assignment was not merely to promote old standard truths like, 'Be good, be loving'. He was sent on a specific mission, which was more about a new age of freedom than it was about the abstract idea of love.

It is still very common to regard Jesus more as a good religious teacher rather than a liberating ground-breaker, the founder of a new era for humanity. But the opinion that he was a teacher and his message was all about love is 2,000 years out of date. It belongs to the old era, not the new era he launched.

2. Are we seriously talking about a physical resurrection, not just a religious vision of a dead person? How unscientific can you get?

Yes, we believe the literal, physical resurrection of Jesus. We agree with the Apostle Paul on this one. If the resurrection is fake news, everything else we are saying about Jesus and religion falls apart (1 Corinthians 15:14).

As for science, 20th century science tried to make rules about what can or cannot happen based on what we know from other theories and observations. 21st century science is coming around to a more truly scientific perspective. Our new technology makes new data available that proves many of our old theories were wrong. But we don't have new theories yet that explain all the new data. In other words, we admit that we don't really know what is going on in some cases and we cannot make any scientific rules about what is or is not possible.

As for philosophy, is the resurrection really that big of an issue? I recall a friend telling me about his undergraduate course in Introduction to Philosophy at a major American university. To his surprise, the well-known professor did not give a panoramic view of philosophy as a discipline. Instead he spent the entire semester dealing in great depth with only one issue, proving that Jesus did not rise from the dead. He apparently believed that the purpose of his intro course was to clear the path to philosophical thinking. He saw the resurrection as the main boulder to bulldoze out of the way.

As for history, especially in an era of fake news, we evaluate all possible explanations in light of what each group has to gain or lose from its version of the facts. Morrison did this with Jesus' resurrection in his book Who Moved the Stone? It was published in 1930 and is still in print.

Morrison was a lawyer who approached the case as if moving the stone from Jesus' burial chamber had been a crime to solve. His investigation was highly biased, aiming to pinpoint the human or humans who had moved the stone and stolen Jesus' body. That would disprove the resurrection theory. Spoiler alert: the evidence forced him to a conclusion he did not want, and the book explains how that happened.

3. What freedoms do I have to give up in order to become a free citizen of the kingdom of Jesus?

The list is really short, just one item. But it is still long enough that many people don't like it.

Jesus had a seal which he stamps into the passports of all free citizens of his kingdom as the sign of our identity in him. The seal was the core of Jesus' identity. It is what showed up plainly in the most agonising crisis time of his life when he knew he was about to be arrested, condemned and executed. On that fateful night in the Garden of Gethsemane he asked God his Father to find another way to accomplish his mission. But, in the end he said the words that I call his seal, the defining mark of authenticity, *'Not my will but yours be done'* (Luke 22:42).

Bearing this seal, we go through life telling God at each crisis point, 'Yes, my King, your way not mine.' In ordinary times, our preferences, comforts and insights often line up with what God wants for us. But we all have some times when they clash. In those crisis moments we lay down our freedom like Jesus did.

That is the only door to free citizenship in Jesus' kingdom. *'Whoever loses his life for me will find it.'* (Luke 9:24). As we lay down the freedom to live life our own way, we discover what real freedom is.

The view from here

God, the Real God, creates a beautiful world with life everywhere. He gives the first humans, Adam and Eve, freedom to enjoy it all except for the fruit of one tree.

An enemy of God cons them into thinking they should be free to eat it and they do. Instantly they lose their freedom--freedom to hold their heads high, to enjoy life without working, to give birth without pain, to live forever and to have face-to-face visits with God. From there, things go down-hill for generations—each generation seeking to regain freedom but none able to find it.

So starting with Abraham, God launches his own freedom restoration plan. Abraham's descendants, will bless the world with the freedom known by people who trust God like Abraham did. Sorry to say, the 'Freedom Tribe' soon gets enslaved and oppressed in Egypt. They can't free anybody, even themselves.

So God frees them his way. Through Moses he sends so many plagues on Egypt that the ruler finally decides the whole Freedom Tribe is a curse. He frees them just to get rid of them.

God gives them victory over other tribes that were living in the land of their destiny, polluting it with vile customs like child sacrifice. For centuries the Freedom Tribe lives there, but their trust in God does not last.

They are carried off as captives to Babylon and God has to free them again, bringing them back to their land after 70 years.

Do you know what keeps them going through all their ups and downs? Their prophets, who tell them that one day God will send the Freedom King, the Liberator, the Messiah, to deliver them. He will be a descendant of their most famous king, David, and he will be born in David's home-town, Bethlehem.

In God's time, it finally happens. The Messiah, Jesus, arrives and issues the Freedom Declaration: 'This is it! God is setting us free now! Follow me and see what I mean.'

Many people assume he is hinting at starting a revolution against the Roman Empire, which ruled over the Freedom Tribe at that time. The crowds love him, but the leaders do not trust him. They arrange with the Roman governor to have him executed for blasphemy and treason.

Instead of rallying his many followers to rescue him, Jesus sacrifices his

Terminus
'All Change'

Rest Stop

7

8 Vision

MESSIANIC
PILGRIMAGE
TRANSIT MAP

Solar Circle
Lunar Ascent
Lunar Link

2 Honour

Mercy

6

Power

5

YOU
ARE
HERE

1

Life

3

Identity

4

Freedom

From Main Line
Station

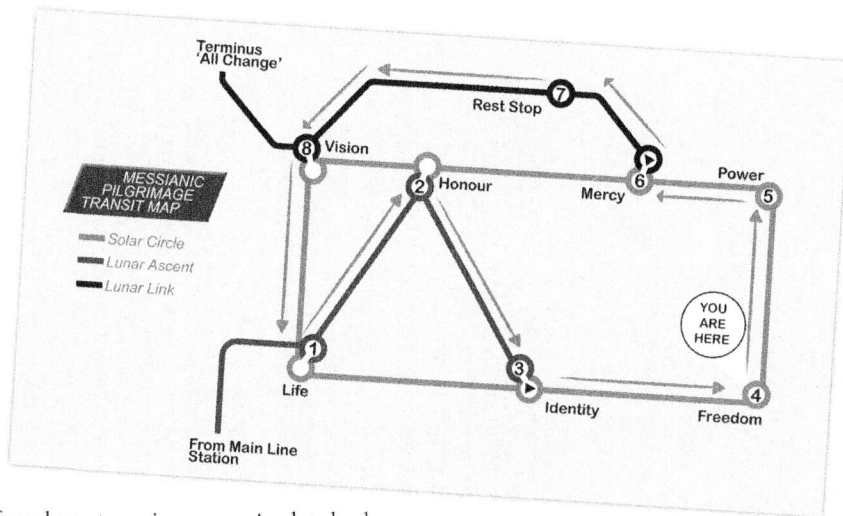

freedom to win ours. And, oh, how he wins it! His death as a willing sacrifice frees us from our sin debt to God, and on the third day, God frees him from his tomb.

Then Jesus takes his liberating mission to a new level. He shows himself alive and well several times before ascending to take his throne in heaven as the Freedom King. Soon he sends his Spirit down into his followers, breaking all their chains and fears. They are so thrilled that they eagerly get to work as freedom activists all over the world and they back up their cause by living freely and graciously.

Some people welcome their freedom message but others, often powerful people, keep pressuring these activists to tone things down. They threaten some, jail some and kill some. It is the same today but the freedom activists do not give up or shut up. They are able to show the mercy and courage of Jesus because his Spirit lives in them.

They also know the secret. Unannounced, the Freedom King will suddenly come back to earth in person to complete the freedom mission. His cause cannot fail.

So that's our story. That's why we live the way we live and tell this story to anybody who will listen. Who are we? We are activists for the new era of freedom in Christ. His cause is our cause. We will do anything, anywhere, any time, at any price to draw more people to pledge their loyalty to the Freedom King and become free citizens of his kingdom.

The 5G flow during Power Season

Ground-breaker
How Jesus sent heaven's power to earth in the first place

What happened?

As the Bible tells the story, Jesus lived and died on earth, was resurrected, lived another 40 days on earth and then went up to heaven without dying again. Once Jesus took power on his throne in heaven his first act was to inject his followers with his power so they could show that the new era he announced is under way on earth. Jesus had taught that the new era of freedom and power would not arrive like a lightning bolt but like a mustard seed or a bit of yeast, starting small, and gradually affecting everything. The power would work little by little.

But as it turned out, Day One of the power era actually was a bit like a lightning bolt. It was a spectacular day that no one could ever forget.

As Jesus' power arrived that day in Jerusalem his followers heard things, saw things and did things that defied human explanation and all this evidence pointed in the same direction—to Jesus as the rightful King, the power holder, making his power visible on earth through his followers for the blessing and uniting of the whole world.

A huge crowd gathered and Peter explained to them that they had made a colossal mistake when they executed Jesus as a fake messiah seven weeks earlier. By raising him from the grave God had declared him the rightful Messiah and now He was on the throne in heaven.

Horrified by their mistake, the crowd knew that Jesus' first act as King could have been to have lightning bolts strike each member of the court that condemned him. That would have got everybody's terrified attention!

But Jesus had a different strategy. Instead of flaunting his power against his enemies Jesus poured out his power on his friends and he did it in a way that gave his enemies a second chance. Peter, speaking for all Jesus' followers, told the crowd they would be forgiven if they would renounce their mistake and welcome Jesus' Spirit, the Spirit of the King, into their lives. Thousands did that on the spot.

Jesus' strategy was also designed to display the global implications of his power, not just the benefits for his own people. The sign of the power that day was not a healing miracle like Jesus had done many times. It was a miracle Jesus had never done in person. Jesus' followers were praising God in languages they had never learned. Foreigners who were present from many other countries understood what they were saying.

The message was that the Messiah's power was going global. Foreigners no longer had to learn a special language in order to worship God properly. By the Spirit of Jesus working in his followers, God has sent his message to foreigners in their own languages. The ground-breaking Spirit had arrived.

Gift
The gift of Christ's power is available now because of the ground-breaker

Each of the Messianic Pilgrimage eight ground-breaking events comes with a new gift for us. The gift we get from Jesus as Power-holder is the privilege of his power working for good in us through his Spirit who moves into our bodies. If this sounds a little eerie, it is, but in a good way.

The good thing about it is that we do not lose our normal consciousness or identity while Jesus' Spirit works in us. We are not in a trance nor possessed by some spirit or force that replaces our normal identity or speaks in a weird voice. As we come under the influence of Jesus' spirit living in us, we stay fully awake and fully ourselves. Yet we are gradually turning into new selves. We also discover that God sometimes works through our new selves in miraculous ways.

Bottom line: in this era of freedom and power, something more than human is happening on earth. We who join the heal, bless and connect campaign get to be walking evidence of it. When we honour Jesus as the spearhead of the heal, bless and connect campaign we have this gift handed to us. His power goes to work in us and through us. It takes a lifetime to open and explore this gift.

Get it
The gift helps us if we get it, if we see why God gave that gift

God has something he wants to prove. His gift of the Holy Spirit is his strategy for proving all over the world that Jesus is still alive, still coordinating the attack that will destroy the forces of darkness on earth and still providing his power to ordinary earthlings like us as we participate in his 'heal, bless and connect' campaign.

We get it. When we are evidence, that is what we are evidence of. When we are witnesses about Jesus, that is what we are witnessing about.

We are not merely evidence that Jesus taught good things and that people become nicer if they follow what he taught. The world knows that already. What the world doesn't know and what God wants to prove is that Jesus is the power centre of the universe. The proof is that Jesus is strategically exercising his power through his Spirit working in his people, the members of his global heal, bless and connect campaign team, also known as his kingdom or pilgrim band.

Human campaigns may disappoint, but the healing, blessing and connecting campaign of Jesus won't because it has what every campaign would love to have:

- a leader so wise he never makes a mistake or miscalculation
- a charismatic leader who can fire up every campaign team member by putting his own Spirit into them
- a leader who can go on forever since he has already come back from death

Jesus actually does what all other campaign leaders only dream of doing.

Even when we do get it that Jesus' power-sharing through his Spirit is God's strategy to prove his point about Jesus as the world's power centre, we still cannot predict exactly when and how Jesus' power will work. We have to discover it as we go along, and different people discover parts of it in different ways. There is no miracle manual because the power of Jesus' spirit is not a predictable technique to learn from a book. It is a life of discovery to be lived.

Go with it
Once we get it, we enjoy the gift and we work so others can enjoy it

Just before he rose to heaven to begin his reign, Jesus said to his followers, '*All power in heaven and on earth is given to me*' (Matthew 28.18). The next verse says, 'So get going!'

In other words, 'I'm the power holder now. I can bring in the era of freedom and power that I was teaching about. This is how I'm going to do it: my campaign team is to recruit more team members (disciples) and train them in all my instructions about campaign work, that is, how to heal and bless the world in my name. And I will go with them on every campaign assignment until this whole thing is over and victory is ours.' (Matthew 28:18-20, authors' paraphrase)

We go with that. Jesus has the power. His strategy is to put some of that power into his team for the good of the world. We are his team. We throw ourselves open to his influence. 'Sync me!' becomes our new catchphrase as we go with the flow of his power.

We watch as Jesus' spirit changes us at deep subconscious levels. This personality repair work is a mystery but we love it every time some new evidence of it comes up to the conscious level and blesses someone.

We watch as amazing things happen when we speak with the power of Jesus' name. The healing work of the campaign goes ahead. Things that could not be healed get healed. People who could never change change. People get over things they were sure they could never get over.

We watch these things happening but we do not take credit for any of them because we know it wasn't really our power at all. Jesus' power is the power that did it. We did nothing to earn that power. We just went with it, and we loved the result.

We don't get arrogant. All we get is more grateful to the Lamb who sacrificed himself to give us access to His Spirit. Our work on the campaign team becomes a pleasure, not a burden, even if it almost kills us sometimes. It is a token repayment on our debt of gratitude.

We gladly keep listening for our next assignment, opening up to more of the Spirit's power so we can do more healing and blessing others, inviting them to discover the power of following Jesus' path. It can work for anybody.

Genuineness
As we go with it, we become walking evidence of God's power for good

What kind of evidence are we? Character witnesses and indisputable evidence.

Character witnesses

The character witness is not our witness to Jesus' character. It is evidence of changes in our own character.

- Old habits and desires break down, though we could never get free of them before.

- When people annoy us, we don't react like we used to.

- New character traits emerge in our lives, like concern about others we never cared about before. We become generous, loyal and exuberant about life .

All this adds up to a genuine character transformation and we can't even explain how it happened. We know it wasn't because we tried harder or we got better at faking it. We say the Spirit is doing it and handing it to us as a gift we are thrilled to get—a new authentic self.

Indisputable evidence

The indisputable evidence is the miraculous part, things that defy human explanation. Even the people who don't believe in God may wonder if they are seeing his fingerprints in these cases.

The Spirit of Jesus mysteriously empowers different people in different ways. Some see many healings happen when they pray in Jesus' name, some know things they had no way of knowing (secrets, things in the future or instructions to do or say a particular thing). Some speak in another language they have not learned, some can translate the spiritual language.

All these things defy scientific explanation. But it is unscientific to deny the evidence that they are happening somehow. Our theory is this: the Spirit of Jesus whom he sent onto his original followers on Pentecost Day, is still at large, still bringing heaven's power to earth, still pointing to the true King of the Universe and still saying to the doubters, 'Over here! Look at this!'

These signs cannot be merely the result of some good truth that Jesus taught. In fact, Jesus didn't teach his campaign team any techniques to guarantee a miracle except to ask in his name that God would do them. But Jesus did teach that he would be with his campaign team members. Where Jesus is, his power is. Character changes. Miracles happen. And it's all good. We are in sync with Jesus' intentions when he sent his Spirit down on his team in the first place.

FAQs

1. If Jesus' campaign team members have all this wonderful power, why don't they routinely use it? Why can't they heal all the sick, stop COVID-19, etc?

Using the power of Jesus' Spirit is neither magic nor science. If it were there would be a way to learn the secret formula or incantation, bottle the power and predict the effect. The Holy Spirit is our connection to Jesus, the leader of our pilgrim band, not an impersonal force or energy. As members of the campaign team, we do not control the campaign leader the way a scientist, technician or sorcerer controls a force. We respectfully make requests.

We try to ask for what we think is the good of the campaign, things that fit with what we know about the King's character and his campaign goals—heal, bless, connect. Some of these, like combatting COVID, are no-brainers. Of course the leader wants it to end. Of course he feels the pain of those who are losing loved ones or are starving because they cannot earn their day's wage. So we ask for our planet to be healed of it, by vaccine and anything else it takes. Meanwhile, we pray that those who are already infected will survive.

Why doesn't the leader answer all those prayers? We don't know. What we know for sure is this—if we stop trusting God when he does not give us a complete explanation for something, we repeat the original most basic mistake of the human race. Adam and Eve did not have a complete explanation for God's warning about the poisonous tree so they stopped trusting him, used their own judgment, ate its fruit and we all lived miserably ever after.

There was no COVID in the Garden of Eden. There is no COVID in the coming kingdom of Jesus, when he visibly rules everywhere. There only is COVID now because the world is out of sync with its past and its future. So we keep on praying for God to bring more of the healing power of the future into the present. And we keep trusting him for an eventual explanation of his timetable.

2. What is the difference between Jesus' power, and power as we know it from history and our personal experience?

We think of power as 'being able to force what I want to happen'. We trust our own judgment and we are sure that everything would be a lot better if we had more power. But look at Jesus. He knows what is good for the world and he has held power for 2,000 years, but he still isn't forcing things. He is not using his power to compel people to do things they don't want to do. He is empowering people to do what their deep inner selves really knew they should do.

This is liberating. On our own, we do not consistently do all the good that our inner self wants. Our dark side interferes sometimes. Jesus' spirit reaches the parts of us that are too deep inside, too far down in our subconscious, for us to reach on our own. The Spirit's power heals and repairs us at that level. Gradually the changes work their way up to the conscious level. When they do, they feel more like discoveries than achievements.

This slow and subtle exercise of Jesus' power fits with the spirit of the Freedom Era that Jesus announced. How could it really be a Freedom Era if people were only in it because they were forced in or terrorised in by power displays?

Earthly power works through force and intimidation. Earthly empires always choose intimidating emblems of power, like a bull, a dragon or a bear. The emblem of Jesus' kingdom is a sacrificed but living lamb, standing on the throne (Revelation 5.6). And the symbol of the one who brings the Lamb's power into our lives is a dove.

When we get the meaning of the Lamb and the Dove, when we realise how Jesus handles his power and how he wants us to handle it, it is like a bomb goes off inside us. It blasts our old idea of power into a thousand pieces and we don't even care. The new idea of power is a thousand times better.

This Lamb-Dove power does not intimidate its subjects. Neither does it corrupt the power holders. Instead it inspires and empowers its subjects, and it purifies those who hold it. This power serves the people it rules, which is what all earthly powers falsely claim they are doing. The Lamb and the Dove get it done.

As holders of this new kind of power, we are more like ambassadors than governors. The Lamb does not delegate his power to certain people to rule certain sections or nations of the earth on his behalf. His strategy is not to consolidate his power over one nation by force and then go on to conquer the next nation.

Instead he covers the whole world at once with his ambassadors, his witnesses. That's what his Power Promise was about (Acts 1:8). His goal is that the whole earth will voluntarily welcome his rule because of what they see his Spirit doing in and through his ambassadors. They are the walking evidence of his friendly take-over of the world. But powers who don't want his take-over see his ambassadors as infiltrators.

3. Wouldn't everything have been simpler if Jesus had announced that he was the Messiah while he was on earth in person? Why did he keep that a secret but then tell his campaign team to tell the secret to the whole world after he left?

Timing is everything. Jesus had to keep the secret for a while in order to change the world's understanding of power. If he had said straight out, 'I am the Messiah', people would have assumed he was going to use his messianic power like all other power holders, forcing enemies into submission. Some of them would have tried to help his cause by starting terrorist attacks against the Roman imperial soldiers in their land, expecting that the Messiah would be pleased with their courage and loyalty. The Roman army would have crushed the terrorists and many innocent suspects with them.

Only after Jesus let his enemies kill him could he let the secret out in a way that would not be misinterpreted.

After that, his resurrection would be the object lesson about power for all time. The lesson is, 'Lay down your power as God asks you to, go through what he puts you through, and watch how he restores every bit of the power you laid down'. (authors' paraphrase)

This is backwards to ordinary views of power, where power is gradually built up and fiercely protected. Nobody throws power away, trusting someone to give them more power on the rebound. It is too risky.

But that is exactly what Jesus did. He showed the world how real power works. A Messiah raised from death is the greatest power the world has ever seen. That's what we are looking at in Jesus, and that changes everything, especially the meaning of power. That is the open secret we are now allowed to tell to the whole human race. With the benefit of hindsight they will not misinterpret it.

4. The miracle of praising God in foreign languages still seems odd. How does one miracle with languages change the game of global power?

It shows that the power of heaven that Jesus is sending to earth is a power for good, not for domination. Its most basic feature is that it will be heard as good news in the languages of all peoples. It is a celebration, not an edict. It is a report about a down-to-earth fact—Jesus is alive again—not a claim about the power of truth and ideas. And it creates peace among the nations without imposing peace through force.

And there's more. This odd miracle was designed to spread this good news throughout the ancient world at great speed. It occurred in Jerusalem during one of the three main Jewish annual feasts attended by pilgrims from all over the world. Imagine the conversations when those pilgrims all got home.

'How was your trip?'

'Great! But the craziest thing happened while we were there.'

'What was that?'

'There was this roaring sound like a strong wind, and then there were a hundred or more locals all shouting excitedly at the same time in lots of different languages. And some of them were shouting in *our language*, even though they had never been here.'

'No way! What did they say?'

That conversation, plus the news of what Jesus' followers had said, would have been repeated countless times in many countries in just a few weeks. Many who heard it, even second or third hand, would have concluded: 'That God over there in Jerusalem speaks our national language, and he has a message for our nation about Jesus. Let's find out more.'

Everybody knows that emperors don't speak your language. They make you learn theirs. So Jesus sends his message to the world—the One who sits on the throne of the universe is not your typical emperor. The power game has changed.

5. Wouldn't Jesus' followers have been able to spread the word about him without the Holy Spirit? They knew his teaching. They understood that his death paid for human sin. They saw him after he rose from the dead. Wasn't that enough?

Jesus didn't think so. Before he left, he had ordered them not to spread the word until they received power from above. If they had gone out right away with their reports and their explanations of the meaning of Jesus' death and resurrection, their focus would have been on what Jesus had already done.

Jesus does not want to be regarded as merely 'a great person in history'. He wants the story of his past to be intertwined with the message that his story isn't finished yet. His campaign to connect, heal and bless the world is not over. His power is not gone. The Holy Spirit keeps bringing it into the members of his campaign team—the ongoing power of Jesus.

Once that power arrived through the Holy Spirit and they praised God in all those languages, every last one of them became walking evidence of God's power for good. From then on they were not just repeating Jesus' teaching or retelling the stories of his miracles, reliving the good old days. They were discovering the good new days of the power of the Spirit.

Individually and together they were exhibits that the new era that Jesus declared was no mere dream for the future. It is a dream they were living, doing things Jesus would do if he were present in person. By seeing them and their power, people who were still stuck in the old era would come to believe that the new era is really here. The game has changed.

When Jesus took power on His throne in heaven His first act was to inject His followers with his power so they could show that the new era He announced is under way on earth.

The view from here

The first human beings had God-given power to rule their beautiful world but they lost it to a liar. He got their power to rule and they fell under a curse. The rest of the story of the world is the power struggle to get that oppressive, manipulative, divisive enemy off their backs.

God has a strategy for that, but it doesn't seem powerful at all. He starts by choosing an elderly couple, Abraham and Sarah, who have never had the power to have children. Through them he creates a whole nation of twelve tribes. Its homeland is right in between the ancient super-powers of Egypt, Assyria and Babylon, like a Chihuahua living between three Rottweilers.

But God keeps sending his messengers to tell his powerless nation about a coming king, a descendant of their great King David. Everything will change when he arrives. He will rescue humanity from evil control and rule the entire world with justice and peace forever.

Centuries pass. Greece takes the nation over, then Rome. Finally a man born in King David's home town declares to this little nation: 'God's ancient promise is coming true in our time! God himself is taking power now. Follow me and see what I mean.'

He shows God's power by healing sick people, driving out demons, multiplying food and doing many things that human power cannot do. Everything he teaches is about God's power arriving on earth. He even empowers his followers to do the same good things he is doing.

The powers of darkness see Jesus as a dangerous person who has to be stopped before he breaks their power entirely. The Jewish religious establishment and the Roman political establishment combine forces to get him executed. They are sure that will absolutely prove to everybody that they are the power holders, not him.

But they have no idea what power they are up against. God does not fight fair! He raises the executed 'criminal' back to life vindicating Jesus and proving where the power really lies.

For forty days Jesus shows his followers that he is alive again but he does not appear to anyone else. He does not strike his enemies dead. He does not strong-arm anyone into believing he is the Rescuer, the Messiah, the rightful heir to David's throne. Then, without dying again, he returns to heaven to take power.

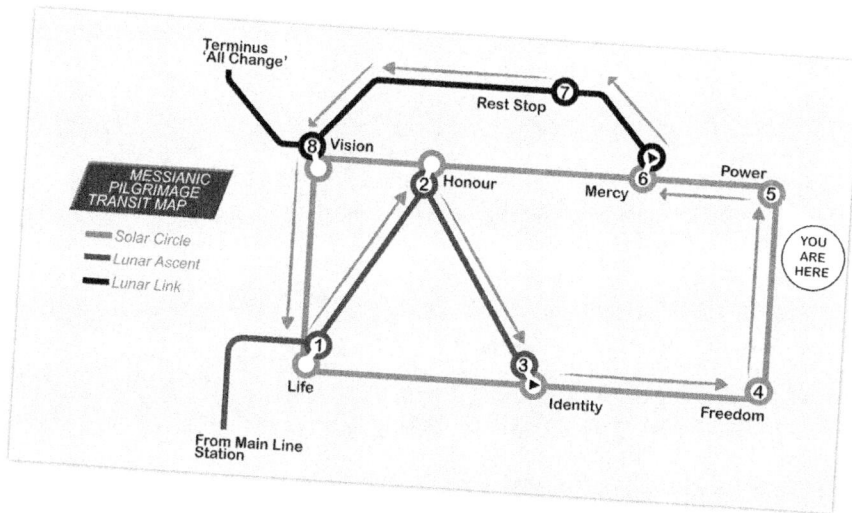

MESSIANIC PILGRIMAGE TRANSIT MAP

Terminus 'All Change'

Rest Stop

7

8 Vision

2 Honour

6 Mercy

Power

5

Solar Circle
Lunar Ascent
Lunar Link

YOU ARE HERE

1 Life

3 Identity

4 Freedom

From Main Line Station

His first act from his throne as King of the Universe is to send his Spirit down into his followers, putting his power for good into them and authorising them to be his ambassadors on earth. Their message is that the power of evil is broken because Jesus is alive and well. They get to show his power to heal the sick and they point people to him and his mercy.

Some people welcome Jesus' powerful representatives; others fight them, especially power holders who feel threatened by them. But the messengers keep working courageously anyway. They know who they are and they know what their mission is. It is not to take over and rule. It is not even to defend themselves. Their mission is only to point everyone to the new era, the new regime of King Jesus, using his power to do good and to bless.

They also know that at the set time the King will come back himself to break the power of his enemies once and for all. He will publicly assert his power, and no one will get away with anything ever again.

Who are we? We are the walking evidence that Jesus is still alive and that his power keeps on working. Our job is to show that Jesus is giving power back to humanity; that is, he has broken the ancient curse on the human race and authorised us to go on defeating evil in his name until he returns to finish the work in person. And that's why we don't grab for earthly power or abuse it if we have it. If we did that, we would not be convincing evidence of his power to transform people inside.

That's our story. That's why we live the way we live and tell this story to anybody who will listen.

SEASON 6

WHO IS MY BROTHER?

The 5G flow during Mercy Season

Ground-breaker
How Jesus' changed everything with his blood

It is easy to talk of God's mercy but it is shocking and humbling to realise what God's mercy led him to do for us.

Suppose you, as a friend, send your son to my house with gifts, but I think he is a terrorist impersonating your son, bringing bombs wrapped as gifts. If I kill him and throw his body in the street, what could ever restore our friendship? I could never do enough to restore it. It would only be restored if, for some unknown reason, you mercifully decided to restore it instead of taking revenge.

God sent his son Jesus to earth, brimming with kindness and goodness, to take his relationship with humanity to the next level. Jesus announced that the reign of God on earth was arriving but humanity rejected his announcement and killed him for asserting during his trial that he was the Messiah. His blood is on our hands as members of the human race. How could humanity ever make up for such a blind, vicious, arrogant mistake?

We couldn't. But God knew we were going to do that. He told Jesus to accept rejection and execution and Jesus kept telling his followers that this would happen.

After it happened, God in his incredible mercy declared that he would treat the execution not as treason against him (which it was) but as a sacrifice. Jesus wiped his blood off our hands and presented it as a sacrifice, just as God in his mercy had planned for us.

Do we see this mercy? God took the stupidest, most horrifying act in human history, the one thing that deserved worse punishment than anything else and transformed it into the means of mercy for us. He transformed what seems unforgivably horrible into what is unforgettably merciful.

Jesus executed God's ancient plan of mercy. He offered himself on the cross as the willing victim and presented his blood to God so we who rejected him could be reconciled to God not executed as we deserved. That shocking act of Jesus as our mediator with God is the basis for the Mercy Season.

The merciless execution becomes a means of mercy and healing. The Messiah is the perfect sacrifice, the perfect mediator and the perfect hero.

Gift

A grace period is available now because of this ground-breaking event

Each of the Messianic Pilgrimage eight ground-breaking events comes with a new gift for us. The gift we get from Jesus as our mediator is mercy, or rather, a grace period to receive mercy. If we take advantage of the grace period, we can have our slate wiped clean, our broken relationship with God restored.

The idea of a grace period may sound odd to many people who think of God in terms of timeless truths. Good has been and always will be good. Evil has been and always will be evil. God's character is reliable, has not changed and never will.

But the timeless view overlooks the fact that the world has a story and it moves through stages. To live wisely in this story, we do have to know the timeless truths but we also have to know which stage of the story we are in and how we got here.

In the story we are in the grace period. The Mercy Season is when we especially remember the grace period. The gift of mercy is within reach of every one of us during the grace period.

Get it

The gift helps us if we get it that Jesus has shown us mercy

If we get it, if we understand God's ground-breaking event and the gift of mercy, that is the 'Aha moment' when something inside us changes.

We get it if we see that by giving up his life and his power, Jesus was actually taking over the world. He was doing something so powerfully persuasive that people would honour him as their King instead of rejecting him as an impostor.

Here is his takeover strategy. He was mercifully removing one debt we could never pay off and replacing it with another one! He removed the debt of our sin, our wanting to live life in our own way without regard for him. That removal is so liberating for us that it causes a debt of gratitude. We can't pay it off but we love to keep trying! We gratefully want to live life his way, in sync with his strategy instead of ours.

Here is the tricky part. Jesus' sacrifice does not automatically cancel our sin debt, the penalty we have accumulated over a lifetime. His sacrifice gives us a window of opportunity for getting our debt cancelled. That window will close either when we die or when the Messiah returns to judge the world.

So what is the opportunity and how do we take hold of it?

The opportunity is to accept the gift, realising what it means.

1. It means we didn't earn it. Gifts are not earned.
2. It means we know how the Messiah will judge us at the end. He will welcome those who accepted the gift of mercy that he made available by his life-blood. He will hold accountable those who rejected it or ignored it as unimportant.

3. It means we agree to become mercy agents, forgiven people who are forgiving people. If we try to receive forgiveness ourselves but are not willing to forgive others, we are trying to work the system. God throws out people who do that.

Caution: We shouldn't get the idea that God calculates our sin debt by weighing our good deeds against our bad and that we only need enough mercy to tip the balance in our favour. Our link with God is an all or nothing thing, like a chain or a bucket. If a chain has 49 good links and one broken link, do the 49 outweigh the one? If a bucket has only one hole in the bottom, do all the 'non-holes' (the solid parts) outweigh the one hole? We all have at least one hole, so even the best of us are totally lost without God's mercy.

Caution: We shouldn't get the idea that accepting Christ's sacrifice is like signing a contract. A contract has obligations on both parties. But Christ's mercy is never presented to us as a contract. It's a favour. A favour comes with hope of a response of appropriate gratitude and respect but this is not spelled out like the terms of a contract. That would spoil the favour. Christ's mercy is not a contract that gives us guarantees and leverage. It is the basis for a connection with Christ and his whole global team of mercy agents.

Caution: We shouldn't get the idea that God only wants to show us that he is merciful and kind. In that case, we are likely to get presumptuous and assume that God's forgiveness means we have permission to repeat the mistake. But God's forgiveness is not a system. We can't learn how the system works, and then work the system.God will see right through that. Jesus was not raised from the grave so that his enemies could kill him a second time!

Go with it
Once we get it, we enjoy the gift and we show mercy to others

We live out what God has done inside us. We become God's mercy agents on earth, working in sync with his strategy.

When we get it, we realise that to have mercy means both to possess mercy and to show mercy. We have it ourselves and we also shower mercy on others. We are in sync with the mercy of Jesus, going along with his plan to flood the world with his mercy.

It is his gentle method of taking control of the world. It may seem like a weak strategy, but nothing else has the transforming power of God's mercy shown in Christ's self-sacrifice.

That is what we represent. We are agents of his mercy, not officials of his government. We do not take control. We only show his mercy and his mercy brings willing people under his control.

This is a great way to live! As messengers of the merciful sacrifice of Jesus, we are the salve for all the wounds and scars of the world. People who were bitter and vengeful can be released. People who were traumatised or abused can benefit from one who has been through worse things than they have. And they can become mercy agents too, so that Jesus' healing and his control spread further.

On the other hand, if we welcome Jesus' sacrifice for us but do not forgive others, we are not going with his mercy and his plan. We are out of sync with his purpose. We are trying to get his forgiveness to work for us without letting it flow through us to others. We are trying to work the system and the King does not tolerate that. We either forgive others or we forfeit his forgiveness ourselves. (Matthew 6:14)

Genuineness
As we go with it, we become mercy agents

We find our authentic identity in Christ because of his mercy. We are 100% genuine people, not having to fake anything or hide anything any more. The blood of Christ has exposed it all and taken care of it all! We become part of God's strategy to heal the world by giving it the mercy it does not deserve.

The world is not kind to us as mercy agents any more than it was kind to Jesus himself. There is a lot of pain and suffering involved. We have to bite our tongues, stop our urge to retaliate and turn to God with our tears.

But nothing is more genuine evidence of God's secret power at work than the way we handle the wrongs people do to us when we represent Jesus to them. There is no human explanation for our good will toward their enemies, our joy that bubbles up no matter what, and our trust in the King who will make everything right in the end.

Only the mercy of God in Christ can account for it. We received it as a gift, and we are giving what we received from Christ, not giving back the evil that people gave us. We are in sync with his intentions on the day he mercifully presented his sacrificial blood to God on our behalf.

God in his incredible mercy declared that he would treat the execution of his son not as treason against him but as a sacrifice.

The view from here

God, the Real God, creates a beautiful world with life everywhere. There is only one rule people have to obey in order to keep everything working and they get duped into breaking it! God punishes them but they don't learn their lesson. Their sons are no better and one ends up killing the other. Things get so corrupt and violent that God destroys all but eight humans in the Great Flood, but not even those eight learn their lesson.

There has to be a better way for people to learn how to live in God's world and so God provides one. We see it in the story of Joseph, who gets sold into slavery by his eleven jealous brothers. Years later Joseph gets a golden opportunity to kill them all but he has mercy on them. He even provides for them and their families.

That event sets the tone for the whole incredible story of God's mercy coming into the world through the 'God Tribe' descended from Joseph's great-grandfather, Abraham. God later sets up an entire forgiveness system of sacrifices and priests through Moses and Aaron. When the tribe abuses the system, God punishes them but never wipes them out.

Centuries later the story of God's mercy comes to a climax. God sends Jesus, the Messiah, the one-of-a-kind God-person to earth through Mary and it's perfect. Even his name means, 'The Real God rescues'. Jesus spreads the declaration: Good news! God's mercy is arriving. God's deliverance is here. Welcome it and follow me! And then the authorities have him executed. That has to be unforgivable, right? They have Jesus' blood on their hands. But there is a twist in the story here. God declares that the senseless, wicked execution of Jesus will be the very thing he uses to reveal how deep his mercy goes.

Instead of paying them back, God raises Jesus to life so he can serve as the agent of mercy for humanity. Then Jesus presents his own blood to God as the perfect, final sacrifice. He declares not Judgment Day, but a grace period. He starts adopting foreigners who accept this incredible mercy into his kingdom (the God Tribe).

The God Tribe becomes the Mercy Tribe, a huge global task force to spread the news of his mercy during the grace period. He gives them all his Holy Spirit so they receive the power to show mercy like he did, and the courage to endure like he did.

from https://syncx.org

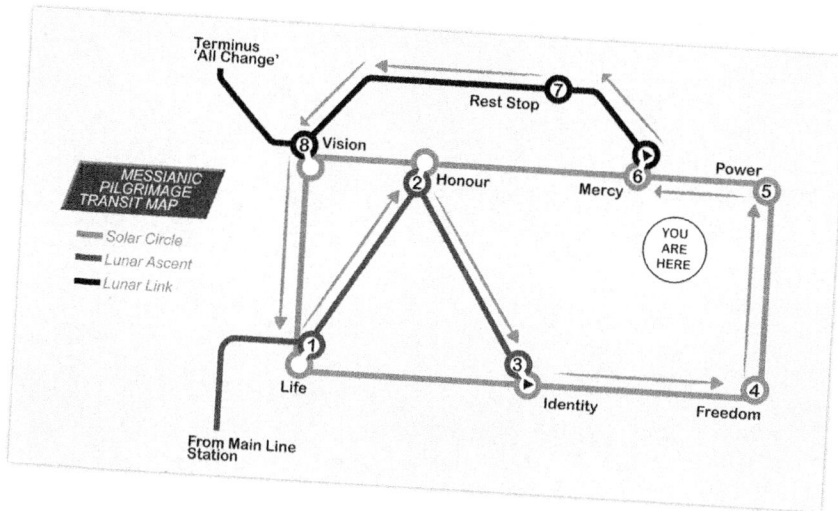

MESSIANIC PILGRIMAGE TRANSIT MAP

Solar Circle
Lunar Ascent
Lunar Link

Terminus 'All Change'
Rest Stop
7
8 Vision
2 Honour
6 Mercy
Power
5
YOU ARE HERE
1 Life
3 Identity
4 Freedom
From Main Line Station

Who are we? We are mercy agents, guilt-busters, taking God's mercy to the world before the grace period runs out. We don't want anyone to miss the deadline! Jesus died to show mercy to all. How could we leave anyone out? How could we fail to let them know?

That's our story. That's why we live the way we live and tell this story to anybody who will listen.

You would think that the whole world would welcome Jesus' messengers of mercy with open arms. But while some do, many are mystified or insulted with the whole idea that they need mercy at all. Some would like to receive mercy, but don't want to be merciful to others; Jesus does not allow that. Some of them try everything to silence the messengers.

That's how things stand for the time being. But it will all change whenever the grace period runs out. No mercy then. Jesus, the Rescuer, will come back to earth in person to rescue the forgiven people from those who refused to accept Jesus' forgiveness or to let his mercy transform them. Evil will be destroyed not forgiven and all the mercy-lovers will live in gratitude forever, basking in the glory of God with no evil to spoil it.

CONTEMPLATING THE ROAD AHEAD

The 5G flow during the Rest Stop

Ground-breaker
God created; then he took a break. Everything changed.

Each phase of our pilgrimage starts with a claim that God did some specific thing that changed the story of the world, affecting everything right down to today. The ground-breaking event we celebrate at the Rest Stop is the day God granted the human race its entitlement to rest.

At the end of his creative process that culminated with the creation of the first woman, God *'saw all that he had made and it was very good'* (Genesis 1.31). Everything was beautifully in place. Humans had been blessed and given their assignment in the whole.

So what does God do the next morning?

A) inspect the creation and do any touch-up improvements

B) start the training program for the humans, who are new to their situation

C) rest

D) something else

What God actually did was C and a little more: *'And God blessed the seventh day and declared it holy, because it was the day when he rested from all his work of creation'* (Genesis 2:3).

'Holy' means 'not ordinary; reserved for a special purpose' and that purpose was rest. In other words, life is not entirely about activity. It is about a rhythm of activity and rest. And this rhythm applies even to God, though he was not tired from all that work of creation. Resting was simply the right thing to do. It set a model for humans and all other creatures tired from the work of life.

Gift
Rest is a gift from God that has other gifts inside it—rhythm, interest and joy.

Human life was supposed to be punctuated with regular pauses to rest; however, rest is not just the full stop in life. It is life's exclamation mark.

When we take time to rest, we create time to look back and draw joy from the good our work has done. We thank God for enabling and blessing our work and for doing things that go far beyond it. We get more interested in life and we become more interesting people. We miss all this if we keep our heads down in our work all the time, anxiously pressing on to get more things done, afraid to take a break.

God didn't make us slaves. He made us his friends.

Get it
We recognise that this gift means that God is for us and has set everything up with our welfare in mind.

God could have created us to be slaves. He could have thought only about how much work he could get out of us, or how many times we could sing songs in his honour. But he didn't make us slaves. He made us his friends.

True, we still have work to do for him, but he sees us as much more than workers. He sees us as friends with needs, like the need to rest and he sets up structures to help his friends. In this case the structure is one day of rest each week. That allows God and his friends to spend some relaxed uninterrupted time with each other because we want to and we can.

If we get that, we will never see God as grouchy, judgmental or unfair again. He is for us. He has been for us since the dawn of the human race, when he showed it by resting. He is not too busy to sit down and 'waste some time' with us and he does not want us to get too busy for him.

Go with it
Once we 'get it' that God is for us, we embrace rest and use it as he intended.

Once we see the big picture that rest is a gift, we go with the flow of what God is doing. He wants us to celebrate the week that just went by. We'll celebrate it. He wants us to remind each other that he is for us. We'll remind each other. He wants us to unload our shoulders and let him deal with all that weight. We'll get rid of our burdens. He wants us to pay attention to his guidance for the week to come. We'll pay attention.

If we don't take the rest that God puts there for us, or if we don't use the rest as he intends, what does it cost us? We become more negative about life, more doubtful about God's goodness, more depressed about our burdens and further out of touch with God's guidance.

Neglect of God-given rest may be the clearest evidence of human stupidity. We have a choice between rest and its results or non-rest (constant work) and its disastrous by-products. Why do so many of us opt for non-rest? Non-rest means unrest, the opposite of the peace we say we seek. Let's go with rest instead.

Neglect of God-given rest may be the clearest evidence of human stupidity.

Genuineness

As we 'go with it', we are joyfully rejuvenated, attractive to potential pilgrims and ready for the next leg of the pilgrimage.

One of the marvels of resting (not working) is that it changes us. If such change happens when we are not doing anything active, it means we did not work to change ourselves. Someone else was working on us. All we did was sit still and give him some time and room to work.

A weekly rest is a bit like a surgeon's anaesthetic, keeping the patient still enough for the surgeon to work properly. As God does his spiritual surgery on us week by week, we become genuine people. Our spiritual cancers get cut out. Our torn ligaments (relationships) get repaired. He may even do some cosmetic surgery to deal with some of our scars and our ugliness. Our souls embrace the results of the surgery and we become healed and whole people, all the way to our core.

By the way, we kept this 5G reading shorter than the 5Gs about other stages of the pilgrimage because reading feels like work to some people. We don't want to make anyone weary at the Rest Stop!.

The view from here

Rest was always supposed to be an important part of human experience. When God created the whole universe, he showed us how to take a day off, doing nothing but soaking life in and loving it.

Humans had restful lives in the beginning. They could just pick life off the trees—no hassle, no stress, no problems sleeping. They faced only one danger but they managed to blunder into it and spoil everything. Now work, pain and all kinds of dangers prevent or wreck our rest.

The story of the world is basically the story of the global rest restoration plan God launched through a person called Abraham about 4,000 years ago. His nomadic life may not make him the poster child for a rest campaign but he did have the key to all rest—enough trust to do what God told him to do even when he couldn't understand the reasons for it. Lack of that trust was exactly what had cost our human forefathers their rest in the first place.

The pattern repeats down through the centuries of Abraham's descendants. Obedient trust in God brings rest; disobedient lack of trust forfeits it.

God laid down the law for Abraham's descendants. Everyone was required to rest on certain days and years and everyone was entitled to rest, including slaves and domestic animals. When the nation kept ignoring his command to rest from farming every seventh year, God used the Babylonian empire to demolish Jerusalem and take thousands of leading citizens away into lives of captivity. This brought life in Israel to a standstill, a rest, for seventy years.

For centuries the prophets had predicted that real rest would come for the nation when God sent his Anointed Leader (Messiah) to take over, throw evil out and bring permanent peace and calm across the world. Finally a prophet called John whips up expectations with his claim that the Rest-bringer will arrive at any minute. Then a person called Jesus goes on a national awareness campaign, telling the whole weary nation, 'God's rest is here. Come on in! Take my burden and feel how light it is'. (authors' paraphrase)

Since he has no official endorsements but crowds still flock after him,

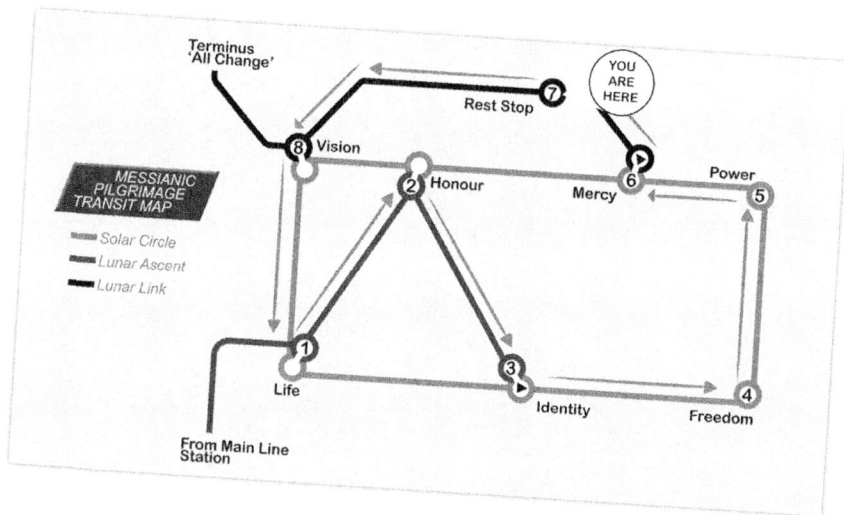

MESSIANIC PILGRIMAGE TRANSIT MAP

Terminus 'All Change'

Rest Stop 7

YOU ARE HERE

8 Vision

2 Honour

6 Power

Mercy

5

— Solar Circle
— Lunar Ascent
— Lunar Link

1 Life

3 Identity

4 Freedom

From Main Line Station

else. They will make things as unrestful as possible for us. But because of the Spirit in us, our indescribable inner peace stays solid as a rock. It is the peace of the future becoming visible in the present, giving a preview of what the Rest-bringer will do when he returns in person.

So that's our story. That's why we enjoy the inner calm we do and bring rest to everybody we can. Who are we? We are rest-bringers, connecting any willing people with the real Rest-bringer, Jesus.

his campaign scares the power holders. They decide it has to be stopped. They give him a death sentence and carry it out so no one will ever look to him for rest again. But God raises the Rest-bringer from the grave and his campaign rolls on.

It is still rolling to this day and he is still leading it. He's not physically on earth any more. He's on the throne of the universe, but he is totally in touch every minute. He has sent his Self (his Spirit) into those who are looking to him as the Rest-bringer for the world, directing them and refreshing them for each next step as they bring rest to the world. They are forgiven and forgiving. They calm things down.

Of course, the spoilers are still out there, stuck in their anti-rest lives, churning with inner and outer conflicts and blaming it all on everyone

TOGETHER FOREVER!

The 5G flow during Vision Season

Ground-breaker
Jesus is coming back to take over the world and create the utopia we thought was impossible.

The ground-breaking event for Vision Season is Christ's return. This is the only one of the eight ground-breakers in the Messianic Pilgrimage that has not happened yet. But so far, God has done seven out of seven, so we have solid reason to trust him this one last time.

The ancient prophecy says, '*As my vision continued that night, I saw someone like a son of man coming with the clouds of heaven. He approached the Ancient One and was led into his presence. He was given authority, honour, and sovereignty over all the nations of the world, so that people of every race and nation and language would obey him. His rule is eternal—it will never end. His kingdom will never be destroyed*'

(Daniel 7.13-14) Jesus claimed to be that person, and he promised to return to fulfill that prophecy (Revelation 22.20) That will be the final game-changer in the story of the world.

At that time, everybody who thought they successfully got away with something will see their secret in the headlines. All unsolved murder cases will be solved. And it will be payback time, except that payback will not come from the victims. It will come from the King, exercising justice.

Those who want to oppose the King and undermine his reign of justice and peace will be destroyed and excluded. Every tactic they have been using to maintain unjust power in the current world will utterly fail in the coming world. They will not be able to mount an attack on the kingdom or infiltrate it to do damage from inside. Their cause will be lost because the game will change.

Gift
The promise of Christ's return is a gift, a solid reason for us to live in hope.

We don't usually think of a promise as a gift. A gift is whatever is actually received when a promise is kept. But if the promise is given by someone who always keeps his word, the promise is a gift in itself. We feel almost like we have the gift already.

The gift we get from this prophecy is a vision of Christ's return and the peace he will bring. No tears. No wars. No death. Not even any lies or gossip.

This utopian vision brings us a paradoxical combination of internal peace and intense motivation. We can relax because we know the story of the world has a happy ending, but at the same time, we can't wait for it to happen. We are motivated to bring as much of heaven to earth as we can, and to do it as soon as we can without trying to force it.

Get it
The gift helps us if we get it that Jesus is more a king than a teacher.

If we see Jesus as a teacher, then the pressure is on us to try to create the beautiful world he taught about. But if we see him as a King who is coming back to create that world himself, the pressure is off. We don't have to force improvements on the world. We just let Christ put those improvements inside us, and we let them spill out to connect, heal, and bless the world.

If we see Jesus as a good religious teacher, we don't get it yet. Teachers may give visions of an ideal world, but it is up to their students to bring those ideals about. The students have to study hard, work hard, and get as close to the ideals as they can. But in the real world, they fall short no matter how grand the ideals are or how good the teacher was.

Politicians and revolutionaries also announce grand visions. They say, 'You are sick. You need surgery. We know exactly how to operate on you. We have the sharpest scalpel that has ever been developed. And we have a wonderful anaesthetic so you will never feel a thing.' But on the day of the surgery they show up with a rusty butcher knife, two aspirin, and 500 excuses.

We get it when we realise Jesus has more than a vision. He has a strategy and the power to execute the strategy. Jesus delivers on his promises. In fact, the name Jesus means, 'God delivers'.

Jesus doesn't watch his vision fall apart and then blame the failure on his followers, 'You didn't work hard enough. You didn't follow the plan well enough.' No, he starts the strategy by laying down his own life, as we saw in Honour Season. Then he takes the strategy into the next phase by putting his power into us, his followers.

Bottom line:
- Jesus was born to connect, heal and bless the world.
- We now do the same three things in his name and with his power.
- He returns to totally do what we are partially doing
- We get it.

Go with it
Once we get it, we live positive, radiant lives.

The natural thing to do is to Go with it, to go with God's non-violent plans for global improvement. We start living like we have one foot in the future. We actually do. We already are free citizens of Jesus' kingdom.

Jesus reigns over us now, giving us some of the joy and peace that will be everywhere when he reigns everywhere. Whatever evil will be eradicated from the world at that time, we want him to eradicate from us right now. Whatever honour and praise the nations will give him then, we want to start giving already. We start 'Living the Dream'.

Jesus, as King, set this up so he could show everyone how well things turn out when he takes over. In this way they could be drawn into his kingdom too. Before they are even born, people everywhere are wired to dream of the world that Jesus is going to bring. When they see us, they should see their dreams coming true.

This is a great way to live! As people with one foot in a guaranteed future, we can re-inspire people who have become cynical about the way the world is going, people who don't even try any more because they think nothing will ever do any good.

We don't let the world self-destruct right now. We don't sit around waiting for Jesus to instantly, magically transform it all when he returns. If we do that, we are not 'going with' his strategy. He gave us the gift of the vision in order to move us to action and to keep us going, even when the action doesn't seem to work. This is no time to sit on our hands.

Genuineness

As we go with it, we become walking previews of the future world that Christ will rule.

We find our authentic identity in Christ the coming King. We are 100% genuine people, locked into the vision of Christ's return to reign. We are not pretending; we are already perfect examples of the coming ideal world, but we are genuinely on the way to that world.

We synchronise with that vision a little more each day. We aren't in the perfect world yet, but we can see it from here, and as we focus on it, its power changes us to be more like Christ the King.

Of course, we are not perfect, complete examples of the future utopia. We do not make the world's dreams come true. That is neither our goal nor our burden because Jesus will do that part himself when he returns. Our role is only to give genuine glimpses into the coming world.

We are only the actors for the trailer for the movie of utopia. If we have seen only the trailer for a movie, we haven't seen the whole movie yet, but we have seen enough to know what kind of a movie it will be. The trailer is a genuine part of the movie even though it can't tell the whole story. In the same way, we don't have to be perfect to be genuine.

We prove our genuineness not by taking power, nor by doing good things that have great impact, but by keeping on doing good even when the impact doesn't look impressive at all. Our persistence shows that we still trust Jesus to complete the vision even when it looks like the vision will never come true. We see the coming world that others can't see yet, and we stay genuinely in sync with the King of that coming world. That is how his kingdom comes and his will gets done—partially now through us; totally later through his return in person.

The view from here

The first humans had it all. There was no way to envision anything more beautiful, pleasant, or satisfying. They even had frequent visits from the Real God himself.

Something has obviously gone wrong since then, and there are all kinds of conflicting ideas about how to fix it. This story sketches one of those visions for the world.

I call it the best vision ever because it is more than wishing, hoping, and trying to be good. This vision is ancient, it is true, it adapts for all ages and cultures, and its followers may die for it but they will not kill to bring it about. Here it is, starting about 4,000 years ago.

An old man with a small family sees a vision that confirms an incredible list of God's promises to him—his descendants will be as uncountable as the stars. God will give them control of a vast area of land, and they will bless every family on earth.

Those promises begin to come true for Abraham and Sarah as their family grows to become a whole nation and gets established in its homeland. God sends prophets like Isaiah who talk of one particular king whom God will send at his chosen time. He will rule the entire world, not just the land of Abraham's nation, and his reign will never end. The nation can't wait for his arrival, but they do have to wait for hundreds of years.

And then, out of nowhere, God moves the vision forward. An angel appears to Mary and tells her she will miraculously become pregnant with the baby who will make the nation's vision come true. That baby, God's son Jesus, grows up to declare: 'The ancient vision is coming true now! God's glory is on the rise!' (paraphrase) He shows it by healing many people, by teaching brilliantly in ways that ordinary people could understand, and by calling people to follow him and trust him absolutely.

Powerful people see that he is on a campaign to carry out his vision, and he will take over everything if they do not stop him. They put him on trial for talking like he is the Messiah, the super-king the prophets envisioned and predicted, and they accuse him of being a liar whose vision will lead his nation to disaster. They sentence him to die on a cross not just to kill him, but to shame him, destroy his reputation, crush his vision, and end his campaign.

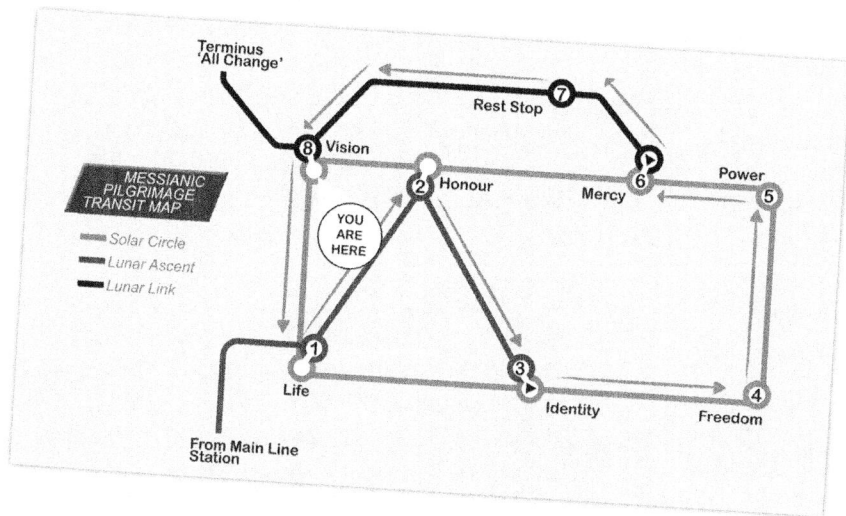

Terminus 'All Change'

Rest Stop

MESSIANIC PILGRIMAGE TRANSIT MAP

Solar Circle
Lunar Ascent
Lunar Link

(8) Vision

YOU ARE HERE

(2) Honour

(7)

(6) Mercy

Power

(5)

(1) Life

(3) Identity

(4) Freedom

From Main Line Station

But it all backfires. All it does is set the stage for the proof that the Real God sent him, and his vision was true. On the third day, God the Father raises him from the grave to carry his campaign on to victory.

We might expect him to claim his throne on the spot, going back to the court to ask them, 'Can you hear me now?' But he does not do that. He returns to his heavenly throne without dying again. Before he goes, he tells his campaign team what to do until he comes back to earth to take total control here and destroy evil.

His team is supposed to embody the vision, not impose it by force! How can they do that? He sends his Spirit to turn them into a new kind of human being. They receive Jesus' mercy and become merciful, showing that his vision works and his campaign is succeeding.

We are the current members of the campaign team. We pick up where previous followers left off, and we hit some of the same obstacles. People who are pushing some other vision for the world do not want any competition from Jesus' vision. Sometimes they trash his vision or try to block us like the powers tried to block Jesus himself. But he lives in us, sticks with us, and gives us the courage to keep going with the campaign even when all hope seems lost.

Who are we? We are actors in a trailer for the movie the world will see when the campaign leader returns to carry out his vision totally. The trailer doesn't tell us the whole story, but it gives us a feel for what kind of a story it is. That's what we do. We already see the vision coming true as he heals, blesses and connects us by his Spirit. We already have one foot in that glorious future! We are living the dream, that is, living part of it and looking forward to the rest.

That's our story, and that's why we keep telling it. How could we ever keep quite about a vision that good?

Images through the book

p.76   Hazmat medical team pushing stretcher by ambulance on street | Storybooks licensed Asset-ID: SBI-300904860

p.79   Gray wolf canis lupus in the green leaves forest detail portrait of wolf in the forest | Storybooks licensed Asset-ID: SBI-325326458

p.80   Mature woman sitting on the bed is scared of a man woman is victim of domestic violence | Storybooks licensed Asset-ID: SBI-305109683

p.84   Gandhi spinning | Unknown author (Public Domain)

p.85   Studio photograph of Mahatma Gandhi, London, 1931 – Elliott & Fry (Public Domain)

p.86   Alice Cooper during Wacken Open Air at Schleswig-Holstein, Wacken, Germany on 2017-08-05 – Sven Mandel | Creative Commons Attribution-Share Alike 4.0 International license

p.87   Alice Cooper band performing live during Halloween Night of Horror at Wembley Arena, London, England on 28 October 2012 – Kreepin Deth (Creative Commons Attribution-Share Alike 3.0 Unported license)

p.88   Unrecognizable vietnamese woman weaving a bamboo mat | Storybooks licensed Asset-ID: SBI-305136951

p.89   Realistic earth closeup render | Storybooks licensed Asset-ID: SBI-301825525

p.90   Balloons | Storybooks licensed Asset-ID: SBI-300617516

        Blue Birthday Background | Storybooks licensed Asset-ID: SBI-300242395

p.91   Tenda do campo de beduínos no deserto do Saara, África ID 162276140 | David Molina | Dreamstime.com

p.92   Group of young smiling students with books and backpacks walking together at university | Storybooks licensed Asset-ID: SBI-302891938

p.93   Dunbar | Jelena Mrkovic (Creative Commons Attribution-Share Alike 4.0 International license)

p.94   Happy business people with their heads together representing concept of friendship and | Storybooks licensed Asset-ID: SBI-300855337

p.96   Native American women dishing out food at a family meal | Storybooks licensed Asset-ID: SBI-346270618

p.97   Beautiful young woman on a pink floral background | Storybooks licensed Asset-ID: SBI-317616619

p.101   Man arrested as a consequence of his crime | Storybooks licensed Asset-ID: SBI-301327025

p.104   Freedom | Storybooks licensed Asset-ID: SBI-300913165

p.106   Refugees on a boat crossing the Mediterranean sea, heading from Turkish coast to the northeastern Greek island of Lesbos, 29 January 2016 – Mstyslav Chernov | Creative Commons Attribution-Share Alike 4.0 International license

p.143 St. Francis of Assisi, Royal Museum of Fine Arts Antwerp – Philip Fruytiers (1610–1666) (Public Domain)

p.144 Kisses from Katie Book Cover| Amazon Advertising

p.145 Daring to Hope Book Cover | Amazon Advertising

p.147 Jesus' parable of the unforgiving servant – Sweet Publishing | Creative Commons Attribution-ShareAlike 3.0 Unported license

p.151 Chohan Rajpoots, Delhi between 1862 and 1868 – Charles Shepherd and Arthur Robertson (Public Domain)

p.152 A hand comes down to save another hand from the ocean | Storybooks licensed Asset-ID: SBI-301080940

p.153 Balloons | Storybooks licensed Asset-ID: SBI-300617516

Blue Birthday Background | Storybooks licensed Asset-ID: SBI-300242395

p.154 Mountainous desert with colorful cloudy sky judean desert in israel at sunset | Storybooks licensed Asset-ID: SBI-300878843

p.157 Young runner in blue jacket sitting on an asphalt path leading through green grass tra | Storybooks licensed Asset-ID: SBI-305226451

p.162 Yoga Meditating Sunrise, Woman Mindfulness Meditation on Beach | Image ID: 74149792 | Copyright Inara Prusakova | Dreamstime.com

p.163 Tourists following a tour guide at Giza | Image ID: 24580730 | Copyright Verdelho | Dreamstime.com

p.164 Easter bread wine and cross on vintage old wooden background | Image ID: 107055980 | Copyright Udra11 | Dreamstime.com

Empty wooden table top | Image ID: 46849225 | Copyright Alexandr Kornienko | Dreamstime.com

p.166 Rabia al-Basri (717–801) – (Public Domain)

p.168 Henri Nouwen | Frank Hamilton – (Creative Commons Attribution-Share Alike 3.0 Unported license)

p.169 Rembrandt, The Return of the Prodigal Son 1662–1669 (Hermitage Museum, St Petersburg) – (Public Domain)

p.171 Side view of serene woman sitting on sandy beach against blue sky outdoors | Storybooks licensed Asset-ID: SBI-300739709

p.172 Relaxed young man at home on balcony | Storybooks licensed Asset-ID: SBI-300818265

p.173 Sailboat on the tropical ocean | Storybooks licensed Asset-ID: SBI-300935935

p.174 Fairuz in Beiteddine Concert 2001 – Wissam Chidiak (Creative Commons Attribution-Share Alike 3.0 Unported license)

p.175 Balloons | Storybooks licensed Asset-ID: SBI-300617516

Blue Birthday Background | Storybooks licensed Asset-ID: SBI-300242395

p.176 Morning sunrise on mountain | Storybooks licensed Asset-ID: SBI-300847108

p.179 Couple hand together touch with love vintage filter tone | Storybooks licensed Asset-ID: SBI-301086055

p.181 Silhouette of a woman during and adventage (sic) climbing and mountain walking | Storybooks licensed Asset-ID: SBI-300996634

p.183 Hands of an unrecognizable woman with bible praying | Storybooks licensed Asset-ID: SBI-305129015

p.184 Photograph of Clive Staples Lewis (29 November 1898 – 22 November 1963) (Wikipedia - fair use under United States copyright law)

p.185 View of the mountains and mourne wall in Northern Ireland – Marksie531 (Creative Commons Attribution-Share Alike 3.0 Unported license)

p.186 Tom Hanks as the title character on the film set of Forrest Gump 1994 – Jesse Kaplan/lakesbutta (Creative Commons Attribution-Share Alike 3.0 Unported license)

p.187 HBO Post-Emmys Party, Pacific Design Center, Sept. 21, 2008 – Kristin Dos Santos | Creative Commons Attribution-Share Alike 2.0 Generic license

p.189 Photo of poster on wall – Stuart Brown

p.191 Watercolor vector illustration hand drawn easter scene with cross Jesus Christ crucified | Storybooks licensed Asset-ID: SBI-305227016

p.192 Wooden bridge over brook in the forest | Storybooks licensed Asset-ID: SBI-324629958

p.194 Balloons | Storybooks licensed Asset-ID: SBI-300617516

Blue Birthday Background | Storybooks licensed Asset-ID: SBI-300242395

p.195 Thailand night view from building fisheye lens | Storybooks licensed Asset-ID: SBI-301087237

p.199 Smiling girl making triangle with her painted palms | Storybooks licensed Asset-ID: SBI-301022675

p.209 Hiking scene with silhouette people walking | Storybooks licensed Asset-ID: SBI-301086155

p.217 Public Domain: Doña María de Aragón Altarpiece – El Greco (1541–1614)

p.221 A city showing the effect of climate change | Storybooks licensed Asset-ID: SBI-326468513

p.229 Two men looking at chess figures on chess board | Storybooks licensed Asset-ID: SBI-305525637

p.237 City scape and network connection concept | Storybooks licensed Asset-ID: SBI-301985213

p.247 Man arrested as a consequence of his crime | Storybooks licensed Asset-ID: SBI-301327025

Icons used in 5G flow articles

Volleyball sport elements glossy icon | Storybooks licensed Asset-ID: SBI-300133843

Download basket elements glossy icon | Storybooks licensed Asset-ID: SBI-300133602

Download elements glossy icon | Storybooks licensed Asset-ID: SBI-300133275

Download elements lite icon | Storybooks licensed Asset-ID: SBI-300133909

Download disk elements glossy icon | Storybooks licensed Asset-ID: SBI-300133254

Footstep Icons

game-icons.bet (Creative Commons Attribution license)

Photographs used on the Cover

Wooden bridge in autumn park | Storybooks licensed Asset-ID: SBI-300875162

Photograph of Stan Nussbaum | Lorri Nussbaum

Photograph of Richard Fairhead | Papandreou Kallisthenis

Printed in Great Britain
by Amazon

57628020R00165